MARRIED WOMEN AND PROPERTY LAW IN NINETEENTH-CENTURY ONTARIO

Until this century, married women had no legal right to hold, use, or dispose of property. Since the ownership of property is a critical measure of social status, the married women's property acts of the nineteenth century were important landmarks in the legal emancipation of women.

Reform campaigns represented the first organized attempts by women in Upper Canada to challenge their status in society. Ironically, emancipation was not the first goal of reformers: their demands reflected a concern with protection from economic instability. The laws granting women new rights and privileges were designed to force men to behave more responsibly and to mitigate the worst hardships imposed upon wives by abusive or negligent husbands.

The most detailed and complete account of married women's property law reform yet written for any North American jurisdiction, this fascinating study will be of interest to those in the areas of law, women's studies, and nineteenth-century social history.

(Osgoode Society for Canadian Legal History)

LORI CHAMBERS is a post-doctoral fellow at McMaster University.

PATRONS OF THE SOCIETY

Aird & Berlis

Blake, Cassels & Graydon

Borden & Elliot

Davies, Ward & Beck

Gowling, Strathy & Henderson

McCarthy Tétrault

Osler, Hoskin & Harcourt

The Harweg Foundation

Tory Tory DesLauriers & Binnington

Weir & Foulds

BENEFACTORS OF THE SOCIETY

Bastedo Stewart & Smith

Roger T. Hughes, QC

The Society also thanks The Law Foundation of Ontario and The Law Society of Upper Canada for their continuing support.

Married Women and Property Law in Victorian Ontario

LORI CHAMBERS

Published for The Osgoode Society for Canadian Legal History by
University of Toronto Press
Toronto Buffalo London

© The Osgoode Society for Canadian Legal History 1997

Printed in Canada

ISBN 0-8020-0854-2 (cloth)
ISBN 0-8020-7839-7 (paper)

Printed on acid-free paper

Canadian Cataloguing in Publication Data

Chambers, Anne Lorene, 1965–
Married women and property law in Victorian Ontario

Includes bibliographical references and index.
ISBN 0-8020-0854-2 (bound) ISBN 0-8020-7839-7 (pbk.)

1. Married women – Legal status, laws, etc. – Ontario –
History – 19th century.   2. Separate property – Ontario –
History – 19th century.   I. Osgoode Society for Canadian
Legal History.   II. Title.

KE0222.C42 1997   346.71304'2   C97-931020-2
KF527.C42 1997

This book has been published with the help of a grant from the Humanities and
Social Sciences Federation of Canada, using funds provided by the Social Sciences
and Humanities Research Council of Canada.

University of Toronto Press acknowledges the financial assistance to its
publishing program of the Canada Council and the Ontario Arts Council.

Contents

Contents   vi

Foreword

THE OSGOODE SOCIETY FOR CANADIAN LEGAL HISTORY

The purpose of The Osgoode Society for Canadian Legal History is to encourage research and writing in the history of Canadian law. The Society, which was incorporated in 1979 and is registered as a charity, was founded at the initiative of the Honourable R. Roy McMurtry, a former attorney general for Ontario, now Chief Justice of Ontario, and officials of the Law Society of Upper Canada. Its efforts to stimulate the study of legal history in Canada include a research support program, a graduate student research assistance program, and work in the fields of oral history and legal archives. The Society publishes volumes of interest to the Society's members that contribute to legal-historical scholarship in Canada, including studies of the courts, the judiciary, and the legal profession, biographies, collections of documents, studies in criminology and penology, accounts of significant trials, and work in the social and economic history of the law.

Current directors of The Osgoode Society for Canadian Legal History are Jane Banfield, Tom Bastedo, Brian Bucknall, Archie Campbell, Susan Elliott, J. Douglas Ewart, Martin Friedland, Charles Harnick, John Honsberger, Kenneth Jarvis, Allen Linden, Virginia MacLean, Wendy Matheson, Colin McKinnon, Roy McMurtry, Brendan O'Brien, Peter Oliver, Paul Reinhardt, Joel Richler, James Spence, and Richard Tinsley.

The annual report and information about membership may be obtained by writing: The Osgoode Society for Canadian Legal History, Osgoode Hall, 130 Queen Street West, Toronto, Ontario, Canada M5H 2N6.

Married Women and Property Law in Victorian Ontario, by Professor Lori Chambers, McMaster University, is a fascinating account of gender relationships in nineteenth-century Ontario as revealed through a series of laws which reflected Victorian attitudes to marriage, property, and power. 'In all common law jurisdictions,' Professor Chambers reminds us, 'marriage, for women, represented civil death.' Her manuscript explains the practical and theoretical implications of this reality for the Victorian family and especially for the married woman.

This important revisionist study requires us to rethink a good deal of the conventional wisdom about gender relationships, the law, and the judiciary in nineteenth-century Ontario history. Of interest to all those concerned about the nineteenth-century origins of Canadian social institutions, it will prove of particular value to students of family, gender, and authority in Victorian society.

R. Roy McMurtry
President

Peter N. Oliver
Editor-in-Chief

Acknowledgments

Encouragement and support for this endeavour came from many sources and individuals. I have benefited enormously from financial assistance provided by the Social Sciences and Humanities Research Council of Canada and by the University of Toronto. Comments and criticisms from my thesis supervisors – Arthur Silver, Jim Phillips, and Sylvia Van Kirk – have been enormously helpful and have forced me to clarify my themes and arguments. Perhaps more important, their faith in me and in the value of this project helped sustain my interest and enthusiasm during the long process of research and writing. Without the considerable aid of Jack Choules of the Archives of Ontario I would have been unable to wade through the enormous volume of unprocessed court documents which he placed at my disposal. In the process of transforming this work from thesis to book I have become indebted to numerous other individuals who have given generously of their time. Michael Grossberg, Ian Radforth, Peter Oliver, Rob Ferguson, Constance Backhouse, and anonymous reviewers at the University of Toronto Press, the Osgoode Society, and the Humanities and Social Sciences Federation of Canada have provided commentaries and raised questions that have greatly helped in the clarification of the arguments that follow. Marilyn MacFarlane has been cheerful and supportive throughout the long process of bringing this book to fruition. Kathy Johnson's editorial changes have also greatly improved the manuscript. I have also benefited from the informal aid of numerous participants at the annual meetings of the Canadian Historical Association and from the encouragement and ideas of members of the Legal History Group in Toronto. Ed Montigny and Mary Jane Mossman have generously shared their research with me, and for this too I am grateful. Teaching colleagues at McMaster and the University of Toronto have also been consistently supportive and encouraging.

Most important, I am indebted to my family. My parents, Kay and Dave Chambers, have provided unfailing support. My sister, Mary-Catherine Chambers, has enthusiastically discussed the themes and ideas explored in this book on occasions too numerous to count. Above all, I thank Michel Bédard. Not only has he read and criticized this manuscript extensively, but his encouragement, his good cooking, and our shared laughter have sustained me and made the completion of this work possible. This book is dedicated to our children, Geoffrey and Catherine. Transformation of the thesis into a book would have progressed more quickly without them, but their arrival has enriched our lives beyond our greatest expectations.

MARRIED WOMEN AND PROPERTY LAW
IN VICTORIAN ONTARIO

Introduction

In all common law jurisdictions, marriage, for women, represented civil death. Nineteenth-century married women's property law reform provided the first tentative legal recognition of the wife as a being separate from her husband, and remedial legislation in Upper Canada was part of a much wider international phenomenon.[1] Before these reforms were enacted, the wife's legal identity was obliterated at marriage and she was entirely under the power and control of her husband. At law, the wife could not hold, use, or dispose of property, whether land, money, chattels, or wages earned by her own labour. Without the right to own property, wives could not support themselves independently of their husbands, a fact that greatly constrained their options in abusive relationships. Although the physical and economic power differential between spouses could not be abolished by legislative fiat, the possibility of property ownership began to mitigate some of the practical problems faced by abused and unhappy wives. In a more symbolic sense, by recognizing the separate personality and interests of the wife, the married women's property acts represented a crucial turning-point in the theory of married women and the law. As the author of one treatise on the law of husband and wife recognized in the early twentieth century, 'personal status is the correlative of disability, and the removal of the latter necessarily creates or restores to a corresponding extent the privileges of an independent person, or in other words of a citizen.'[2] By recognizing, albeit indirectly, the citizenship of wives, the married women's property acts provided the theoretical justification for further legal reform for the benefit of all women. For this reason, the acts, and the beliefs that inspired them, are of enduring importance for feminist scholars.

Property and personal status are intimately linked in Anglo-American culture, and the extent to which women own and manage property is, as Marylynn Salmon has argued, 'an important baseline for learning how men and women share power in the family.'[3] This study examines the gradual expansion of the property rights of wives in Ontario between 1837 and 1900. Although marital property law reform varied in its specifics from province to province, this case study of Canada's most populous region suggests the limitations inherent in the married women's property acts. It fills an important void in Canadian historiography and provides a basis for comparing reform in Canada with legislation in both the United States and Great Britain.[4] Despite their enduring symbolic importance, the married women's property acts did not revolutionize the economic structure of most families; women had a theoretical right to own and ·control property, but many lacked the means of acquiring either money or immovable assets. It is argued throughout this work that although the right to own property created the possibility that men and women would 'share power in the family,' in practice little changed for most wives.

Reform was enacted slowly and incrementally in Ontario, beginning with the introduction of the Court of Chancery in 1837 and culminating in formal legal equality for wives under the Married Women's Property Act, 1884. None of the acts was motivated by any desire to emancipate women. Instead, the guiding intent of legislation was to 'better protect'[5] women from the potential coercion and cruelty of their mates, to allow women to support themselves and their dependent children when husbands were absent, abusive, or economically irresponsible. Reform was popularly justified by the belief that women, being 'weak and liable to be imposed upon by their husbands,'[6] required special legal protection, not equal rights based on their equal humanity. For women who had previously been denied any legal representation separate from their husbands, recognition itself was a crucial step forward. However, the chivalrous ideal of protecting helpless women was less than empowering. Also – and not surprisingly, given the motivations that underlay reform – formal legal equality, established in its essentials in 1884, did not challenge the economic and social inequality central to nineteenth-century marriage. The separate property regime allowed wives to keep their wages and inherited property, but gave them no claim on family property held in the name of the husband. In a society in which economic opportunities for married women remained extremely limited, most wives continued to work in the privacy of the home. They were not paid for such labour and most women could also not expect to inherit estates adequate for their independent support. In this context, the theoretical right of ownership of property was of little practical importance for the majority of wives. In spite of their limitations, however, the acts represented a radical departure from the common law concept of marital unity – the belief that husband and wife were one person – and therefore both a potent symbol of married women's citizenship and a crucial building-block for future feminist reform. This study is intended to illustrate both the importance and the inherent limitations of these acts and of the separate property regime itself.

This work draws upon sources neglected by earlier legal historians. Not only were legislation, newspapers, legal treatises and commentaries, and the provincial law reports consulted, but all extant unreported cases for the period 1837 to 1900 were examined.[7] The vast majority of cases in Ontario, at least those involving married women's property law, were not reported, and can be reviewed only by the slow process of sifting through the uncategorized court documents at the Archives of Ontario.[8] In the nineteenth century, in contrast to the present, the rules for court reporting were not firmly established, and much depended on the discretion of individual court reporters, the lawyers who took notes and transcripts during hearings and trials. The law reports were, as James Snell has argued, 'the chief means by which members of the legal profession communicated with each other.'[9] The law reports served an educative function for practising lawyers and, indirectly, for the public at large. Cases were selected for reporting often as much because they dealt with exceptional points of law or circumstances as because they set important precedents. In this context, reported cases involving family law must be viewed as intended lessons not only on the specifics of law but on gender roles and marital expectations. The scripts in reported cases were structured in such a way as to legitimate and reinforce specific standards of conduct and to illustrate that deviance from such ideals would be punished. Adulterous or deserting wives received no sympathy from the court, and their cases were disproportionately likely to appear in the law reports. Such cases, however, were exceptional. In the vast majority of unreported cases it was men who had violated gender and marital norms in some manner, and the court was not hesitant to deny such husbands their common law rights over the property belonging to their wives.

Received wisdom in this field, based exclusively on an examination of reported cases, has pitted women seeking new legal freedoms against a conservative male judiciary determined to thwart them.[10] Unreported cases, however, suggest that this model is too simplistic. While judges opposed female independence, particularly within marriage, this did not prevent reformers and conservatives alike from supporting measures intended to protect individual women from mistreatment.[11] The contrast between reported and unreported cases illustrates the exceptional nature of the cases that found their way into the law reports in the nineteenth century and highlights the dangers of relying exclusively upon reported cases when studying the impact of law. Throughout this work an attempt is made to balance the evidence from unreported cases, cases that illustrate the day-to-day working of the law, and to explain why certain cases were considered worthy of preservation for posterity in the law reports.[12]

Evidence from unreported cases also suggests that protection from mistreatment, not emancipation, was foremost in the minds of women themselves. In cases in which women were suffering abuse at the hands of their husbands, this should not be surprising; their priority was safety, not independence. Although they may have been playing to the perceptions and biases of the court, women used the language of supplicants when they addressed the bench. In rare cases, by their behaviour or language, some women defied stereotypes of helplessness and dependency and, not surprisingly, received from the bench not sympathy but stern lectures about female duty within marriage. Such cases were reported in disproportionate numbers. Interpreting women's own views of their rights and responsibilities within marriage is the most challenging task one faces in the study of these legal sources. The women do not ever speak directly, but instead their voices are filtered and mediated through the court process. Women had to structure their claims to meet the specific provisions of legislation and the demands of the judicial system itself and those who interpreted the female voice – lawyers, judges and court reporters – were themselves all male and their personal views not only constrained women's speech in court, but 'coloured the selection of cases reported and the elements in the case that were emphasized.'[13] Although the nature and comprehensiveness of case files varied widely, some were extensive, containing multiple depositions by various parties, and concrete evidence – letters, police reports, medical files and property inventories – that provides an unusual window into the private sphere. Despite the problems and biases inherent in these sources, an attempt is made throughout this work to recover female voice and agency by considering not only the arguments articulated in court, but the meaning of the actions of women, men, and the neighbours and family members who intervened in domestic struggles.[14]

Using these sources, this study seeks to explain and illustrate the motivations that propelled reform, the interpretation of legislation in the court, and, most important, the impact of reform on the lives of individual women. The women who came before the court were, no doubt, exceptional; women had to own property for the law to be meaningful for them. Property legislation primarily benefited those women who inherited money, or could earn, through education or other skills, significant wages. This said, however, the law did not in any overt way distinguish between the gentlewoman and the factory girl, or between women of various ethnic or religious backgrounds, and it is assumed throughout this study that women, despite important differences of class and race, are a distinct group, 'for which there are established patterns of behavior, special legislative restrictions, and customarily defined roles.'[15] To argue that the law did not recognize or acknowledge differences between women is not to diminish the double burden of poverty or racism under which some women laboured. Although the law impinged differently upon the lives of individual women, it limited and constrained the options of all wives; an examination of the working of law reveals the restrictions beyond which all women's freedom to act could not go. Because of the exceptional nature of the cases under study, this work remains heavily oriented towards understanding the internal intricacies of law; legal sources, while they illustrate the limitations placed upon women's action, do not tell us much about the nature of marriage itself, or about social relations between the sexes except in the particular cases under study and with regard to the ideal encoded in law. This book, therefore, is a study of married women's property law, its origins and limitations, not of marriage itself.

To set the stage for the reforms that would be enacted at mid-century, the first chapter of this work examines in detail the myriad disabilities imposed upon married women by the common law fiction of marital unity – the belief that husband and wife were one person and that the one person was the husband. This chapter also illustrates the changing social and economic circumstances in Upper Canada that encouraged a reconsideration of the law of marriage and property.

Reform began in 1837 with the introduction of the local Court of Chancery, or Equity, under whose jurisdiction individual wives could gain access to alimony and could protect some property for themselves through the use of trusts. Since statutory reform in 1859, 1872, 1873, and 1884 was based upon precedents established in this court, 1837 provided the point of departure for primary research in the unreported case files. Alimony, the subject of chapter 2 of this work, provided some of the most desperate of Upper Canadian wives with a means of escaping from abusive partners. The chancellors were sympathetic to the plight of such wives, and few women had their petitions for alimony denied; those who were denied relief by way of alimony had themselves violated the marriage bargain in some overt way, and their cases were particularly likely to be reported. In a society in which women had limited employment opportunities and no means by which to obtain ready cash, judicial sympathy for innocent wives wronged by their husbands proved to be of little practical value; husbands could readily abscond with all family property long before their wives could bring them to justice in court. Taking one's husband to court for alimony was a courageous act, and while women emphasized their proper wifely obedience in petitions to the court, they simultaneously defied feminine stereotypes that demanded subordination of women's needs within marriage. Alimony, however sympathetically it might be interpreted in the court, was an inherently limited remedy for women's grievances because it entailed only a right of maintenance out of the family property that still legally belonged entirely to the husband.

In Upper Canada, unlike in England, the chancellors adjudicated both alimony cases and disputes involving marriage settlements, also referred to as trusts or separate estates. Under marriage settlements wives could own property, but not control it. Such property was placed in the hands of a third party, the trustee, who was obliged to use the property for the benefit of the wife and to provide her with a regular disposable income. The trustee could be held accountable for his actions in the Court of Chancery. Evidence presented in alimony cases revealed the extent of the problem of marital violence; in this context, the local chancellors recognized the inherent power differential in nineteenth-century marriage. While they did not wish to undermine the hierarchical nature of marriage, they simultaneously retained a pervasive fear that all husbands were potentially abusive, domineering, and coercive. In England, by the nineteenth century, trustees served a nominal purpose only. However, because of their experience in alimony cases, when interpreting marriage settlements, examined in chapter 3, the Upper Canadian chancellors were adamant in their insistence that wives could not control their separate property themselves. If wives were allowed to control their own separate property, it was feared, husbands would simply kiss or kick them into placing the property at their disposal. Instead, trustees were perceived as a necessary protective shield against the common law power of husbands. Since the chancellors had the power to force trustees to behave in a responsible manner, by the careful use of judicial discretion they could protect the material interests of wives without granting women themselves independent powers of control over their property. This fact would have an enormous impact upon the shape of legislative reform in 1859; not only did the contrast between law and equity provide incentive for property law reform, since only the wealthy had access to marriage settlements, but it was chancery precedent that was ultimately generalized and democratized.

The act of 1859, discussed in chapter 4, granted wives the right to own, but not to manage or to alienate, the property that they brought to marriage or inherited during coverture. As in the Chancery model upon which reform was based, wives themselves could not control such property. Since the court could not appoint individual trustees to serve for each wife, the husband became trustee over his wife's statutory separate estate. It was assumed that his behaviour could be controlled by recourse to the court. In contrast to Chancery, however, wives did not have control over the income derived from their separate estates, a fact that limited the practical usefulness of such property. Without the right to control or dispose of their property, even money and chattels, it remained difficult for wives to use their separate estates to establish independent households when husbands were abusive. Also, by this act a mechanism was created by which any wife who would be eligible for alimony could retain control over her wages by obtaining a protection order from a local magistrate. It was hoped that these provisions would shelter wives against the economic impact of speculation on the part of their husbands and provide abandoned women of the working class with the legal means to support their families without interference. The women of the province mounted an extensive petitioning campaign that was of central importance in ensuring the passage of this act, and chapter 4 presents substantial new evidence illustrating the existence of an informal protofeminist reform network in the colony in the 1850s.

In 1872 the Ontario legislature granted wives the right to manage and dispose of their personal property, since money and chattels are of little use without rights of disposition. This made statutory separate property more exactly parallel to separate estates in Chancery. Also, the wages of all wives were hereafter to be considered part of the statutory separate estate. This was a crucial step in reducing the husband's potential coercive power over his wife; she could now, at least in theory, support herself with her own wages, although the earning potential of women, particularly married women, remained very limited in Ontario during this period. In 1873 the passage of the Married Women's Real Estate Act confirmed that wives had not yet been granted dispositive powers over their land, and provided a mechanism by which deserted or abused wives, those eligible for alimony, could petition for the right to alienate such property when necessary for the support of themselves or their families. These acts are discussed in chapter 5.

The acts of 1859, 1872, and 1873 failed in their central purpose – the 'better protection of married women.'[16] As trustee over his wife's separate property, the husband retained powers of control that did little to reduce his scope for coercion and abuse; confusion about the rights of disposition granted to wives over their personal property, but denied with respect to their land, undermined the protective intent of the legislation. Moreover, this confusion created the potential for fraud when wives and husbands acted in collusion. It was difficult for creditors to deal with married women with any sense of security since wives did not have full liability on contract and husbands controlled and managed separate property. Wives who required protection from coercive and abusive husbands found inadequate relief under these acts, and, ironically, some wives who had more egalitarian relationships with their spouses used the legislation to participate actively, and dishonestly, in the market, defying the belief that women had little aptitude for business. Both of these problems were exacerbated by the position of the husband as trustee over the separate property of his wife. These themes are discussed in chapters 6 and 7.

The act of 1884 abolished the role of the husband as trustee over his wife's separate estate. Mounting evidence of fraud by married couples, the failure of the acts to protect needy wives, and remedial legislation in Great Britain ensured the passage of this liberal legislation. This act was of great symbolic importance because the elimination of the trustee meant that the wife was no longer treated as a 'child, lunatic or criminal – a legal incompetent.'[17] The wife herself was hereby granted the right to manage, encumber, and dispose of her property in the same manner as if she had remained unmarried; by this act married women achieved formal legal equality with men and single women. Despite the achievement of formal equality, the act of 1884, discussed in chapter 8, did not aim to make the husband and wife equal players in the marketplace or the home. It was still assumed that the husband was responsible for family maintenance and protection, even though he would no longer control his wife's property, and the wife was given no claim on goods accumulated through the joint labour of spouses. The continuing belief in the necessary authority of the husband and father, despite the passage of legislation granting husbands and wives equal rights over their separate property, is clearly reflected in the fact that under this act wives could, under exceptional circumstances, apply for control over the wages of their minor children. Under normal circumstances, however, children, and their productive power and wages, remained the exclusive right and responsibility of the husband. Not surprisingly, this Act failed to solve all of the problems that had emerged under earlier legislation.

Without joint ownership of family property and joint liability for family debts, creditors remained at the mercy of unscrupulous husbands and married couples; even once the husband was denied rights of trusteeship over his wife's separate estate, husbands and wives could transfer property from a liable to a non-liable spouse, misrepresent who actually owned what property, and evade debts with impunity. The myriad ways in which fraud continued to be committed are documented in chapter 9, and these cases suggest that information about legal changes was diffused rapidly amongst a surprisingly legally literate populace.[18]

More important, from a feminist perspective, without joint ownership of family assets the majority of wives were denied the theoretical benefit of separate property. In a context in which most wives continued to labour in the home, without economic remuneration, they lacked adequate ready money to leave abusive partners. The ownership of a significant amount of separate property, narrowly defined as wages or inherited property, was impossible for most married women. The married women's property acts did not acknowledge the economic value of women's domestic labour. Marriage, despite the nineteenth-century rhetoric of domesticity and the veneration of motherhood, was not considered an economic partnership, and the contribution of the wife as mother and homemaker was not granted legal recognition. Wives were not granted any claim on the property accumulated by the joint labour of spouses. Without access to ready cash while in the home, without any claim on family property, and without any place of refuge, many wives remained trapped in abusive and unhappy marriages despite the protective intent of legislation. The legislation, therefore, failed in its central objective – protecting unfortunate, supposedly exceptional women from irresponsible and violent men. This failure is documented in chapter 10, but may have been much less apparent to contemporaries. The rhetoric of equality – and the fact that better-off women could use the legislation to their own advantage – may have reduced the incentive for further examination of the impact of property law reform in the period after 1884.

The overwhelming theme to emerge out of this study is that despite considerable judicial sympathy for abused and abandoned wives and popular support for property law reform, the new laws did not serve women's needs. I have sought to understand not only why this was the case, but also the ways in which women attempted to use the legal system, despite its flaws, to their individual advantage. Some of the women whose stories are told in the following pages suffered severe mistreatment at the hands of men, but they were not simply passive victims. They courageously asserted their right to decent treatment and sought punishment for irresponsible and violent husbands, making the court a forum for the articulation of new standards of manliness. Some of them, moreover, astutely manipulated the statutes, acting as partners in fraud, defying stereotypes of feminine behaviour and thereby illustrating for posterity the potentially enormous variation in nineteenth-century marital behaviour.[19] The law, as these cases illustrate, is not a dry subject removed from everyday life. Despite the theoretical importance of these acts that acknowledged the wife's separate legal identity, and despite the fact that some individual women used the acts to their personal advantage, married women's property law reform left an ambiguous legacy for the twentieth century. Under the various married women's property acts, judges retained enormous discretion in determining cases between husbands and wives. The outcome in such cases continued to hinge not on a sense that women were entitled to independence, but on 'the perceived significance and character of the victim and the offender,'[20] of the wife and the husband. The central ideological presumption that underlay these reforms – the notion of chivalry – legitimates male control and protection of women on the basis of the belief that women themselves are weak and defenceless. The responsibility for such protection simply passed from family patriarchs to male representatives of the state. As Kate Millett has eloquently asserted, 'while a palliative to the injustice of women's social position, chivalry is also a technique for disguising it.'[21] The concept of chivalry has yet to be eliminated from law and society. This study illustrates the limitations of formal equality in a society still permeated by economic inequality and a belief in the necessity of feminine dependence. It should also serve as a salient reminder that property law is of real importance only to those in society able to earn and to own.

Although the focus of this study is historical, it is simultaneously informed by a concern with the present state of the law. Inherent in the arguments that follow is a belief that feminists ignore law – both in theory and in practice – at their peril.

1

'So Entirely under His Power and Control': The Status of Wives before Reform

The symbolic importance of married women's property law reform is only clearly elucidated against the backdrop of the common law treatment of the married couple. Under the common law doctrine of marital unity, in the words of the eminent eighteenth-century jurist, Sir William Blackstone, 'by marriage the husband and wife are one person in law: that is, the very being or legal existence of the woman is suspended during the marriage, or at least incorporated and consolidated into that of the husband: under whose wing, protection and cover she performs everything.'[1] As Blackstone also made clear, marital unity, or coverture, was based explicitly on subordination: 'the wife is regarded as distinct from her husband, but so entirely under his power and control that she can do nothing of herself, but everything by his license and authority.'[2] Unity was achieved only by the obliteration of the legal personality of the wife. The legal assumption that husband and wife were one person and that the one person was the husband informed social beliefs and values and imposed a myriad of practical disabilities upon the average wife, of which the inability to own and control property was only one. Perhaps more importantly, it reinforced and legitimated a way of thinking about marriage that was extremely hierarchical and restrictive for women. It is important to note, moreover, that it was not gender, but marital status, that ensured a woman's subordinate legal status. Single women had most of the civil rights of men and could own, manage, bequeath, buy, and sell property, had full rights of contract, and could sue and be sued in their own names; they lost all these rights, however, upon marriage.[3]

Men and women approached marriage as theoretical equals, but the decision to marry was, for women, the most important decision in life. Because the husband was legally obliged to support his wife, and because women had limited employment options, all of which offered rather meagre wages, for most women marriage 'was life's most promising material enterprise.'[4] Marriage, at least potentially, offered significantly greater material security than remaining a spinster, most likely in the family home under the watchful eye of parents. However, because the wife lost all her civil rights upon marriage, her future happiness depended entirely upon the husband's temperament and sense of responsibility. As one author asserted in 1828, 'in the fate of a woman, marriage is the most important crisis, it fixes her in a state of all others the most happy or the most wretched.'[5] Marriage was the central institution that shaped most women's adult lives and was celebrated as a woman's highest calling. It is ironic, therefore, that marriage represented civil death for the wife.[6]

The wife's subordinate status in marriage was fundamental not only to the common law, but to Western religion, philosophy, and culture. The Judaeo-Christian heritage provided much of the theoretical basis for the common law fiction of marital unity.[7] Blackstone's assertion that 'by marriage the husband and wife are one person in law'[8] had a clear scriptural basis: 'man leaves his father and mother and is united with his wife, and they become one.'[9] Marital unity had a parallel in the canonical doctrine of the unity of the flesh. The husband's ultimate authority in marriage, the fact that his wife could do nothing except 'by his license and authority,'[10] was also consistent with Christian teaching. St Paul enjoined wives to 'submit yourselves to your husbands as to the Lord. For a husband has authority over his wife just as Christ has authority over the church.'[11] He also instructed husbands to 'love [their] wives just as Christ loved the church and gave his life for it.'[12] This relationship, while hierarchical, implied mutual responsibility; according to St Paul, a husband should 'love his wife as he loves himself. No one ever hates his own body. Instead he feeds and takes care of it.'[13]

Under the common law, as in Christian teaching, the husband was expected to use his authority in the manner of a benevolent despot. In theory, the disability of the wife was balanced by the responsibility of the husband for her maintenance and protection, the husband's duty to 'feed and take care of [her],' and in this the relationship between husband and wife paralleled those between master and servant, father and child, and lord and vassal, and reflected the feudal origins of the common law. By marriage, the wife assumed her husband's name and by extension his rank and social status. The husband, taking responsibility for his wife's care and maintenance and assuming liability for her debts, also gained control of all her property, assets, and the potential products of her labour. It was presumed that the husband 'by his education and manner of life, has acquired more experience, more aptitude for business, and a greater depth of judgment than the woman,'[14] and was therefore better prepared than the wife to provide for the family and to ensure its financial viability. Legal treatises emphasized the responsibilities attendant upon husbands, not their rights.

When husbands behaved in accordance with scriptural dictates and the common law assumption of maintenance and protection, the wife's lack of legal identity was not oppressive in practice. For this reason, the common law probably worked tolerably well for many early nineteenth-century Upper Canadian families and its flaws are more evident in retrospect, in the context of an individualistic society concerned with gender equality, than they would have been to contemporaries of Blackstone.[15] In happy marriages decisions were potentially made jointly, irrespective of the state of the law. The husband, however, had the power to be a despot if he so desired. Despite the importance of a woman's labour in a frontier community, ownership of family property was the sole right of the husband.[16] For this reason, it was a simple matter for the husband to evade his common law responsibilities; he could refuse to support his wife and children, desert his family, or mistreat and abuse his dependents until they fled. The problem with the common law system of marital relations was not its emphasis on family unity, which simply reflected not only religious beliefs but also the fact that most families did labour jointly to accomplish common economic and social goals, but that the rights of the husband were absolute and unfettered. The law assumed the good faith of the head of the household, and the wife – like the other subordinate members of the family unit – had no means by which to protect herself when her legal guardian failed to act responsibly.

Under the unreformed common law, married women were extremely vulnerable, particularly in Upper Canada, for two central reasons: marriage, once entered into, was not any ordinary contract, but was indissoluble; and wives could not own property and thereby support themselves even in the case of separation unsanctioned by state and church. Wives could not sever their formal ties to their husbands. Access to divorce throughout the Anglo-American world was limited; in Upper Canada it was virtually nonexistent. In England, a wife could apply to the Ecclesiastical Court, one of the church courts with long-established authority on questions regarding the validity of marriage and concerning the sexual morality of the family, for an order for a divorce *a mensa et thoro*, a divorce from bed and board without the right of remarriage. A divorce *a mensa et thoro* could be issued upon certain limited grounds such as extensive physical abuse, adultery, and desertion, and the Ecclesiastical Court could also grant such a wife alimony. The ecclesiastical courts, however, were administered exclusively by the Church of England and, because of the religious plurality that characterized Upper Canada, were not established here. For this reason, legal separation and alimony were unavailable to Upper Canadian wives until 1837, when the new local Court of Chancery was granted jurisdiction over 'all cases of claim for alimony that is exercised and possessed by any Ecclesiastical or other Court in England.'[17] Even after 1837 the collection of alimony remained difficult; perhaps more importantly given the centrality of marriage in women's strategies for achieving material security, without the right of remarriage a separated woman faced bleak economic prospects. In Britain, until 1857, a divorce as we understand it, with rights of remarriage, could only be obtained by a private act of Parliament, an expensive and cumbersome process; this exception to the general indissolubility of marriage was intended primarily to provide relief for rich men who might otherwise be cuckolded and find themselves legally responsible for children born of their wives' adultery. The English Matrimonial Causes Act of 1857 established divorce courts separate from Parliament and made divorce affordable for a larger, although still limited, percentage of the population, but retained a gender imbalance in terms of when the remedy of divorce would be deemed appropriate. Women could petition for divorce only on the basis of aggravated adultery – adultery accompanied by abuse, bestiality, sodomy, or desertion; simple adultery, even on a single occasion, sufficed to justify a husband's petition.[18] This distinction was based upon the belief that 'the wife's infidelity is followed by results of a graver character than those which follow the infidelity of the husband.'[19] Ultimately, this created 'in favour of the male sex a monopoly of justice and redress.'[20] However limited the relief it offered women, the Matrimonial Causes Act was itself not even adopted by the Parliament of the United Canadas. Any expansion of access to divorce was opposed in Catholic Canada East. At Confederation, in 1867, divorce became a matter for federal jurisdiction, but the continued opposition of Quebec and a widespread perception that the liberalization of divorce law south of the border had unleashed immorality ensured that divorce reform would be controversial and therefore avoided.[21] Although provinces that had adopted some form of divorce procedure before Confederation were enabled to continue existing practice, provinces without any pre-Confederation mechanism for divorce could not establish divorce courts without federal approval. This ensured that the history of divorce in Canada, as Wendy Owen and J.M. Bumsted have asserted, is 'a veritable quagmire of inconsistencies and contradictions.'[22] Legislative divorce remained the only means, for Ontario couples, of permanently ending a marriage and of providing the former spouses with the legal right to remarry. As had been the case in England, such divorces were expensive. Although the first legislative divorce in Upper Canada had been granted as early as 1839, no woman was granted legislative relief until 1877. After this time the proportion of wives to husbands increased, and in the 1888 case of Eleonora Tudor-Hart the legislature departed from British precedent and granted the wife a divorce purely on the basis of the adultery of her husband.[23] Despite this, however, divorce remained rare well into the twentieth century, and no divorce court was established for the province until 1930, ensuring that divorce remained a privilege of the élite, not the democratic right of all grieved spouses, a fact that had particularly harsh consequences for wives.[24]

Of course, even without access to formal divorce procedures, couples could and did separate by mutual consent or by unilateral desertion, but property regulations provided a formidable barrier to independence for women whose husbands were abusive, irresponsible, or merely opposed to separation. Since the husband was legal owner of all property that his wife might earn by her labour, inherit, or bring to marriage, even if the couple ceased cohabitation, women faced enormous obstacles in supporting themselves, let alone any dependent children, outside a functioning heterosexual family. The common law granted the husband extensive powers over his wife's property on the basis of the fact that he was legally responsible for her maintenance and support. As one observer of the law argued in the Toronto *Daily Mail* in 1872, 'it may be stated generally that all her lands and chattels pass on marriage to her husband for their joint lives. The maintenance and protection afforded by the husband are considered sufficient compensation for such surrender by the wife.'[25] These provisions, of course, provided little security for women whose husbands failed to maintain and protect them.

Upon marriage all the wife's real property, her land, was transferred to the direction and management of the husband. Although he could not dispose of the land his wife brought to marriage without consulting her, all profits from it were his absolutely. The land could only be alienated if both the husband and wife consented to this action and signed a joint deed of conveyance. When such conveyances were executed, the wife had to be examined separately by a magistrate to ensure that she was signing such a deed 'freely and without coercion or fear of coercion.'[26] As one critic of the law of married women and their property later argued, however, 'so far as the protection of the wife's interests was the object of this ceremony, it was well understood to be useless. If the execution of the conveyance was procurable by coercion, the acknowledgment or assertion of freedom from coercion was procurable by the same means.'[27] Although the separate examination was intended to ensure that a husband would not abuse his power and sell his wife's property against her will, only to leave her destitute, nothing guaranteed that the profits from a sale to which a wife was forced to agree, or the profits from crops or other products of the wife's land, would be used for her benefit.

If a woman outlived her husband, the land that she had brought to marriage reverted to her control and was not inherited by the husband's relatives. She also had a legally recognized one-third inchoate life interest – a right of use but not of alienation or disposal – in all the lands that her husband had owned during the course of their married life. Upon her husband's death, the wife became entitled to this life interest, known as her dower.[28] Consistent with common law provisions for the married couple during cohabitation, dower extended the husband's responsibility for his wife's maintenance beyond the grave.[29] Common law dower was intended to provide the wife with security against the interests of her husband's heirs and creditors and to prevent poorer widows from becoming a public liability.[30] As the *Upper Canada Law Journal* argued in 1857, dower was, in principle, equitable; it provided 'for the support of a widow out of the lands of her deceased husband ... for the sustenance of herself and the education of her children.'[31] In practice, however, the dower portion often failed to provide widows with adequate support because it gave the wife a life interest in realty, a right to enjoy but not to alienate such land; it did not give her a claim on any personal property or the money or chattels owned by the husband. In 1857 the editors of the *Upper Canada Law Journal* lamented the problems that the law of dower posed for the average widow in a farm-based community:

She claims dower. What is that? The third part of her husband's lands for life. Of what use is the third part of 100 acres without a house upon it, to a widow without means? Sell it ... she cannot. Till it ... she cannot. Eat it ... she cannot. Truly, the widow asks for bread; but the law gives her a stone. She wants 'sustenance' or that which will provide sustenance for her – in other words she wants money. The law does not provide that she shall recover money. It provides that she shall recover an estate in land which is not convertible to money. So far the law practically fails to give that which it professes to give – the required relief.[32]

More important, dower only became operative upon the death of the husband. During marriage or coverture a wife could make no such claim on her husband's lands, even if he abandoned her and left her destitute.

In the case of the wife's death, the husband had a life interest in the lands that his wife had brought to marriage only if a child had been born of the union. This interest was referred to as the curtesy of England. Curtesy provided an inheritance for children of the marriage, and the fact that the husband had only a life interest in such land ensured that it would not be squandered. When no children were born of a marriage, the wife's real property reverted to her own family, as to allow the husband to continue to control such land would be to risk that it might be inherited by the children of a second marriage. The rules regarding curtesy stand in stark contrast to the law of dower, and reveal the unequal status of husband and wife within marriage. Wives were believed to require support whether or not children were born of the marriage, while it was assumed that a man could be responsible for his own maintenance.

The wife's personal property – her furniture, money, farm animals and implements, and all other non-land forms of property – was not even accorded the minimal protection evidenced in dower, but was acquired absolutely by the husband. He could dispose of these goods without her consent and could bequeath them, even to the exclusion of her children. With her husband's formal legal consent a woman could bequeath her personal property, but her husband had the right at any time to revoke such approval. These provisions applied to all money and chattels that a wife brought to marriage except her 'paraphernalia,' her clothes and intimate personal items. These could be sold during the husband's life, but they could not be willed to anyone but the wife. Because the wife owed services to her husband, even the wages that she might earn by her daily labour belonged to him. A particularly unscrupulous husband could inform an employer that his wife's wages were to be paid directly to him. Because all the wife's chattels and money belonged legally to the husband, even property that she might accumulate during a period of separation could be sold without her consent and the profits retained by the husband.[33] The husband's ownership of the labour of his wife and children undermined the ability of female-headed households to ensure their own survival. The common law provisions regarding family property also created a tremendous problem for parents who distrusted prospective sons-in-law; gifts at marriage and inherited property became vested in the husband, and parents could not ensure that any such land, money, or chattels would be used for the benefit of their daughters or potential grandchildren.

The wife was a legal nonentity. The husband was responsible for his wife's physical well-being, and was 'bound to provide his wife with necessaries by law, as much as himself.'[34] Yet it remained difficult for women to force their husbands to live up to the responsibilities imposed upon them by the common law. Under a primitive theory of agency, the common law recognized the right of the wife to enter into contracts as the representative of her husband, imposing upon him the obligation to pay any debts she might thereby incur. In happy marriages this might give women considerable scope for economic activity and involvement in the wider community; even in such cases, however, the wife acted only as the deputy or representative of her husband. Blackstone argued that the wife was thereby assured of support, since 'if she contracts debts for them, he is obliged to pay them.' However, the proviso that 'for anything besides necessaries, he is not chargeable'[35] illustrates the powerlessness of the wife. The husband and the court, not the wife, had the power to determine what items were necessary; moreover, the right of agency was discretionary and it was not uncommon for men to advertise that their wives were not to be granted credit for any reason. Over the course of the nineteenth century hundreds of Upper Canadian husbands placed notices in local newspapers that they would not 'be accountable for any debts she contracts from this date, nor will I allow any of my debtors any money they pay her on my account.'[36] Such notices had the force of law and served to absolve the husband of any further legal responsibility for his wife; the wife, without legal rights of her own, was thus left in a state of legal limbo.

The wife was more than a legal nonentity; she was, in essence, the property of her husband. The husband had a proprietary right to all his wife's services, including her sexual services,[37] and if she was injured because of the misconduct of a third party, he could sue for damages.[38] Moreover, he had powers of physical control over his wife that indirectly encouraged abusive, or at least domineering, behaviour. Because the husband acquired, upon marriage, legal responsibility for all his wife's actions and debts, he had the right to restrain her, theoretically to prevent her from contracting debts, or committing criminal acts, for which he might later be held liable;[39] as Blackstone put it, 'the law thought it reasonable to intrust him with the power of restraining her, by domestic chastisement, in the same moderation that a man is allowed to correct his apprentices or children.' According to Blackstone, this right of moderate correction was limited to nonviolent acts.[40] In the privacy of the home, however, such limitations were difficult to enforce. Not only did this legal hierarchy ensure that women were physically and economically vulnerable, but the language of law, by classifying women with children, apprentices, and other legal incompetents, was in itself insulting.

Obviously, not all wives suffered equally under the disabilities imposed by the common law. Even when husbands were gentle and loving, however, such a legal regime reinforced and perpetuated an extremely hierarchical vision of spousal relations. And the absolute power vested in husbands left women who had unwittingly married irresponsible or abusive men very vulnerable. A married woman had no legal identity and no means of protecting herself or her children. Her husband bore this responsibility, despite the fact that in some cases it was from her own mate that a woman was most likely to require protection. In this context, the nineteenth-century demand for married women's property law reform entailed a radical critique of the patriarchal ordering of the family. By seeking the right to own property themselves, women asserted, albeit obliquely, that they were no longer willing to be property.

Despite the problems faced by wives under the common law, in Blackstone's estimation, 'even the disabilities which the wife lies under, are for the most part intended for her protection and benefit. So great a favourite is the female sex of the laws of England.'[41] By the mid-nineteenth century, however, few Upper Canadian observers of the common law would have agreed with this assertion. The beginnings of the first industrial revolution and the remarkable growth of towns and cities that occurred at mid-century may have contributed to the perception that common law provisions for wives were becoming archaic. As early as the 1850s the pull of urban centres such as Toronto and Hamilton, for the native-born as well as for immigrants, was becoming apparent, particularly since available land for farming sons was dwindling.[42] In an urban setting, the dependence of families on wages rather than on the produce of the land increased the opportunities for husbands to misappropriate family money and chattels. On the farm, the produce of the land assured the families of even the most parsimonious and abusive of men at least the means for subsistence; in the urban setting, however, cash was necessary for basic survival, and husbands had legal control over money, which was much more readily squandered or alienated than a family farm.[43] The husband could appropriate the wages of his wife and minor children, refuse them support, and waste all family earnings on mistresses, booze, and riotous living; his family had no recourse. Moreover, the easy mobility and transciency that characterized non-land-owning families made desertion an ever-present and increasingly visible problem.[44] After desertion, or even informal separation by mutual consent, the wife and any dependent children found themselves in legal limbo. Whatever property they might accumulate still, at law, belonged to the absent husband, who might return and reclaim such goods without warning. In some cases, no doubt, unhappy couples separated by mutual consent and husbands continued to support their wives, or at least allowed them to support themselves without interference. Even these women, however, remained dependent upon the goodwill of men, a precarious situation at best. These conditions made the problems inherent in the common law doctrine of marital unity both visible and disturbing, and the fear that female-headed households would become a drain on the public purse undoubtedly contributed to a growing sympathy with the plight of deserted wives.

Of equal importance, beliefs regarding the proper behaviour of spouses within marriage were changing during the nineteenth century, a fact that encouraged a re-evaluation of the common law provisions for wives. Marriage in the middle ages, when the common law provisions for spouses were established, had been a political, economic, or social strategy, and marital property law reflected the importance of dynastic control of land. As the importance of kinship ties and economic considerations in the choice of a marriage partner declined, companionship came to be seen as the cornerstone of the marriage relation.[45] Moreover, in both the United States and the United Kingdom, the two great sources of immigration into Upper Canada in the early nineteenth century, liberal and democratic ideology had gained new momentum; in particular, Jacksonian democracy, abolitionism, and the rise of liberalism in Britain brought legal inequality of all kinds under greater public scrutiny. While much of the rhetoric of democracy and equality continued to exclude women, it could not help but influence attitudes towards relationships between individuals within families. The men and women who settled the vast lands of Upper Canada brought these changing ideas and ideals with them. Arguably, also, the obvious importance of female labour on the family farm, the most important economic institution in a frontier community, encouraged greater respect for women's traditional domestic labour.

Although the rise of companionate marriage contributed to the willingness to reconsider property law, the choice of a partner on the basis of modern, romantic, or companionate ideals did not in itself ensure that marriage would be egalitarian. In his controversial work on the evolving family, Edward Shorter has defined the idea of companionate marriage as 'the hallmark of contemporary family life, the husband and wife being friends rather than superordinate and subordinate, sharing tasks and affection.'[46] This definition, however, overemphasizes the ideal of spousal friendship and obscures the inequality that continued to characterize much of the discourse surrounding marriage and, undoubtedly, the reality of many marriages.[47] Companionate marriage softened patriarchy but did not eliminate it. The ideal of friendship between husband and wife did not necessarily undermine the husband's position as the 'superordinate' partner in marriage. The ideal wife as portrayed in romantic and Victorian literature – and advice manuals – was not an independent and assertive individual, but rather a giving and docile helpmate, who 'revere[d her husband] and minister[ed] unto him.'[48] Moral, spiritual equality is not the same thing as social equality, and nineteenth-century liberalism emphasized the difference between these two concepts.[49] The companionate ideal of mutual love and respect was not incompatible with the belief that wives should not only esteem their husbands, but also 'submit themselves completely to [them].' The wife was exhorted always to 'behave obligingly' to her husband, to 'avoid contradicting' him, 'to command his attention by being always kind to him, to preserve order and economy, and never to forget that a wife owes all her importance to that of her husband.'[50]

While the companionate emphasis on love and respect did not eliminate hierarchy within the family, it did encourage rising expectations within marriage and create new standards of acceptable masculine behaviour. New definitions of manliness imposed an obligation on the husband to treat his wife with dignity, reverence, and love. As the editors of the Toronto *Daily Mail* argued in 1876:

Coarseness, rudeness and tyranny are so many forms of brute power, of what it is man's particular glory not to be. The obligations of gentleness and kindness are extensive to the claim of manliness. These three qualities must go together.[51]

Such beliefs did not challenge the fundamental right of the husband to direct and manage his household and dependants, but the means by which it was deemed acceptable for a husband to enforce his authority in the family became increasingly circumscribed. As one author asserted in the Toronto *Daily Telegraph*, wifely obedience and subordination would be more likely if men treated their wives with respect:

Let a husband be the true and pure guardian of his family, labouring always to adorn himself with the godlike gems of wisdom, virtue and honor; let him bear himself in relation to his wife with gracious kindness towards her faults, with grateful recognition of her merits, with steady sympathy for her trials, with hearty aid for her better aspirations, and she must be of vile stock if she does not revere him and minister unto him with all the graces and sweetness of her nature.[52]

Affection and patriarchy, as this passage illustrates, could and did coexist; moreover, the ideal of the husband and wife being friends was not always reflected in reality. None the less, evolving beliefs about marital relations encouraged a reconsideration of the common law rights and responsibilities of spouses. Particularly when husbands were negligent in their performance of marital duties, good wives could increasingly be viewed as deserving of aid and relief.[53]

The hierarchy still implicit in the evolving companionate family was reinforced by the gender-based division of labour that characterized the nineteenth century and that ensured that wives, even those who worked for wages, remained economically dependent upon their husbands. As the economy became more complex and as production moved from the home, the companionate family came to be seen as a 'haven in a heartless world,'[54] and woman's place was increasingly circumscribed within the confines of the home. The development of the sentimentally viewed nuclear family and of new standards of acceptable masculine behaviour coincided with the rise of what has come to be known as the 'cult of domesticity,' a widespread veneration of women and of their importance as mothers and keepers of the hearth.[55] As the Reverend Robert Sedgwick, a popular Canadian speaker on the subject of the domestic sphere of women, argued in 1856, men and women were believed to have complementary social roles and responsibilities:

Woman is the equal of man, alike in the matter of intellect, emotion, and activity, and ... she has shown her capabilities in these respects ... It would never do, however, from these premises, to draw the conclusion that woman ... is bound to exert her powers in the same direction and for the same ends as man. This were to usurp the place of man – this were to forget her position as the complement of man and assume a place she is incompetent to fill, or rather was not designed to fill.[56]

Above all other aspects of women's domestic role, motherhood was revered and eulogized; the editors of Montreal's *The Witness Weekly Review and Family Newspaper* asserted in 1846 that 'a mother's teaching, example, precept, training, throw a weight into the scale which counter-balances all other human influence. Then, of man, in general, it can be said, he is what his mother makes him.'[57]

Not only were women actively encouraged to seek solace and their life's work and satisfaction in the domestic sphere and in the service of others, but the economy and social beliefs combined to deny them other viable opportunities and options. What wage labour did exist was primarily designed for single women and was paid at a rate that precluded independence.[58] Wage labour was, moreover, available primarily in urban centres.[59] Many working-class wives, while still responsible for child rearing, did not have the luxury of refusing wage employment and performed piecework or laundry and other domestic services in their homes; but such work was anything but liberating.[60] Even employed wives, moreover, remained financially dependent upon their husbands, since women could find work only in the lowest-paying job ghettoes and because their wages belonged, at law, to their husbands. The most common strategy for working-class survival when husbands' wages were inadequate, the hiring out of older children, also did little to liberate either children or their mothers. Fathers owned the productive capacity and wages of all minor children. The domestic ideal of exclusive concern with home and children coincided with reality most closely for women of the middle class.[61] Even for the middle-class women for whom domesticity was a reality, however, this ideology was less than emancipatory. As Nancy Cott has argued, domesticity 'articulated a social power based on [women's] special female qualities rather than on general human rights.'[62] Women's domestic labour, performed increasingly in isolation in the home, was denied economic remuneration; while the popular idealization of the home may have given wives a sense of gratification and the confidence to start seeking greater social power, it did nothing to provide them with economic independence or to allow them to escape from marriages that were less than ideal.

The decline of economic concerns as a reason for marriage helped to make feudal property law appear archaic; moreover, individual husbands who failed to conform to evolving standards of manliness, to fulfil their responsibilities under the common law, were increasingly perceived as undeserving of the rights attendant upon such responsibility. Greater respect for wives and mothers, however, had not been translated into legal rights, a fact that encouraged women to publicly demand decent treatment and protection from irresponsible and abusive husbands, protection that would allow them to enjoy their rightful and important domestic sphere. A growing minority of articulate men and women saw the harsh provisions of the common law as an affront to the integrity and dignity of all wives and mothers.

It is in this context that married women's property law was incrementally reformed. The reforms in Chancery and the various married women's property acts described in this book were intended to protect women from the worst consequences of their husbands' potential misbehaviour. As several authors have illustrated, however, such changes did not emancipate women but transferred male responsibility for dependent, weak members of the family unit – women and children – from the husband and father to the state, particularly the judiciary.[63] In cases of male irresponsibility or abuse of power, the male-defined and male-dominated state took it upon itself to provide chivalric protection for women who were still perceived as unable to protect themselves. Moreover, the impact of reform was limited by class as well as gender bias. Legislators, judges, and the literate members of the middle class who advocated reform perceived male irresponsibility as primarily a working-class failing, closely associated with intemperance; as female reformers asserted in a petition to the legislature in 1857, 'unequivocal is the injury sustained by women of the lower classes ... she may work from morning to night to see the produce of her labour wasted in a tavern.'[64] The married women's property acts can be considered another aspect of the multifaceted middle-class response to urbanization, industrialization, and growing class consciousness.[65] Although a critique of patriarchal property relations is inherent in reform rhetoric, any radicalism was muted by the biases of class and gender that shaped the world view of reformers and of the judges who interpreted legislation in the courts. These ideas simultaneously provided an incentive for change and limited the shape that reform could and would take.

2

'A Life That Is Simply Intolerable':
Alimony and the Protection of Wives

In 1835 Ellen Fitzgerald, an illiterate farmwife from Niagara, with the aid of more fortunate and literate members of her community, submitted a dramatic plea to Lieutenant-Governor John Colborne. Her husband had recently been released from prison and was threatening her life:

Since the return of my husband from Toronto, where he was, as well as here, imprisoned for a supposed murder, I have not had one days peace with him often beating and abusing me in a shameful way. That on Sunday last he beat and abused me out of all character as a wife and on Monday he beat, kicked and took one of my hands and held it in the fire until it was severely burnt, choaked and undertook to cut my throat with a razor he took out of his hat, which he would have effected had he not taken compassion for the prayers of a little one of mine when he desisted from his horrid purpose. That I have made or had cause to be made, applications to several magistrates to bind him over to keep the peace all which proved fruitless since which he has threatened to take my life and I have not the least doubt that he will do it if he can get the opportunity. Therefore I humbly pray that your majesty will have the goodness to direct or command some one of the magistrates here to attend to the subject.[1]

The outcome of this case is not evident from the file, but Ellen's predicament stands as a telling indictment of common law marital regulations and of the legal fiction of marital unity. Ellen had no legal rights separate from the husband who threatened her life. The farm that she had maintained during her husband's absence belonged exclusively to him and she had no right to exclude him from the premises. She herself could flee, but she did not have rights of custody over her children and could not receive legal sanction for separation from her husband or claim support in the form of alimony. The common law assumed that all husbands protected and cared for their wives and denied women any recourse when men failed to perform such duties. For these reasons, Ellen sought special dispensation and petitioned for mercy. It is unclear what specific solution Ellen believed the lieutenant-governor could provide for her problem, but her petition illustrates that she understood her own powerlessness under the law and looked upon the head of state as a patriarchal arbiter of justice.

Although Ellen's case was particularly extreme, before 1837 and the establishment of the Court of Chancery the legal prospects for all abused and abandoned wives in Upper Canada were bleak. An abused wife could seek a peace bond from a local magistrate to restrain her husband from beating her, but the practical availability and impact of such orders, as Ellen's case illustrates, was limited.[2] While anyone who had supported a separated woman could sue the woman's husband for maintenance costs, such suits had no guarantee of success, and the wife herself could not sue her husband.[3] The right of the husband to control all family property meant that a deserting husband could easily abscond with any and all family resources, leaving his wife and children destitute. A wife could not sever her legal connection to her husband, even when cohabitation had ceased, and he retained all rights to her person, property, and children. A particularly vindictive or greedy husband could seize and squander any property that his wife managed to accumulate during a period of informal separation. Economic opportunities for married women outside the family were very limited, and if a woman could find employment her daily wages belonged at law to her husband.[4] Most women who left their husbands, therefore, had to depend upon the charity of family, neighbours, or friends for simple survival. Unhappy couples could arrange out-of-court separation agreements, but contracts between husband and wife could not be enforced in the courts of common law, leaving the wife dependent upon the goodwill and sense of responsibility of her estranged husband for her future maintenance, a precarious situation at best.[5]

The failure to establish any proceeding by which a wife could receive legal sanction for separation and claim alimony against an errant spouse left Upper Canadian wives excessively vulnerable, even by comparative nineteenth-century standards; in England and in most of the American states, separation and alimony were available. For this reason, under the Chancery Act of 1837 the newly established court was given 'authority and jurisdiction in all cases of claim for alimony that is exercised and possessed by any Ecclesiastical or other Court in England.'[6] This directive, however, was ambiguous. The English Ecclesiastical Court granted alimony only in conjunction with a judicial separation – a *divorce a mensa et thoro* – and the Upper Canadian Court of Chancery was not given jurisdiction over divorce in any form. The chancellors had the right to enforce support payments, but not to give legal validity to separations themselves. This legislative failure to provide the court with a clear mandate for action could have been used to nullify the legislation. Instead, the Upper Canadian chancellors applied this directive in its broadest possible sense and asserted that they had an obligation to provide relief to the battered and deserted wives who sought their protection.

The jurisdiction of the court to grant alimony was explicitly challenged in 1851.[7] Hannah Soules had proved to the satisfaction of the court that her husband's ill-treatment and threats rendered it 'unsafe for the plaintiff to reside with him,'[8] and that she was therefore entitled to alimony. Counsel for the defendant did not challenge the evidence and freely admitted to violence, 'but he contended that the court had no jurisdiction to grant the relief prayed.'[9] Admitting that the legislation did not give jurisdiction to deal with questions of divorce, Chancellor Blake none the less asserted that the authority to grant alimony, and thereby *de facto* recognition of separation, was implied by the enabling statute. He also argued that if his extension of the powers of the court were erroneous, it 'must be corrected by a higher tribunal.'[10]

This call for a clear mandate through unambiguous legislation was echoed in 1852. Again, counsel for the defendant challenged the right of the court to grant alimony. Blake reiterated his belief that 'the state of the law upon this subject, second to none in extent and importance, must be admitted to be highly unsatisfactory.'[11] Despite this admission, alimony was granted. The intention of the chancellor was to push the legislature to clarify and confirm the jurisdiction that the court had already acted upon. In 1859 the legislature responded with an amendment to the act regulating the Court of Chancery. The jurisdiction of the court in alimony litigation was clarified, and cruelty, desertion, and adultery – the bases which in England would entitle a wife 'to a divorce and alimony as incident thereto' – were confirmed as the bases upon which a woman could petition for such spousal support in Upper Canada.[12]

Under the amended Chancery Act, alimony cases were heard in several county centres on a rotating basis throughout the year,[13] but before the hearing a bill of complaint had to be served to the central Chancery office in Toronto. The bill of complaint had to be prepared by a solicitor and delivered to the court, and a duplicate delivered to the woman's husband or his attorney. All of this could be quite costly.[14] It was the rule of the court, as Chancellor Blake asserted in *Soules v Soules*, 'that the wife has a right to have her costs at all times. The reason is, because there are no other means of obtaining justice, since the marriage gives all the property to the husband.'[15] Costs to the plaintiff, however, were not awarded until the case had been brought to hearing and the amount of such costs could be determined; ready money, therefore, remained a substantial obstacle to successful prosecution. Without cash of her own, a wife who was unable to obtain financial assistance could easily be forced to drop her charges. The procedure, moreover, was clearly beyond the means of many wives, since unless husbands had substantial property or income there was little point in attempting to claim support.

In this context, it is not surprising that although the occupations of the husbands in these cases varied widely, all had achieved at least moderate economic success.[16] The financial constraints women faced in prosecuting their husbands are also predictable, since under the common law family property belonged only to husbands. Wives' options were also constrained by the limited job prospects available to women in the nineteenth century. Few of these wives were themselves employed. Only ten of the three hundred wives who petitioned for alimony between 1837 and 1900 mentioned their own employment as a potential source of support: four of these women claimed to work at odd labour in order to put food on the family table; one wife was a washerwoman; one worked as a milliner; one ran a boarding-house; another was a private teacher; one ran an inn; and one had been driven in desperation to enter domestic service. In seven of these cases, the husbands in question were in the habit of claiming and appropriating their wives' earnings, often using such funds for alcohol and thereby undermining mothers' desperate attempts to feed their children. Most women, not surprisingly, were housewives, many on farms, with limited access to cash, a fact that constrained their ability to leave abusive spouses, particularly if they had young children.

Instead of alleviating the financial problems that wives faced, court procedure exacerbated them. The length of alimony proceedings favoured the interests of men. After a bill of complaint was filed, a husband had 40 days in which to respond with a statement of defence. The fact that notice of a suit had to be filed with the husband or his solicitor provided husbands with warning and opportunity to sell family property and to abscond before the law could catch up with them.[17] Even when their petitions were successful, therefore, women remained at the economic mercy of their husbands.

Despite these problems, alimony represented an important theoretical improvement over the common law. No longer did desperate wives such as Ellen Fitzgerald have to seek justice through *ad hoc* petitions to the government. The existence of a legal remedy in cases of male irresponsibility and abuse allowed women to articulate new standards of acceptable marital conduct. While wives still had to petition an all-male audience to seek justice, they could at least now do so in a context in which, under clearly defined conditions, relief was viewed as a right, not a privilege. The chancellors explicitly acknowledged that, at least in some cases, the interests and needs of the wife could be diametrically opposed to those of her husband; the court had an obligation to protect the interests of the wife against the common law power of the husband.

That women negotiated these new rights in language that simultaneously emphasized their acceptance of domesticity and the imperative of wifely obedience should not be surprising. Nineteenth-century definitions of femininity emphasized women's natural motherly love, capacity for forgiveness, and moral superiority, and reinforced the values that encouraged women to put up with abusive husbands. The cult of domesticity reflected a division of labour that kept most married women out of the paid work force and economically dependent on their husbands, severely limiting their options within abusive relationships. This fact illustrates the central contradiction that would plague much nineteenth-century reform. Women sought protection from abusive men, and judges and reformers attempted to enforce new standards of chivalrous conduct, but women were still considered incapable of protecting themselves; they were not believed to be the equals of men in general, of their husbands in particular. In this context, petitioning the court for a decree of alimony was a courageous act. In order to challenge the rights of their husbands, wives had to make their private lives very public. In articulating new standards of masculine behaviour, these women presented an inherent, if obliquely articulated, challenge to notions of femininity that demanded silence and self-denial, particularly within marriage.

Petitioning the court was also an act of desperation. Battered, betrayed, or deserted by the very men who, the law assumed, would protect and care for them, these women, despite the sympathetic response they would receive from the chancellors, would have found little that was comforting or reassuring in the physical environment of the court. The chancellors were wealthy, educated, and privileged men drawn from the ranks of the élite established families of the province;[18] most of the women who came before this court were from much more modest economic and social backgrounds. Many of them lacked even a rudimentary education; of the 311 cases examined,[19] it is clear that at least 25 wives were illiterate and signed their legal documents with an X. This should not be particularly surprising, since many of these men and women would have reached adulthood before the introduction of public and compulsory schooling.[20] Illiteracy did not provide a fundamental barrier to economic success in a farm-based economy.[21] It would, however, have contributed to the awe, and perhaps the fear, inspired by the judicial process. The nineteenth-century court was the exclusive domain of men; women could not serve as either lawyers or judges. The formal rituals of court and the robed and wigged majesty of judges would only have served to heighten women's perception of the class- and gender-based differences that divided judge from judged.[22] Recourse to the court was usually the final step in a long-standing process of informal negotiation. Wives hoped that the formality of the court would inspire awe and fear in their husbands and that the chancellors would be able, where social and family pressure had failed, to force husbands to pay support or to resume cohabitation.

Despite these hopes, the court, while sympathetic, was usually ineffective; even when granted alimony, few wives received support from their estranged husbands. But to acknowledge the problems of the legislation should not be to argue that the chancellors were unmoved by domestic violence or male abuse of economic power.[23] The chancellors consistently took the side of women; the nineteenth-century belief that wives were the moral superiors of their husbands placed the onus on the husband to disprove his wife's charges. Even in cases in which husbands contested their wives' complaints with counter-complaints of violence, ill temper, neglect of household duties, and drunkenness, the chancellors rejected their assertions that such behaviour justified either abuse or desertion. They argued instead that 'under such misconduct of either of the parties, for it may exist on one side as well as the other, the suffering party must bear in some degree the consequences of an injudicious connection, must subdue by decent resistance or by prudent conciliation: and if this cannot be done, both must suffer in silence.'[24] The chancellors deliberately extended their mandate to deal with domestic problems and broadened strict legal definitions of adultery, desertion, and cruelty.[25] Few women –

only 5 of the 311 extant cases – were denied relief, although winning in court did not in itself provide any guarantee that women would actually receive the money that was owed to them.

The chancellors were authorized to grant alimony on the bases of adultery, desertion, and cruelty, and in each of these types of cases they acted with consistent sympathy and support for women. Adultery, particularly in cases of bigamy or venereal disease, was perceived by wives and the chancellors alike as a fundamental denial of the basis of marriage itself.[26] The chancellors did not expect wives to passively accept male promiscuity, particularly when it was accompanied by other behaviour that was harmful to the wife. For example, in 1869 Ellen Conroy petitioned the court for alimony on the basis of her husband's sexual transgressions before their marriage; she had no evidence that her husband had committed adultery. She asserted in her petition that previous to their marriage, and unbeknownst to her at the time, John Conroy had had 'considerable intercourse with prostitutes.' After seven months of cohabitation, Ellen contracted venereal disease. John Conroy insisted that the symptoms from which she was suffering were caused only by a cold; he refused to allow Ellen to see a doctor and instead provided her with 'the same medicine the doctor had cured him with.' Ellen's condition did not improve, and John became increasingly defensive and abusive, locking Ellen in the house and refusing to allow her to see family and friends. She finally escaped, had her fears confirmed by a doctor, and sought refuge from John's abuse with her sister. Shortly after submitting this petition, Ellen was persuaded to return to her husband. In court again in 1876, however, Ellen won her case. Despite John's vehement protestations of his innocence and his complaints that Ellen did not 'fulfil her duties to him as his wife,' the court granted Ellen relief. Ironically, John Conroy complained specifically that his wife did not fulfil her sexual duties within marriage; she countered that he forced her to perform 'unnatural acts' that had caused her undue psychological suffering.[27] Clearly the chancellors did not agree that the wife owed sexual services, particularly 'unnatural' ones, to a husband who had transmitted venereal disease to her, although it is unclear whether relief was granted in this case because of John's adultery, his sexual 'deviance,' the violence he inflicted upon his wife, or the three combined.[28]

Similarly, men who deserted their wives had failed in their primary duty as breadwinners. The chancellors recognized that, for the wife, financial support was of central importance within the marriage bargain. By English precedent, a wife could not claim to have been deserted until her husband had refused to cohabit with her for a period of two uninterrupted years; in practice, this meant that a husband could live apart from his wife, refusing to support her, and return for a few days each year only to prevent her from initiating proceedings against him. The Upper Canadian chancellors, however, accepted petitions from wives immediately after their husbands' desertion. They were willing to define desertion in broad terms, arguing that extreme cruelty on the part of the husband that necessitated the departure of the wife, and 'the exclusion by the defendant of his wife from his house,'[29] constituted cases of legal desertion. Desertion was a very public offence.[30] The greatest problem that deserted wives faced was not convincing the chancellors that they were deserving of relief, but bringing their husbands to trial. Deserting husbands, because of the power they wielded over family property, could plan their escapes in advance and sell, convey, or lease property before their departures, effectively leaving their wives without legal remedy. When her husband fled the country, a wife's most practical course of action was probably to form a new, technically illicit, marriage, rather than to take any form of legal action against her lawful spouse.[31]

Most important, the chancellors accepted masculine authority in the family, but they did not sanction domestic violence. Wives were beaten, kicked, slashed with cooking knives, scalded with kettles full of boiling water, threatened with loaded revolvers, half-strangled with ropes, bedsheets, and riding-whips, and often were left bruised and bloodied to tend to their wounds without assistance. The chancellors viewed such treatment with disgust. Men who abused their wives indulged in behaviour that the chancellors characterized as 'reckless and unmanly cruelty'[32] and which proved them unfit to fulfil the responsibilities placed upon them by the common law. The chancellors asserted that with the privileges accorded to men in marriage came heavy responsibility. The state, as a surrogate and protective father, was willing to punish its errant sons-in-law.

Cruelty was potentially the most difficult branch of alimony litigation, largely because in most cases abuse took place within the privacy of the home and in the absence of witnesses. It was also the most common complaint made by wives; the majority of women – 201 of 311 – sought alimony in order to escape what they described as the 'gross cruelty' of those who had sworn to love and honour them. It is in this area of litigation that judicial innovation is most striking and important. The definition of cruelty inherited through British litigation was limited and strict:

The law as laid down in the more modern cases, as well as in the older ones, lays upon the wife the necessity of bearing some indignities, and even some personal violence, before it will sanction her leaving her husband's roof ... There must be actual violence of such a character as to endanger personal health or safety; or there must be the reasonable apprehension of it ... The ground of the Court's interference is the wife's safety, and the impossibility of her fulfilling the duties of matrimony in a state of dread.[33]

Despite this restrictive definition, the chancellors overwhelmingly supported the petitions of women who sought relief from the cruelty of their husbands. They relied increasingly on the idea of reasonable apprehension of violence – the belief on the part of the wife that violence would be a certain result of cohabitation – as a justification for granting abused women alimony. They also rejected the British rule that condonation of cruelty prevented women from claiming abuse as a reason for alimony. In cases of adultery, condonation of the offence implied permanent and irrevocable forgiveness, but the chancellors acknowledged that 'cruelty is cumulative, admitting of degrees, and augmenting by addition, so that it may be condoned and forgiven for a time and up to a certain point without any bar in sense or reason to bringing it forward when the continuance of it has rendered it no longer condonable.'[34] In both these ways, they transformed the legal definition of cruelty itself.

The contempt that the chancellors felt for abusive husbands is well illustrated by the case of Margaret Haffey. In her 1867 petition, Margaret asserted that she had married John Haffey in 1844 and had borne six children, 'doing all incumbent upon her to do as such wife.' She argued that she had 'always conducted herself in a proper and becoming manner,' yet she had been subjected to violence, bad language, ill temper, and unreasonable conduct. On many occasions her husband had forcefully evicted her from their home, leaving her in the chill of winter without clothing or protection. She had miscarried their third child after being beaten 'until senseless' and kicked down the stairs of their farmhouse. She had been threatened with brooms, whips, and farming implements, and had suffered in silence for over 20 years. She claimed that in the last few months before her petition the violence had intensified and that her life had been in 'constant danger.' None the less, she emphasized her willingness to return to the defendant 'if he would receive her and comport himself as a husband should.' Margaret Haffey asserted that she had a right to be treated decently, to be a companion to her husband, and to be treated with dignity and respect.

Her husband, however, rejected the rhetoric of companionate marriage. In his written answer to these charges and in the hearing that was conducted by the court, John Haffey delineated a view of marriage that was explicitly hierarchical and used these beliefs to defend his actions. Haffey was a successful farmer who had served both as a police magistrate and as a local justice of the peace in Simcoe County; his knowledge of the law of husband and wife was extensive, and other women seeking peace bonds against abusive husbands would clearly have met with little success in his court.[35] He emphasized the common law right of the husband to control and chastise his wife, children, and apprentices, and denied that he had ever ill-treated the plaintiff. He admitted that he had, on occasion, locked his wife in their house and had used physical force to restrain her. He argued, however, in a statement that echoed William Blackstone, that his behaviour was within the realm of reasonable and moderate correction:

If I have on a few occasions struck the plaintiff, it was never with violence or with the intention to injure her and only when I was utterly exasperated by her and that the correction was moderate and just and such as a husband has a right under the circumstances to give. I deny that I ever abused or ill-treated her.

Although Haffey's children had also fled the farm in fear, had suffered extensive abuse themselves, and had given telling testimony in favour of their mother, he asserted that his wife had no just reason to be 'in fear of her life' and that her claims were exaggerated:

I don't believe that my wife was afraid of me because I was a police magistrate and knew the law. I don't know that she was afraid to take proceedings against me because I was a JP and I don't believe it. I gave the rest of my family no cause to leave me. I don't believe it was my bad temper that drove them off. I don't know what my temper is, but I have not got a quick one.

In an attempt to discredit his wife's testimony, Haffey argued that she was 'of a very violent temper' and 'often refused and neglected to cook my meals.' Asked to explain the source of their marital conflict, John Haffey asserted that 'the causes of complaint I have against my wife are bad treatment, bad temper, bad food, jealous minded, contracting debts without my consent.' His central source of anger, however, was his wife's alleged habit of 'countervening my orders and directions.' Questioned directly about his beliefs regarding the role of his wife, Haffey admitted that he 'had no complaint of her housekeeping if she would have left me alone.' She 'interfered with business' by helping a neighbouring woman during her confinement, which took her away from his home, and by her interaction with the children. Haffey did not accept the rhetoric of companionate marriage; in his view, his wife should serve as his personal servant and should not expect to be respected by him or to take any part in the moral upbringing of her own children:

Q: What do you consider her business was?

A: To keep the house clean and comfortable, attend to my wants, and cook the victuals.

In this contest of character, John Haffey was perceived by the chancellors as an unmanly bully, and Margaret was awarded $240 *per annum* in permanent alimony.[36] Despite the sympathy of the chancellors, however, it is not surprising that Margaret Haffey was married for twenty-three years before she gathered the courage necessary to leave her abusive spouse. She was economically dependent on him, and had been terrorized by his daily brutality and hostility and taunted with the fact that 'she had no rights at law' to family property or to her children. Also not surprisingly, all her children were grown and had left home by the time she finally confronted her husband in court; in fact, she was living with a grown daughter and son-in-law at the time of her suit, and without such a place of refuge escape might not have been possible. Despite such support, Margaret did suffer from economic problems in attempting to bring her case to hearing. At one point in her proceedings, Margaret's solicitor sent a letter to the court stating that Margaret 'could not proceed unless the necessary disbursements for interim fees and other expenses were paid by the defendant.' It is unclear how Margaret obtained the money necessary to continue proceedings; perhaps her husband paid up when threatened by the court, or her children helped her; or perhaps her solicitor, sensing that she would win, agreed to delay payment pending the completion of the case. It is ironic that Haffey had to be threatened regarding the payment of interim alimony, for ultimately he was one of the few men in the extant cases who did pay the permanent support awarded by the court. Possibly, given his self-assurance regarding his interpretation of the law of marriage, he failed to flee or to insulate his property from seizure on the assumption that Margaret's suit would be unsuccessful.[37] If so, his confidence was misplaced. Margaret had unquestionably proved that the violence to which she had been subjected was frequent and life-threatening. This case was not a precedent-setting one, and it was not reported. The existence of many similar files in the unreported court documents, however, suggests that at least some nineteenth-century judges were sympathetically disposed towards abused wives, not abusing husbands.

Increasingly, moreover, such strict evidence of repeated abuse was deemed unnecessary. *Rodman v Rodman*, a reported case heard in 1873, forever altered definitions of legal cruelty in Ontario and codified a growing judicial reliance on apprehension of violence, rather than violence itself, as a sufficient justification for granting wives alimony. Ann Rodman petitioned the court for alimony, alleging as her cause physical violence on only one occasion and habitual drunkenness. According to strict legal definitions of cruelty, while clearly reprehensible, the actions of Ann's husband were neither sustained nor life-threatening and would not have been sufficient to warrant a decree for alimony. Despite this, Ann won her case.[38] Viewed in conjunction with unreported cases, *Rodman v Rodman* emerges as the most significant alimony case to be heard in Ontario in the nineteenth century. It set a new, and much more reasonable, legal definition of marital cruelty.

The Rodmans had been married for over eighteen years, and Ann Rodman's husband was a habitual and notorious drunkard. Although he had not physically abused her before the week of their separation, his behaviour had been menacing and she had come to live in fear. He frequently threatened his wife with physical chastisement to enforce his will, and she claimed that his drunken rantings were incoherent. She finally left his home after a particularly disturbing episode following a drinking spree:

I left the last day of August last. I have not lived with him since. I left on account of his ill-treatment, and I was afraid of my life stopping with him. I left on a Saturday. On the Thursday previous he had been at Little Britain. He brought some beer home, and before night was the worse of liquor. He went down into the cellar where the beer was kept. I was sick and did not wish him to make so much noise. I was afraid of him when he was in liquor.[39]

Ann then fled in fear but returned the next day, in the presence of two male friends, to talk to her husband, 'to see if he would give up drinking altogether, and throw away what he had, and then I would continue to live with him. If he had promised I would have gone back.'[40] In response to this ultimatum, in the words of one of Ann's male witnesses, the defendant 'went towards her, picked up a rod from the grass, found fault with her, and went at her and struck her a few times. She screamed and ran behind us, and then down into the field, and he told her to begone.'[41] From this day onwards, Ann refused absolutely to return to her husband.

At the circuit court level, the case was heard by Vice-Chancellor Strong, who awarded Ann alimony. The case came to be reported because Mr Rodman appealed this decision, claiming that the court did not have a mandate to grant alimony on the basis of only one incident of violence. On full hearing in chambers in Toronto, Chancellor Spragge and Vice-Chancellor Blake upheld Strong's decision and thereby transformed the legal definition of cruelty in Ontario.

Spragge held that Ann's 'apprehensions of personal violence and for her personal safety were genuine, and were unhappily too well founded ... Her request that he would abstain from drink was perfectly reasonable.'[42] She could expect that, should she return to her husband's house, future abuse would be likely to follow, and 'the law does not put it upon the wife to continue to fulfil the duties of matrimony when her personal safety is compromised.'[43] It was the duty of the court to protect the weak and the innocent:

It is well to consider what we must hold if we refuse relief in such a case as this. We must hold a wife bound to submit to blows, to be kicked at, to be held by the arm with her husband's fist threatening her face; to be told to begone and such other like violence and indignities as a husband brutalized by drink may inflict; and still be bound to live with him and endure it all, and live, in short, a life that is simply intolerable. The law of England, in its care that husband and wife should not be separated on slight grounds, has gone far enough in exacting endurances from the wife.[44]

Spragge implied in this summation that the law, in its concern for the family, showed insufficient interest in the wife.

The ruling was also upheld by Vice-Chancellor Blake, although he defended his decision in more conservative terms than did Spragge. He was concerned with the example Rodman had set for his children and with the fact that Rodman had banished his wife from his home, and he was clearly influenced by the rhetoric of the nascent temperance movement:

[Drink] which so completely unfits the husband for the duties which he has, as such, undertaken – which turns him, who is bound to be the protector and guardian of his family, into a being incapable of holding this position, whose conduct leads them into that which he should teach them to shun, and opens the door in others to a freedom and laxity, the effects of which may be seen in the ruin of his children, should have been considered as a sufficient cause for grounding a temporary separation.[45]

Blake expected a wife to obey her husband, but this belief in the ultimate authority of the husband within marriage was not incompatible with the rhetoric of companionship and mutual respect. Blake demanded that a husband use his power in a responsible and loving manner, and would have expected an extensive forbearance on his part had it been the wife who was the drunkard. When the husband, the natural 'protector and guardian of his family,' failed in the performance of his duties, the court was willing to intervene in the privacy of the home. Despite this sympathy, however, Ann Rodman later lost a court battle for custody of the children she had left behind when she fled her husband's home. She was deemed to have insufficient income to support her family, and since her husband had never threatened the children themselves, he was not believed to be an unfit parent. It is unclear whether or not she returned to her husband's home at this point in order to be with her children.[46] While this case, therefore, highlights a growing judicial revulsion at domestic violence, it also illustrates the limitations of alimony as a solution to the problems faced by abused wives.

Cases heard after the Rodman decision illustrate that the chancellors used this new, more inclusive, definition of cruelty to the benefit of the women who sought their protection. For example, in 1881 Georgina Malloch petitioned for alimony after four years of marriage. She had previously taken proceedings against her husband in Manitoba, but the defendant 'by promises of amendment prevailed upon the plaintiff to stay the proceedings.' Georgina asserted that 'she had always conducted herself as a wife should,' but that her husband had threatened her and had used abusive language. He had publicly humiliated her by attacking her virtue, calling her a 'whore and a slut.' She argued that he provided a pernicious moral example for their three-year-old son, whom he had threatened to remove from her custody. She did not claim that he had ever committed any acts of physical violence and she was not afraid for her life. She was miserable, but she was not, by any legal definition, an abused wife. Despite this, Georgina won her case. An order preventing her husband from disturbing her custody of the children was issued by the court and she was granted $600 in maintenance for the year. The only limitation the court placed on this decree was that it was temporary. After

the one-year period had elapsed, the court would review further develop-
ments and determine whether or not permanent alimony was warranted.[47] The court had clearly overstepped its jurisdiction in two ways: it
did not have a mandate to provide decrees of temporary alimony, and
according to established precedent Georgina had not presented a cause
that would provide legal justification for leaving her husband's home.
The court's definition of cruelty had evolved beyond recognition from the
strict terms inherited from English litigation. Unfortunately, no further
documents relating to this case could be found, and it is unclear whether
the couple again came before the court. Perhaps they continued in their
separation by mutual consent, or Georgina was again convinced to return
to her husband on promises of amended behaviour. It is also possible that
further court documents have been lost or that her husband failed to pay
the money awarded by the court, and that she simply lost faith in alimony as a solution to her problems.[48]

As these cases illustrate, the chancellors displayed a consistent sympathy for abused and abandoned wives, and used judicial discretion to
expand the scope of legislation; alimony, despite this fact, was of limited
practical value for many women. Recourse to the court was outside the
means of many women. Financial vulnerability – concerns related to children and the relative ease with which men could abscond – ensured that
the majority of the petitions during this period (168 of 311) were dropped
by wives before cases could advance to hearing. This ensured that many
separated wives, particularly those with *de facto* custody of dependent
children, would live in poverty.

In theory, the court protected women and alleviated their financial
problems by granting interim alimony to all wives. The policy that
'where the marriage is admitted, or proved, interim alimony will be
granted as a matter of course, and notwithstanding that defendant
swears he is willing to receive and maintain the plaintiff' was established
in 1866. Refusal to grant such interim alimony, it was acknowledged by
the court, was tantamount to forcing the wife, who could be deserving of
relief, to return to her spouse, a potentially dangerous prospect.[49] In
practice, however, this measure was difficult to enforce. In 24 of the 168
cases that failed to advance to hearing, interim alimony payments that
had been granted by the court are known to have been outstanding; this
may have been true in other cases, as in the majority of files no reason is
given for discontinuing proceedings. Inability to collect interim alimony
would not only have discouraged the belief that a decree for permanent
alimony would ensure economic support, but could also have forced

women to abandon litigation because they could not pay the fees required by their solicitors. One complainant outlined this problem explicitly in 1875:

I am utterly without means to take the cause to hearing at the said sittings. Pursuant to my undertaking, when undertaking was given it was so given on the faith of the Defendant paying the interim alimony awarded and in the absence of his paying the same I have no means of obtaining money for the purpose of supoenaing witnesses and retaining counsel for the Hearing.[50]

Not surprisingly, this suit did not come to trial.

Even when wives had alternative sources of funds, court proceedings could prove fruitless. Husbands could deliberately place their property in the hands of friends and relatives and then claim that they were unable to pay the interim or permanent alimony awarded by the court. For example, Julia Holmes had married in 1880, and at the time of her marriage her husband had been a clerk in his father's store. Shortly after the marriage her father-in-law had taken her husband in as a partner in the business. His monthly proceeds from the store had averaged $60. The partnership had ostensibly been dissolved in 1883. Her husband, she argued, was being paid 'a salary of $30.00 a month ... but always received from his father much more than that amount.' She asserted that the partnership had deliberately been dissolved in order to avoid the possibility that her husband might have to pay her alimony, as she had threatened to leave him because of his abusive behaviour:

No satisfactory reason for the dissolution of the said partnership was ever given and I then believed and am of the opinion still that such dissolution took place and the defendant was put upon a minimal salary for the purpose of defeating me in any claim I might make for alimony as shortly before the dissolution of the said partnership my father, Henry S. Bermes, told the defendant's father of the defendant's cruelty to me as I am informed and believe and also of the possibility of my taking legal proceedings if such cruelty was not discontinued.

This case provides a tantalizing glimpse into the extralegal social pressures that were imposed upon husbands in an effort to change abusive behaviour. These pressures and ultimate recourse to the court, however, were of no avail, and although Julia was granted interim alimony of five dollars a week, she never received any payment and eventually dropped her suit. Her parents had funded the petition, but on the husband's refusal to pay even interim alimony, and in the light of her father-in-law's collusion with his son, they probably decided that further prosecution would be both ineffective and costly.[51]

Even when wives did successfully complete the process of prosecution, husbands could ignore court orders with impunity. For example, Frederick Fell had subjected his wife to severe and frequent abuse. He failed to respond to her bill of complaint, and the case was decided against him. But Frederick had conveyed his lands to a son from a previous marriage, and all writs of seizure, issued to enforce the payment of alimony, were unsuccessful. In September 1877 Frederick, who was living in Barrie and was therefore still within the reach of the court, was ordered to Toronto for an accounting of his real estate. Under examination he asserted: 'I have made up my mind not to answer any questions as to what I have done with my money or to whom I have lent it or where it is.' Although the court issued a warning that if he continued to neglect the alimony order, 'you will be liable to arrest by the Sheriff and you will also be liable to have your estate sequestered,' this was an empty threat. Having already vested his property nominally in others, Frederick had no property that could be seized, and under the Insolvent Act of 1869 a debtor could not be imprisoned merely for an inability to pay his debts.[52] Not surprisingly, Frances did not receive her alimony. This case helps to illustrate the myriad ways in which the structure of law was inherently antithetical to women's interests. In such a context, alimony, despite the sympathetic hearing women received in Chancery, was of limited value.[53]

Many men simply disappeared in order to evade alimony orders. The planning that some husbands put into their escapes is evident in the case of Amelia and Arthur Richardson. Amelia was granted permanent alimony of $150 *per annum* in November of 1878 on the basis of cruelty. By this time, however, it was too late for such a ruling to be of any practical value to her. In a letter to his solicitor dated April 1878, Arthur Richardson outlined his plan to abscond before the trial could come to hearing:

I have the sanction of my family and friends and shall dispose of all I do not want with me when I get word from you. Marriage consists in the union of man and woman as to their love and interests, not in the mere legal sanction. Since the feeling, I may say, has altogether gone between my wife and self, I feel relieved of any responsibility to her and in consequence cannot see why I should waste my time and my happiness for no justifiable reason. I shall be better elsewhere when I can commence again and make myself a good income and another home ... If out of her reach I can build up again, I shall seek the love of another who will throw some sunshine into my life ... I have but one life to live and I intend to get all I can in happiness and prosperity.

Knowing her husband's intentions, Amelia applied for and was granted a writ of arrest. Arthur's brother posted bail of over $800 and secured his release from jail. Once free, Arthur transferred nominal ownership of all his property to his brother. He then left the country. Not surprisingly, Amelia was unable to make good on the alimony awarded her. Although Arthur's desire for marital happiness and a fresh start are understandable, he deliberately denied his wife the benefit of property that she had helped him to accumulate during a seventeen-year marriage; his use of the rhetoric of companionate marriage, in this context, is highly ironic.[54] The ease with which Arthur avoided repsonsibility for the maintenance and protection of his wife illustrates the limitations of alimony.

Failure to pay alimony awarded by the court was an endemic problem; only in 9 of the 78 cases in which alimony was granted is it certain that such money was received by the wife. In many cases the records do not reveal whether or not alimony was actually paid, but evidence from other court proceedings suggests that nonpayment was the rule rather than the exception. For example, in one case for which no decision is extant in the alimony documents, other litigation proves that alimony was awarded, but that the husband refused to pay. In 1873 Helen Melville was awarded permanent alimony. Her husband never paid the money owed to her, and she supported herself and the couple's blind daughter by working as a schoolteacher. It was explicitly noted by the court in this case that Helen Melville was 'a negress,' the only woman of colour to appear in any of the cases found in the unreported files.[55] Helen was very successful in supporting herself, and she eventually purchased a home with her earnings; given the overwhelming racism of the time, her achievements were remarkable. Her lawyer erroneously included her husband's name on the deed of ownership of her home. When her husband learned of this mistake, he threatened to sell the property and to use the proceeds to support his second wife, with whom he was living in the United States in a bigamous marriage. The husband himself was struggling to survive on his wages as a vaudeville performer, and the possibility of claiming this property must have been very tempting. Helen was granted a *lis pendens* to prevent him from alienating the land, and ultimately her sole title to it was confirmed. Her husband then returned to the United States and expressed no further interest in his wife or their child.[56]

Not only was it difficult to enforce collection, but alimony was only a right of maintenance, parallel to dower; it did not provide any inalienable claim on the property accumulated during marriage by the joint labour of spouses. The work that women performed in the home, on family farms, and in other enterprises was not acknowledged in law; all property accumulated during marriage belonged exclusively to the husband, and the wife's only possible claim was for basic support. The hardship that these beliefs could create for wives is clearly illustrated in the case of Mary Ann Watts. Married in 1850, Mary Ann had worked with her husband at an unspecified trade until he deserted her in 1873. She claimed to have 'contributed greatly to the accumulation of their common property'; at law, however, 'common property' did not exist. Before leaving for England, Isaac Watts had sold most of their land and had cleared $4,000 of stocks; he also took with him all of the savings upon which Mary Ann had counted to support her in her approaching old age. Isaac defended his actions by arguing that 'the plaintiff has only worked with and assisted me in the way any working man's wife is accustomed to work with him and assist him by managing and attending to his household duties.' As a self-proclaimed 'responsible husband,' Isaac had left Mary Ann in possession of one of his houses in Toronto. He acknowledged that, as his wife, Mary Ann had a certain claim on him for minimal support; he rejected out of hand, however, any arguments for compensation due on the basis of labour that had helped him to accumulate property. Domestic labour and assistance as required in a trade were, according to this view, simply part of the duties that a wife owed her husband.[57] Although the chancellors were sympathetic with regard to the abuse Mary Ann had suffered, they did not question the validity of Isaac's assessment of her role as his wife. The economic dependence of wives on their husbands, a dependence that greatly increased wives' vulnerability, was central to nineteenth-century definitions of femininity. The cult of domesticity eulogized the role of women as mothers and keepers of the hearth, but did not carry this veneration to its logical conclusion and recognize the economic importance of female contributions to family survival. The economic vulnerability inherent in the doctrine of separate spheres and domesticity could not be more clearly illustrated, and in this context alimony could never hope to provide an adequate remedy for wives' legitimate grievances.

The economic dependence of married women was reinforced by the presence of children in the family home. When wives, in fear of their lives, fled from the marital home, they could be refused access to their children entirely, since this left husbands with de facto custody. In five of the petitions brought before the chancellors, women complained that their husbands had denied them visitation rights with their children since separation. Even more frequently, violence against children accompanied wife abuse. Wives stayed with abusive husbands, often suffering extra hardships because of their efforts to protect children. For example, Jane Bavin was granted permanent alimony of ten dollars a month in 1895 and had suffered through thirty years of abuse at the hands of a drunken, tyrannical husband. One labourer who had worked for her husband and boarded with the family testified that she had put up with this violence in order to protect her young children:

I left because I considered him a dangerous man and I considered it dangerous to live with him. I did not consider it safe for the plaintiff or any of their children to live with him ... I found that he was in the habit of carrying a loaded revolver and I also found that he was a very passionate and abusive man ... They had an 11 year old son and I understood the plaintiff was remaining there to try to protect him and I have seen the defendant swing the revolver in the house and the little fellow crying in fear and the plaintiff pale and trembling with fright.[58]

Another mother complained that her husband 'strikes and beats the said children and they are in dread of the said defendant insomuch that they fear to eat or speak in his presence.' Hannah Lalonde, the mother in this case, petitioned the court twice during this period. Not only was her husband physically abusive with her two young sons, but he had sexually molested their two teenage daughters. He had been cleared of rape in these cases because, she claimed, at the last minute the daughters refused, due to fear, to testify against their father, despite the fact that the youngest daughter had borne a child of this incestuous relationship. Her husband also had a fourteen-year-old concubine living in the family home.[59] A woman's love for her children would have encouraged such mothers in the belief that it was a woman's duty to remain in an abusive relationship, as another mother described it, 'for the sake of the children and to avoid depriving them of a home and protection.'[60] As one mother testified, so that the children would 'not be deprived of a mother's care, she has borne with the defendant's conduct longer than she would or ought to have borne with the same.'[61] Clearly, she assumed that she would be unable to take her children with her if she fled the marital home.

The case of Caroline Scott provides a particularly poignant illustration of the obstacles that young mothers had to confront when attempting to leave abusive husbands. From early in her marriage Caroline had suffered physical abuse at the hands of a domineering husband. In July 1871 she had her husband arrested and bound over to keep the peace, but he broke the peace bond and from the time of his arrest his treatment of her worsened. She finally left him and sought refuge with a friend because he was 'keeping her in constant terror.' After filing her bill of complaint, however, she was induced to drop her suit. Her youngest child, whom she had taken with her when she left her husband, had become ill. Unable to pay for necessary medical treatment, Caroline returned to John because he had the financial resources necessary to save the child, but he refused to do so as long as Caroline remained apart from him.[62]

Without access to family resources and lacking opportunities in the job market, married women faced enormous obstacles in supporting their children outside the family unit. This problem was compounded by custody law. Under the new custody provisions of 1855, upon proof of abuse or negligence on the part of the husband, a wife could be granted custody of children under the age of twelve.[63] However, these provisions were not intended to equalize the custody rights of husband and wife. It was still considered undesirable to disrupt the husband's custody rights except in the most extreme circumstances; as the editors of the *Upper Canada Law Journal* put it, 'if the protection of the children can be obtained consistently with the common law right of the father to the custody of his child, that right ought not to be interfered with.'[64] In six petitions women accused their spouses of cruelty or incest and sought custody as well as alimony. Unfortunately, only one of these cases advanced to trial. Significantly, the wife in this case was granted both alimony of $600 per annum and custody of the children. The father was given minimal visitation rights of two hours on each last Saturday of the month and during vacations and illnesses. The plaintiff was forbidden to remove the children from the province.[65] As the Rodman decisions illustrate, however, even wives who were successful in their alimony suits could not be assured that they would be granted custody. It appears that custody was more likely to be granted if the wife included this demand in her original petition for alimony, since abuse of the wife herself was not considered relevant in custody hearings. In this context, not surprisingly, abusive husbands used the threat of custody battles to dissuade their wives from leaving. Luke Beatty's wife petitioned the court three times during this period and was each time induced to drop her charges and return to her husband. Beatty countered his wife's charges of cruelty with the assertion that she had left him without 'just cause' and had removed his child from his care 'without my permission.'[66] His implication that he would sue for custody of their son should her alimony suit meet with success was quite possibly one of the factors that convinced her to return to him.

It is not surprising that many wives waited until children were grown before leaving abusive spouses; over forty wives, all of whom had children, were married for more than twenty years before they filed for alimony, and in seven of these cases it is clear that mothers had taken refuge in the homes of adult children in order to prosecute their husbands. In five of these cases such married children had also funded their mothers' petitions for alimony. The most extreme example of such self-sacrifice is perhaps the case of Hannah Strong. Married for fifty-three years, Hannah stayed in her marriage to protect her children and only took refuge in the home of her grown daughter in 1880, at the age of seventy-five, when 'age and infirmity render[ed] it impossible for her to suffer in silence any longer.' In a sad conclusion to this tale, Hannah died before her case could be brought to hearing.[67] Unless their own parents were willing and able to help them, wives with young children did not have any such place of refuge.

Husbands could use their powers over children and financial resources to induce wives to drop litigation and return home or to nullify decrees for alimony that were granted. Despite these problems and limitations, however, alimony proceedings represented a significant improvement over the common law. Although it was relatively easy for husbands to plan their 'escapes,' those who deserted their wives more impulsively, and who failed to insulate their property by selling or conveying it, could find such property seized under writs of execution. For example, Mary Ann Turner's husband had abandoned her after twenty-five years of marriage to elope to the United States with a younger woman, but had failed to sell all of his property before absconding. She was granted $300 a year in permanent alimony, and she issued a series of writs against the property that her husband had failed to sell. Between 1877 and 1880 she collected $650 of the money owed her. At this point her writs of seizure ceased, presumably because no further property existed out of which the judgments could be paid.[68]

Perhaps more important, if a husband wished to remain in his community it was more difficult to insulate property from seizure. Alimony litigation reflected very poorly on the husband. In this context, for some husbands settlement with the wife was the best option. Afraid of the scandal that would follow an alimony suit, eighteen husbands are known to have settled out of court to avoid the cost and publicity of litigation. This may also have occurred in other cases; settlements had to be drawn up by solicitors but did not have to be filed with the court. The threat of alimony proceedings could itself be a powerful weapon. As one husband asserted in 1882, he had entered into an agreement with his wife 'with a view to avoiding the mortification of a public trial in which his domestic affairs would be exposed in public in a manner painful to himself and his relations.'[69]

Solicitors representing defendants in alimony cases were aware that the sympathy of the court lay with wives, not husbands, and that alimony was likely to be granted if a suit advanced to hearing. While some solicitors, as Arthur Richardson's case illustrates, may have provided their clients with advice as to how to evade payments by absconding or by conveying property, many would also have counselled defendants to avoid extra court costs by settling amicably with their wives. Solicitors representing plaintiffs in these actions used the acknowledged sympathy of the court in their attempts to force recalcitrant husbands to support their wives:

She is your wife, and as the law always looks to the reconciliation of these unhappy differences we trust you will in the meantime remember your obligation to her ... She now only asks that you will provide her with a fair allowance and permit her to live in peace ... We are sure it cannot benefit either party to have any of these things made public. Mrs. Coulson has expressly instructed us to exhaust every probable method of settlement before commencing a suit. We think your own judgment will lead you to conclude it will be for your benefit especially to have such matters kept quiet. An alimony suit usually has but one ending, and the legal proceedings are expensive.[70]

It is interesting to note that the wife in this case ultimately dropped her suit. She admitted that she had used the threat of alimony in an attempt to convince her husband to provide her with separate maintenance, although he had never behaved violently. Her bluff did not work, but this case raises the possibility that women used the threat of alimony as a way of forcing men to accept separation, even when marriages were simply unhappy. In adopting this course of action, they would have been aided by the fact that solicitors on both sides of these proceedings took it for granted that women who could prove adultery, desertion, or cruelty would be granted the alimony they requested.

For the same reason, the majority of cases in which alimony was granted were not considered worthy of being reported. For the period between 1837 and 1900, 311 alimony cases were found in the unreported court documents. Of these, 168 cases were dropped before they reached hearing; in 18 cases settlement is known to have been reached out of court; in 76 cases the alimony requested was granted; only in 5 cases was relief denied, and in the remaining 44 cases the outcomes are unknown. Between 1869 and 1881, the period for which the unreported court records are most complete and therefore provide the most accurate comparison with the law reports, 38 of 112 petitions for alimony reached hearing in the Court of Chancery. Of these, 33 were successful. In the five cases in which women's petitions for alimony were denied, four of the women had been proved to have committed adultery. In the fifth case the wife admitted that she had deserted her husband without legal cause. Men would not be forced to support wives when it was women who had violated their marriage vows. Perhaps more importantly, all of these wives had subsequently established common law relationships and were being supported by other men.[71] Of the 33 cases in which alimony was granted, only 3 appear in the reports;[72] in contrast, 3 of 5 of the cases in which alimony was denied were reported. These cases were reported because they were exceptional, not representative, and clearly any study of alimony and of judicial attitudes towards domestic violence is incomplete and potentially misleading if unreported cases are ignored.[73]

The establishment of alimony proceedings represented an important improvement over the common law. Women seeking support from irresponsible spouses received a favourable hearing from the chancellors. Recourse to alimony would have done little to protect Ellen Fitzgerald from a husband who was determined to stalk, threaten, and possibly kill her. The existence of even a limited legal weapon against marital violence, however, provided relief for some women whose husbands were less singleminded. Moreover, it helped to transform the discourse surrounding marriage itself; women could begin to think of decent treatment as a right, not a privilege. Women still had to appeal to men for relief, and the legal system had by no means undergone a feminist-inspired revolution. Recourse to alimony, however, represented a significant theoretical advancement for wives, and the chancellors sought to enforce mutual respect and forbearance within marriage. Although men who wished to do so could evade the payment of alimony with impunity, the threat of alimony proceedings none the less provided women with legal ammunition against abusive husbands. Men incurred significant social costs when they fled family and community to avoid payment. Despite the theoretical importance of alimony and the relief it provided in some cases, alimony litigation left an ambiguous legacy for posterity. Alimony was of little value to a woman whose husband did not own property or earn decent wages, and without some form of state assistance such wives remained locked in abusive relationships or were forced to separate without the sanction of the state and to live in perpetual poverty. Without improvements in other areas of the law, particularly the enforcement of peace bonds, some women continued also to live in perpetual danger, whether they left their husbands or not. Moreover, while alimony cases illustrated the need to mitigate the absoluteness of the husband's powers over his wife, these cases simultaneously reinforced the judicial perception that women were incapable of protecting themselves within marriage. The court was seen as the essential intermediary enforcing marital responsibility; property law reform at mid-century would incorporate this machinery of judicial patriarchy.

3

'To Properly Protect Her Property': Marriage Settlements in Upper Canada

In 1824 Hannah Snider's father, concerned about her husband's 'unsteady habits,' conveyed to her a life estate in fifty acres of land. Under the common law, however, the management and benefit from the property devolved upon her husband, Henry Nolan. Within a short period of time Nolan abandoned his wife, but he retained his interest in what was ostensibly her property, leasing it for profit until he sold it, without obtaining Hannah's consent, in 1856.[1] From the time of the desertion until her husband's death in 1864, Hannah lived 'dependent more or less on the charities of those who were acquainted with her, having none of the comforts of the home that her father hoped he had provided for her.'[2] For over thirty years the court was powerless to protect her interests; when Henry Nolan died, however, the court held that her life interest – her right to dower – reverted, and the property was removed from the individual to whom her husband had sold it.[3] In the interim, however, Hannah had suffered enormously.

Under the common law a father could give his daughter property before marriage, but such property automatically became vested in the husband and therefore did not provide the wife with income or security if her spouse proved to be reckless or abusive. In England, wealthy families could avoid this calamity by placing property in trust for wives in the Court of Chancery. Chancery or Equity, a separate body of law, had originated in England in the middle ages in the idea of the king's discretionary pardon, and had expanded gradually as a less formal system of law that supplied a corrective in cases in which the common law was too rigid. The chancellors saw themselves as the 'guardian[s] of the weak and unprotected.'[4] The court classified married women – along with lunatics and children – as legal incompetents who were 'weak and unprotected' under the common law. The trust in Chancery provided a mechanism by which families could ensure the future security of daughters. Legal title to property was not given to the daughter, or thereby the husband, but to a third party, the trustee. The trustee was obliged to manage the property in the interest of the daughter/wife and could be held accountable for his behaviour in the Court of Chancery. Trusts were expensive and cumbersome, and in practice were used only by the wealthiest members of the community, but even this limited protection was unavailable to women in Upper Canada until the establishment of the local Court of Chancery in 1837.[5] Before this time, when individuals came to Upper Canada with marriage settlements, such documents could not be enforced in the courts of the common law. Despite a knowledge, at least on the bench, that 'such a court [was] a most essential part of our establishment and many cases of hardship and instances of failure of justice must occur until it is established,'[6] considerable resistance to the introduction of a Court of Chancery in the colony had to be overcome. This opposition is perhaps attributable to the reputation of the English Court of Chancery for delays, outrageous expenses, and other problems. As John Spragge, later the chancellor of Upper Canada, asserted, 'it was from no love of a Court of Chancery that it was introduced, but in spite of many and strong prejudices.'[7] In this context, before 1837, Upper Canadian wives were excessively vulnerable, even by comparative nineteenth-century standards.[8]

With the introduction of the Court of Chancery in 1837, parents, at least those who were sufficiently well-to-do and legally astute, were provided with the means to prevent their daughters and potential grandchildren from being reduced to conditions of poverty. The new court was explicitly given jurisdiction over 'all matters relating to trusts.'[9] Marriage settlements, enforced by this court, placed property in the hands of a third party, the trustee, who was obliged to use the estate and any proceeds therefrom for the benefit of the married woman protected under the agreement. In England and in the American states wives could control their separate property themselves; the role of the trustee had, by the nineteenth century, become largely symbolic. In Upper Canada, however, trustees retained powers of control, management, and alienation over all separate property, real and personal. Despite the comparative conservatism of Upper Canadian marriage settlements, such arrangements denied the husband financial control over his wife, and the possession of separate property provided individual women with enhanced security and the possibility of escape from brutal spouses. Marriage settlements, however, were available to only a small minority of women. Despite this rarity, the procedure and theory of equity provided the most accessible and well-understood alternative to common law rules regarding marital property. The legislative reforms of mid-century that expanded wives' rights over their property were based upon local Chancery precedent. From 1837 onwards, the chancellors unwittingly influenced the course of statutory reform. For this reason, an understanding of how marriage settlements were viewed and enforced by the local courts is a necessary prerequisite to any examination of the various married women's property acts.

By 1837, the rules governing the acquisition and management of married women's separate property, both in England and in the American states, were comparatively liberal; married women could not only own but also actively manage their separate estates. This, however, had not always been the case. Rights of management and disposition had developed only gradually and under pressure created by an enormous volume of litigation. In the sixteenth century, when settlements were first recognized by the English chancellors, they were deemed valid only in cases in which there was good reason for the trust – for example, when the husband and wife were separated, or when the husband was known to be abusive or profligate. It was not until 1769 that the first settlement without a trustee was recognized in England.[10] Even after this time many restrictions remained on the wife's powers over her separate property. Until the late eighteenth century, women enjoyed powers over their separate property only to the extent that they were spelled out in the deed that created the estate. Each power – for example, the right to dispose of property by will or by contract between individuals – had to be explicitly enumerated in a separate clause in the deed. Restraints on anticipation, clauses that prevented the wife from selling or otherwise disposing of her estate, were widely used. It was feared that should the wife have absolute title to her property without the protection of a trustee or restrictions on alienation, the husband would be provided with the means to kiss or kick her into using the property for his own benefit.[11]

Gradually, despite these concerns, the powers of married women over their separate estates were expanded. In both England and the American states, several problems, made evident by an enormous volume of litigation, encouraged an enlargement of the rights of married women. One such problem was that the ambiguous position of settled property – property that the wife owned but that neither she nor her trustee could dispose of or alienate – created an inducement to fraud. While the wife controlled the income from her estate, but could not alienate the property itself, she might enter into contracts beyond her means, and her creditor could not force her to liquidate her property. As Richard Walkem later argued, 'it was strongly felt by the Court that there was great injustice in protecting a married woman, and allowing her to deprive others of their property, by entering into engagements which she must have known herself unable to fulfil in any other way than out of her separate estate.'[12] Moreover, husbands could give gifts of property to their wives, which would render the property inalienable and deprive their creditors of redress. Also, many cases of abuse of trust arose in which trustees misapplied funds to their own benefit; property was placed in the hands of individuals who were often less competent or less interested in the management of estates than wives themselves would have been. In the various American states the expansion of wives' rights of control over their separate property was also, Marylynn Salmon argues, linked to the liberalization of divorce laws. A woman who could divorce an abusive spouse had no need for protection from coercion; a husband's marital rights over property would cease upon divorce or judicial separation. Salmon also argues that the nineteenth-century companionate ideal of marriage caused a decline in judicial fear of coercion and that this allowed the chancellors to reduce the limitations placed upon married women's control of their separate property. As a result, Chancery 'destroyed the legal idea that husbands possess unusual and even secret means of influencing their wives.'[13]

For all of these reasons, by the beginning of the nineteenth century, in England and most American states wives could dispose of and manage their separate property:

A married woman now has an absolute power of disposition by act *inter vivos*, or by will, over her personal property, settled to her separate use, whether in possession or reversion, and over her life interest in the rents and profits of her real estate ... She may bind her separate real estate by contract so as to entitle the person with whom she deals to enforce specific performance of her agreement; and she may also make her separate estate responsible for her general engagements, provided such engagements are made with reference to and upon the faith or credit of, that estate.[14]

Not only was a trustee no longer necessary, but Chancery reversed the assumption that a woman's powers over her separate estate had to be clearly delineated in the settlement. Instead, wives were now assumed to have all rights of management over their property unless such rights were explicitly limited by the terms of the agreement.

None of the factors encouraging reform elsewhere, however, was evident in Upper Canada, and it is not surprising that liberal precedents were not adopted by the local chancellors. The volume of litigation in Upper Canada was very limited, and despite the evidence of fraud and abuse of trust that had arisen in other jurisdictions and of which the chancellors were aware, few such cases appeared in Upper Canada. Divorce remained unavailable throughout this period, leaving wives without the option of ending their husbands' marital rights over the property that they had brought to marriage or earned through employment, even when spouses were no longer cohabiting. Perhaps more important, the Upper Canadian chancellors may have been unusually aware of the extent to which coercion was a problem in many marriages; evidence from alimony cases in other jurisdictions not heard by the chancellors reinforced the belief that many husbands did not hesitate to use physical power to intimidate their wives.[15] The companionate ideal of marriage demanded that husbands act, as the editor of the Toronto *Daily Telegraph* asserted in 1868, as the 'true and pure guardian[s] of [their] families.'[16] The chancellors, however, were all too aware that the reality of marriage could be very different. Instead of assuming that all marriages were 'ideal' and 'companionate,' they sought to protect women who, without any rights or recognition under the common law, were exceptionally vulnerable when husbands refused to behave in a properly loving and respectful manner. In Upper Canada the development of the companionate model of marriage, therefore, did not 'destroy the legal idea that husbands possess unusual and even secret means of influencing their wives.'

Concerns about abusive husbands encouraged support for methods of safeguarding a woman's separate property, but they simultaneously precluded any great expansion of the wife's own rights of control over her land, chattels, and money. With a limited volume of litigation, the chancellors believed that by their own vigilance and discretion they could prevent problems of fraud and abuse of trust and still avoid the liberalization evident in England and the American states. They harboured a fear that liberalization created the potential to undermine the purpose of settlements by giving husbands new scope for coercive behaviour. In safeguarding women's interests against the power of husbands they were largely successful. Women's material needs could be and were protected without granting women rights as individuals; in the minds of contemporary legal and lay commentators, the most obvious problem with trusts was not their conservatism, but the undemocratic nature of the remedy.

Separate estates were undemocratic because most families simply could not afford them. Settled property was usually inalienable and therefore could not be used for the day-to-day support of the family; most frontier families required all resources to ensure survival. It is impossible to know exactly how many marriage settlements were established in Upper Canada and/or how much money was involved in each case. While in many American states the registration of marriage settlements was required to render them valid and binding,[17] in Upper Canada no such formality was enforced. Unless the settlement was challenged, therefore, little evidence of its existence can be expected to remain. For this reason, information regarding settlements in Upper Canada is limited and sketchy.[18] Few cases of litigation involving separate estates appear in Grant's Chancery Reports, and for the period from 1837 to 1905 only twenty-one unreported cases involving marriage settlements were found in the unreported Chancery files.[19] As in other jurisdictions, marriage settlements seem to have been used in Upper Canada only by the well-to-do, and even amongst the élite by fewer families than elsewhere; as one advocate of reform argued later in the century, 'such things were not common in Canada.'[20] More important, it is clear that Upper Canadian settlements were more conservative than settlements elsewhere. In each of the cases found in the unreported court documents, and in all which appeared in Grant's Chancery Reports, settlements involved trustees.[21] These were not passive trusts; trustees had managerial powers, and the powers of the wife, particularly those of disposition other than by will, were limited.[22] This suggests that the conservatism of the chancellors mirrored a wider social belief that the purpose of marriage settlements was protective and that protection was best ensured by the use of a trustee. Despite the rarity of marriage settlements, they are important because of the influence Chancery precedent would have on popular beliefs, demands for reform, and the ultimate form of remedial property legislation.

The terms of one agreement, drawn up in 1840, illustrate the chivalric purpose of marriage settlements and the means by which benefactors deemed it prudent to ensure women's protection:

Between Miss Margaret Nelles and Dr. William Ferris, Henry William Nelles, trustee ...

Marriage being intended (between the first two parties) it was agreed that the

said Margaret Nelles should assign and transfer all her right, title and interest in and to the said land and tenements, money and bank stock [lands in Grimsby inherited from her father, and 13 shares in the Upper Canada Bank] unto the said Henry William Nelles upon the trust and to and for the uses, ends and intents and purposes hereinafter expressed and declared and concerning the same ...
That the said Henry William Nelles, as executor or administrator do and shall permit and suffer the said Margaret Nelles as touching and concerning the afore-mentioned lands to occupy, possess and enjoy or otherwise have, receive and take the rents, issues and profits thereof and any part thereof for the term of her natu-ral life ... and to make valid any disposal by will by the said Margaret Nelles to any person or persons whomsoever ... And also upon the further trust and confi-dence that in case no such will or disposal of the said lands and tenements, mon-ies and bank stocks then the same shall go to and be equally divided between the issue of the said intended marriage be the same male or female ...

[The property] is not to be subject at any time to the debts, control or engage-ments of the said William Ferris...

[Henry William Nelles shall have] power of investment over monies and bank shares to place out and invest every such sum or sums of money or so much thereof as they shall think fit.[23]

The terms of the settlement precluded abuse of the property by the hus-band by placing it in the control and management of Margaret's brother, who could presumably be trusted to behave in her best interest. The property provided the wife with a guaranteed income, but denied her dispositive powers over the settled property itself; this ensured her secu-rity should her husband be unwilling or unable to support her, gave her scope for independent purchases and pleasures, and precluded the possi-bility that the husband might coerce his wife into alienating the property against her will, although he might still persuade her to use her income in his interest. The wife and the husband were also protected from the potential improvidence of the husband in the use of his own property, for the income from her lands would always provide them with a adequate means for survival; marriage settlements, in other words, had potentially important benefits for husbands themselves, particularly those involved in speculative businesses. The property was also preserved intact for potential children of the marriage. Under this settlement the wife did have a right of disposition by will. Rights of alienation by acts inter vivos – between two or more living individuals – were believed to be danger-ous, since they would provide the husband with access to the property by deceit or coercion; the right of disposition by will, however, did not create the possibility that the husband might deprive the wife of the benefit of her estate during her own lifetime. The settlement precluded the possibility that Margaret would be left, as Hannah Snider had been, impoverished and 'dependent more or less on ... charit[y].'[24]

When interpreting and enforcing marriage settlements, the chancellors were motivated by a desire, – similar to that of benefactors, – to protect women from the potential coercion of their husbands and from the hardships and poverty that such coercion, or simple financial mismanagement, might create. In 1881, in *Hillock v Button*, a 'suit instituted by a married woman seeking to have a settlement of her property made upon her marriage canceled, and the property delivered up to her,'[25] the wife's request that management of the estate be removed from the trustees and granted to her was refused. Vice-Chancellor Proudfoot held that since the trustee was not in breach of trust in his management of the property, and because 'the settlement gives larger powers to the plaintiff than are often found in such instruments,'[26] her desire to manage the property was insufficient reason to overturn the specified terms of the settlement, terms to which she had agreed at the time of her marriage. By such an action the purpose of the agreement might be thwarted. The trust had been carefully designed by the plaintiff's guardian and trustee to provide her with a regular income and to protect the property from possible dissipation by the husband:

Some time, how long does not appear, before her marriage, Mr. Farewell [the guardian and trustee] suggested to Miss Wells' [the plaintiff's] sister the propriety of having Miss Wells' property settled on her approaching marriage. And three days before the marriage Miss Wells and her sister called at Mr. Farewell's office and gave instructions for preparation of the settlement. At this interview Mr. Farewell seems to have explained the usual objects of such a settlement. He spoke of the provisions for the children, should there be any, and how the money was to go in that case, that it should go to the child, and that it was advisable to protect the child's interest from the husband ... The intention was to protect the plaintiff from her husband.[27]

Vice-Chancellor Proudfoot approved of the terms of this settlement, which gave the wife an income necessary for her survival should her husband prove to be abusive or irresponsible, but denied her managerial power over the settled property itself. Such provisions protected the wife from the possible secret coercive power of a husband who might attempt to denude her of her estate or to convince her to use it in his interest. It also allowed her some scope for personal purchases and protected the property for the children of the marriage and for the collateral relatives of the wife from whom the estate had originally come:

The settlement provides that during the coverture of the plaintiff the trustees were to pay the rents, interests &c to the plaintiff. In the case of the death of the plaintiff during the life of her husband, the trustees were to pay to such persons as she should by her last will order and appoint, and in default of such appointment then to hold and be possessed of the moneys (settled) for the heirs of the body of the plaintiff. And in the event of the death of the plaintiff intestate and without leaving issue surviving her then to pay to the husband the interest &c during his lifetime and so long as he should remain unmarried, and from and after his marriage after the plaintiff's death, then to pay to the next of kin of the plaintiff ... and in the event of the husband not marrying again and dying, then upon trust for the next of kin of the plaintiff. In the event of the plaintiff surviving her husband the moneys were to be paid to her, and the lands conveyed to her and the settlement to be at an end.[28]

Should the husband die before the wife, the settlement would no longer be necessary so long as the wife herself remained unmarried, for the 'intention was to protect the plaintiff from her husband.' As long as the husband was living, the purpose of the settlement could only be served by maintaining management in the hands of a competent trustee, despite the wife's express desire to control her own estate. As the provisions for the wife upon the death of the husband reveal, the trustee was necessary not, at least primarily, because the wife was considered incompetent to manage her financial affairs, but because the physical and legal power differential between husbands and wives made coercion an ever-present possibility within marriage.

Vice-Chancellor Proudfoot's summation suggests that he perceived even the limited powers that had been granted under this settlement as potentially subversive of its intent. Mrs Hillock had the right to devise her property, and she had executed a will leaving it to her husband. It was at least conceivable that this will had been obtained through deceit or coercion. While the court could not declare the will invalid, the chancellors could, by their insistence on the use of a trustee, ensure that the wife would not be deprived of the benefit of the property during her lifetime. This case reveals the enduring importance of coercion as a legal concept and the reluctance of the Upper Canadian chancellors to eliminate trustees as a protective shield against husbands.

Perhaps the greatest testament to an enduring belief that wives required protection is the fact that many families continued to use marriage settlements after the married women's property acts had abolished the common law disabilities of wives. Before reform, equity had served to mitigate the absoluteness of the common law and to preserve some family property against the claims of the husband and his creditors. After reform, marriage settlements served to mitigate the absoluteness of statutory regimes that gave women full rights of control over their separate estates. Although ironic in terms of women's rights, this is consistent with the protective purpose of settlements. The 1905 settlement between Arthur and Dorothy DeBruhl illustrates this theme.

The DeBruhls had been married in 1902, and since the marriage Mrs DeBruhl had inherited a considerable fortune from her late father. No marriage settlement had been drawn up at the time of the wedding, and Arthur DeBruhl himself was anxious that his wife's fortune be protected from his potential creditors: 'It is desirable [to make a settlement] in the interest of the petitioner, in order to properly protect her property, and to make provision for the issue of the said marriage.' Although a marriage settlement that outlined Dorothy DeBruhl's property would have been sufficient to protect it from creditors, all her lands and stocks were placed under the management of trustees. Until the age of twenty-one she was to have an income of $100 a month from the trust fund, and after that 'the income of the said trust fund for her separate use but so that she shall have no power to anticipate the same.' The trust also stipulated that on her death the property was to be placed in trust for her children and provision was to be made from it for their support, maintenance, and education.[29]

The chancellors were able to continue to emphasize the protective role of trustees since they were presented with negligible evidence of the two problems – fraud by married couples and abuse of trust by trustees – that had created the impetus for liberalization in other jurisdictions. Cases of fraud were rare in Upper Canada, and the chancellors believed that judicial vigilance could provide equity for all parties. The chancellors asserted that it was their primary duty to protect the interests of wives. Money and property inherited from relatives and friends, and even gifts from the husband to his bride, were all considered legitimate objects of protection under marriage settlements. The chancellors recognized, despite the potential for fraud in allowing a husband to give property to his wife, that often such gifts were an essential part of the marriage bargain itself. Even when husbands were guilty of attempting to protect property from seizure by legitimate creditors, if the wife herself could not be proved to have actively and knowingly committed fraud, her interests could not be sacrificed. It would be unfair, the chancellors asserted, to retroactively deny the wife the security that she expected in her marriage. As Chief Justice Draper argued in 1868,

It is the policy of the law to give paramount force to the consideration of marriage, unless the marriage itself be a mere fraudulent contrivance for defeating creditors; the doctrine ... at equity has been to support a settlement of the husband's property when it appears to have been made previously to, and in consideration of, an honest marriage, and this notwithstanding the embarrassed circumstances of the husband at the date of the settlement.[30]

The chancellors were also hesitant to believe that wives themselves were party to fraud, probably at least in part because the rhetoric of domesticity emphasized women's purity, superior morality, and lack of interest in worldly affairs. Despite the fact that this emphasis on the rights of wives had the potential to undermine the legitimate rights of creditors, the chancellors assumed that by the judicious exercise of their discretion the interests of all parties could be protected. As long as the volume of litigation remained limited, such assumptions and goals were reasonable.

The judicial creativity that was necessitated by these beliefs is illustrated by a case that came before the court in 1867. Israel Bowman had been in a partnership that eventually fell into insolvency. In the period before the business declared bankruptcy, but during which the financial difficulties of the firm were evident, he made a settlement of land upon his intended wife and began construction of a house upon this property. Vice-Chancellor Spragge upheld the right of the husband to create an antenuptial settlement, and stated that since the wife could not be shown to have entertained any fraudulent intent, her interests must be protected:

I must take the marriage to be a valuable consideration for the conveyance. It is contended that the building of the house was a voluntary gift. So much as was built before and so much as was built after the marriage admit of different considerations. As to that part of it which was built before; suppose it had been completed before the marriage, I do not see how I could in that case separate the house from the land. I must have held both settled upon the wife before marriage, the conveyance of the land, though before the building of the house, being effectual for that purpose, and if so, an incomplete house must follow the same rule.

As to the expenditures upon the building after the marriage they were voluntary and amounted to a post-nuptial settlement by an insolvent husband. If they had not been erections or additions to that which was already the property of the wife, I should have no difficulty. The difficulty is created by there not being practically separable from that which is the property of the wife, and there being no fraud in the wife allowing them to be added to her estate...

I have to choose between allowing a wife to retain as against creditors a voluntary gift from an insolvent husband, and charging the wife's estate with its value. I cannot but see that doing the latter is onerating her estate with a charge not contracted by her, and may operate as a hardship upon her. But it would open the door to great fraud, to hold that because a wife has land by a conveyance before marriage which is not impeachable, she must therefore be entitled to hold as against creditors, whatever an insolvent husband might place upon it.[31]

Spragge recognized the difficulties inherent in this case, but chose protection of the wife over protection of the rights of creditors: 'The Court ought to give effect to the right of the creditors, when it can see its way to do so without doing practical injustice to the wife.'[32] Spragge believed that allowing the creditors to have redress out of the 'value of the improvements made upon the wife's estate after marriage' provided an equitable solution to this problem.[33] *Jackson v Bowman* was reported because cases of attempted fraud were rare; justice was at least partially served in this case because the chancellors could fashion an individual, discretionary decision.

The dangers for creditors inherent in such interpretations of marriage settlements are made evident in *Royal Canadian Bank v Mitchell*. Isabella Mitchell, wife of Charles Mitchell, was entitled to a life estate in lands. She and her husband were sued in 1868 with regard to a promissory note that both had signed. The creditors sought to seize the property held under the trust. Vice-Chancellor Spragge was aware of the English and American precedent that a married woman could be held liable upon contracts made by her with regard to her separate estate, but he stated that such precedents were destructive of the protective intent of marriage settlements:

It is indeed obvious that the making of the separate estate of a married woman liable upon her contracts does somewhat infringe upon the disabilities of a married woman, and upon the protection which the law throws around her. It gives effect to her contracts, and it exposes her to the loss of the use of her separate property, through contracts which may have been obtained by intimidation or other means used by the husband, and this without the safeguards which the law provides in relation to her parting with her property of any other nature ... This false position of the wife, as I think it may fairly be called, is now generally prevented in

England by the clause, which finds a place in most well drawn instruments, against anticipation.[34]

Spragge equated the disabilities imposed upon married women with their protection, and he did not approve of settlements that failed to include a restraint against anticipation – a clause preventing the wife from disposing of the property. The separate estate held in trust by Isabella Mitchell was not an estate that could be attached by her creditors because the trust agreement did not explicitly grant that 'absolute use shall be in the wife,' nor was the husband 'excluded in terms.'[35] Without such a clause giving the wife a clear and absolute right of disposition free from the claims of her husband, Spragge asserted that it was to be assumed that she had a power only to hold and enjoy her estate, not to alienate it. To hold that the wife possessed only those powers that were explicitly enumerated in a marriage settlement was directly to oppose the majority of contemporary decisions in both England and the United States. The Upper Canadian chancellors displayed an overwhelming concern to protect the wife from 'intimidation or other means used by the husband,' even explicitly at the expense of legitimate creditors. Evidence from a later case involving this same couple proves that Charles Mitchell was an abusive, domineering husband, and in this context it is entirely possible that Isabella had only signed the promissory note under duress and that the intervention of the court was justified; to make this assumption in all cases, however, provided much scope for collusion and fraud. Although the danger to creditors inherent in such decisions is evident in retrospect, the limited volume of fraud litigation with which the chancellors were confronted enabled them to continue to emphasize the protective intent of marriage settlements and to believe that judicial vigilance would prevent injustice to creditors.

Similarly, although in other jurisdictions cases of breach of trust demonstrated the flaws of a system that denied women full control over their property, in Upper Canada such cases were unusual. This rarity encouraged the chancellors in a continued belief that trustees usually behaved responsibly, that dispositive powers for wives were therefore unnecessary, and that in rare cases of abuse of trust judicial discretion could be used, as in cases of fraud, to protect wives and to remove irresponsible trustees from their positions of power. Again, in the majority of cases, these assumptions proved to be correct. The chancellors were not hesitant to assign a new trustee for the benefit of the wife when it could be proved that a trustee had been negligent.

Perhaps the greatest evidence with regard to the chancellors' confidence in their own ability to enforce the terms of trusts is the fact that, despite the pervasive fear of coercion that was central to marriage settlements themselves, when trustees were not named in settlements the court constituted the husband as trustee for his wife. In this the chancellors followed established English and American precedent: 'It is not necessary that the trustee should be a stranger. The husband himself may be the trustee; and if property be settled to a married woman's separate use, and no trustee be appointed, the husband will be considered as such.'[36] Marylynn Salmon has argued that such a precedent reveals a decline in the importance of coercion as a legal concept:

According to standard common law and equitable rules on coercion ... this viewpoint was absurd. How could a man act as an intermediary to protect a woman from his own coercion? If such were the purpose of a trustee, a husband could not serve as one for his own wife. Clearly, equity courts had ceased at some point to regard trustees as primarily protectors of women. Instead, Chancellors saw them as unnecessary and perhaps dangerous interlopers who could be eliminated safely.[37]

The evidence from Upper Canada does not justify such conclusions. The chancellors were willing to make husbands trustees not because they had ceased 'to regard trustees as primarily protectors of women,' but because they believed that the court itself could serve the purpose of intermediary. The court, in such cases, would be the ultimate arbitrator of family disputes, the overriding patriarch bestowing benevolent, discretionary justice. Such protection was not available to women who did not possess separate property because the husband's ownership and management of his wife's property were absolute under the common law. All settlements, however, even those in which the husband served as trustee, outlined limitations on the uses to which the trust property could be put. The chancellors could force even a recalcitrant husband to comply with the terms of a trust or remove him from his position as trustee to be replaced by someone in whom they could place more faith.

It was this course of action which was taken by the chancellors in 1862 when Mrs Tripp, who had been abandoned by her husband, who was a trustee under her marriage settlement, applied to the court to have new trustees appointed:

One of the trustees, Henry Tripp, is now as appears in evidence, resident out of the province; and the other declares in his answer that he desires to be discharged from execution of the trust. The husband left this province in November 1856, leaving his wife in the province, where she has ever since resided; the husband has not been heard of since May 1857 ...

The trust appears by the terms of the settlement to be exercisable only by two trustees, so that Mr. Martin, the only trustee in the province, would not be competent to execute it. Further, in the absence of the husband, whose concurrence is required in the appointment of a new trustee, no new trustee can be appointed without the intervention of this court.[38]

Vice-Chancellor Spragge used the discretionary right of the court to appoint new trustees who would serve the interests of Mrs Tripp. Although it was and is a general rule that no trust shall fail for want of a trustee, it is revealing that even with her husband out of the province and therefore unlikely to subject Mrs Tripp to ill treatment or to force her to part with her property against her will, the court did not authorize her to take control or management of the estate herself. Since divorce was unavailable to Mrs Tripp, it was always a possibility that her husband might return and enforce his marital rights over his wife and her property. Vice-Chancellor Spragge also expressed regret that the settlement had been drawn up so that the rents, issue, and profits from the property were to be paid jointly to the husband and wife. Under these circumstances, half of the rents and other profits were to be paid by the new trustees to the wife, and the other half paid into the court in trust for the errant husband: 'I confess that if I felt that the court had a discretion to exercise in the matter, I should be disposed, under the circumstances, to give the whole of the rents and profits to the wife.'[39]

Not only did trustees occasionally disappear, they also attempted to defraud married women of the benefits to which they were entitled under trust agreements. An unreported case involving Charles Mitchell, who had earlier tried to defraud creditors, illustrates the potential problems for wives when their property was managed by trustees. In 1884 Charles Mitchell, supposedly on behalf of his wife, was again before the court, this time to issue a petition to have George Lizard removed from his position as trustee under the marriage settlement. Charles Mitchell claimed that the trustee had 'only accounted to them for a portion of the rents and profits of the said estate and he has refused to show in what way he has disposed of the balance of the same.' In his defence, George Lizard countercharged that the suit had been instituted against the will of Isabella Mitchell, a woman 'who is 75 years of age and under the influence of the said Charles Mitchell and easily imposed on by him.' The property in question was a farm, rented to a son of the plaintiff and Isabella Mitchell, who had been allowed by Lizard to pay the rents due on the property directly to Mrs Mitchell. Instead, he was acting in collusion with his father. Moreover, Charles Mitchell was 'largely indebted to the defendant' and sought to nullify these debts by the claim of breach of trust. George Lizard asserted that he 'was willing to assign the estate to any person who would protect the interests of the said Isabella Mitchell and who was not in collusion with the said Charles Mitchell.' The court appointed a new trustee, but refused to give any power to Charles Mitchell or to the Mitchells' son.[40] Cases such as this would only have confirmed the chancellors' fear that without the safeguard of trustees married women stood to be denuded of their estates through coercion on the part of their husbands.

Although the chancellors were successful in preventing Charles Mitchell from dissipating his wife's property, it is not surprising that the only case in which the intent of a trust was thwarted occurred when a husband served as trustee over his wife's separate estate. Mary Torrance, the unfortunate wife in this case, had inherited property from her father and her husband had been assigned as trustee. Although he was not the legal owner of her property, he had 'lately assumed to treat them as his own and ha[d] refused an accounting to her and threaten[ed] to sell and use the proceeds for himself.' He had converted over $25,000 into ready money and, at the time of the court hearing, was making preparations to desert his wife. In his statement of defence Henry Torrance claimed that the money had been used for the proper support of their family and that his wife's suit was a result of his refusal to grant her a separate maintenance out of the trust fund to enable her to live apart from him. Up until this time, he claimed, 'she had permitted the defendant to deal with and manage her estate almost with as little interference as if the property were his own – the defendant was very cautious and prudent in money matters and of a very economical disposition and the plaintiff was satisfied that he would manage her estate to the best advantage and better than she could herself owing to these characteristics.' In the separate examination conducted by the court, Mary Torrance showed little knowledge of business but asserted that she wanted her husband's powers as trustee revoked because 'circumstances have rendered him unfit,' and that 'Mr. Torrance is so tipsy and behaved so badly that I was ashamed to have the servants see him ... he was ill-treating me and doing those things through drink.' The chancellors were disgusted with evidence that overwhelmingly proved that Henry Torrance was frequently drunk and habitually abusive; they unhesitatingly revoked his powers as trustee, but this relief came too late to be of practical benefit to Mary Torrance. In an affidavit submitted one year after the case had been heard, Mary's accountant asserted that no money had been received from Mr Torrance, who was no longer residing in the province. Not only had Henry Torrance prevented his wife from using her separate property to live separately when she desired to do so, but he had managed to abscond with the majority of the property, leaving her with reduced means, dependent upon the largesse of their grown children.[41]

In every case but this one the interests of the wife were served by the enforcement of the terms of the marriage settlement. When carefully drawn and when managed by competent, responsible trustees, marriage settlements could provide wives with financial security and protection against the irresponsibility or coercion of their husbands; control by the wife herself was not necessary for the successful protection of her property. When settlements were drawn up individually, the powers of trustees could be limited and judicial discretion could be used for the benefit of wives. It is significant, however, that the only case in which the chancellors proved unable to protect the interests of the wife was one in which the husband served as trustee over his wife's estate. For parents to be certain that a trust would provide a daughter with security, it was best that the trustee be someone other than her spouse. Not surprisingly, given the overall success of the chancellors in protecting women's interests, the precedents set in Chancery served as the model for statutory reform of marital property regulations in 1859. Also not surprisingly, the problems of fraud and abuse of trust, muted in Chancery, became much more evident and troublesome under generalized legislation, particularly since the husband became trustee over his wife's statutory separate estate.

4

'If the Laws Were Made More Salutary':
The Act of 1859

Without any cash or resources of their own, without control even over their wages, wives without marriage settlements were at the complete mercy of their husbands. While this might be of minimal import to women married to loving and responsible men, this absolute financial dependence left married women in a most vulnerable position and was not conducive to marital happiness. One anonymous woman made this argument explicitly in an open letter to the Hamilton *Spectator* in 1858:

Respecting the woman who has a bad husband, with no law to protect her whilst he lives ... and taunted with her very helplessness by him who ought to be her comforter, she is to be pitied. They talk a great deal about slavery. I think the laws for married women are almost as bad. If the laws were made more salutary there would be more happy marriages in the world.[1]

This was not an isolated opinion. Systematic pressure from women, and sympathetic men, was central to the passage of remedial marital property legislation in 1859; the lobby group that petitioned Parliament throughout the 1850s for property law reform represents the first organized effort of women in Upper Canada to improve their own status.[2] The efforts of women were successful because there was broad public, legal, and judicial agreement that the common law afforded married women insufficient protection against the coercive power of husbands. This popular consensus is illustrated by the frequency with which property law reform was discussed in provincial papers and by the fact that, despite the deep political divisions that characterized this decade, married women's property law was not a party issue.[3] Popular discontent with the state of the law was not the only factor encouraging reform. Property law changes in the United States and Great Britain illustrated the ways in which the common law might be modified. A volatile economic climate also provided an essential backdrop to reform; by shielding some family property from seizure by creditors, separate property protected families, not just wives. As passed, the Married Women's Property Act of 1859 democratized the practice of the Upper Canadian Court of Chancery and made all inherited property the statutory separate estate of the wife; since the court could not assign trustees on an individual basis, the husband was constituted as such a trustee. This act also provided protection for working-class women by creating a mechanism by which wives could control their own earnings when husbands were irresponsible, abusive, or absent; women whose husbands were too poor to pay alimony would at least be enabled to support themselves without interference from abusive spouses. The new law was greeted with widespread approval as a necessary and just change for the 'better protection of married women.'[4]

Reform was intended to provide relief in cases in which the common law had created injustice and hardship. By the 1850s, the common law's provisions for married women were perceived as inadequate and archaic, at least among progressive segments of the community:

There can be little doubt that the old English law, which, with very slight modifications, prevails in Upper Canada, is too much tinctured with the old doctrine of the feudal ages, that woman is the servant, not the equal, of her lord; that she owes fealty and service to him, and might be locked up in strong castles or treated as captive by her 'Baron' whenever he might deem such discipline necessary.[5]

In particular, 'the state of the law in regard to property, as affected by the marriage relation, is not satisfactory.'[6] Dower provided some security for widows, but during the lives of their husbands wives were 'debarred from the command of one solitary shilling.'[7] Not only were wives denied the right to make purchases except as agents of their husbands, they also lost the control of their own property at marriage and were not guaranteed any compensation through adequate support. It was considered manifestly unjust that a husband could squander the money his wife had inherited or brought to marriage, leaving his family destitute. This, however, was believed to be a much less common consequence of the law than the plight of the working-class wife abused or abandoned by a drunken husband. In a commentary rife with class bias and motivated by the assumption that only lower-class men could be drunken and abusive, the *Upper Canada Law Journal*, the voice of the legal community, lamented the failure of the common law to afford protection to such women: 'The wife, earning by her skill and her industry that which she has no right at law to call her own, which may, at any moment, be carried off by the man who deserted her, or who, continuing to live with her, leads an idle and dissolute life, supported by her gains, while he leaves her and her children in want ... is to be pitied.'[8]

Not all women, of course, suffered equally under the disabilities imposed by the common law. When marriages were happy, the question of who legally owned family property could be irrelevant to day-to-day life, whatever the economic status of the family. Wealthy wives, moreover, could protect themselves through the use of marriage settlements, which, the editors of the *Globe* asserted, provided individual married women with 'better securities for personal liberty against the acts of tyrannical husband[s].'[9] Although it is unclear how many wealthy wives actually made use of Chancery, the glaring contrast between law and equity was manifestly unfair to poorer wives. The Court of Chancery provided an accessible alternative model of family property relations upon which sensible and, it was believed, effective reform could be based; marriage settlements, experience in Chancery had proved, worked. As the editors of the *Globe* argued in 1857, all women should be provided with equal protection under the law – the provisions of equity should be democratized:

A husband under the law as it now stands upon marriage and the birth of a child acquires a life estate in all his wife's real property, unless there was a settlement or an ante-nuptial contract to prevent that result. The life estate which he acquires as tenant by the curtesy, in legal phrase, may be seized and sold under an execution against lands to satisfy the husband's debts, even though contracted before marriage. The wife may then be stripped of her property for life, unless she outlives her husband. This is manifestly an injustice, and to say that a wife may protect herself against such a consequence by a contract signed and sealed before marriage, or that her parents and friends may by deed or will, limit the property given to her to her 'separate use,' is simply to say that if every young woman, or every father, understood the laws of real property, and the mysteries of every conveyance, and, amid the excitement, the bright hopes, the joyous feelings of the anticipated wedding day, could sit down and coolly and cautiously prepare the deed, or give instructions to the lawyer, and then, with the forecast of Iago, and the exacting spirit of Shylock, present it to her intended for his signature as a condition precedent to the response 'I will,' her property would be placed out of the reach of her husband or his creditors. We hold that if there be a general principle or a rule, which by common comment, should govern the property relations of husband and wife, that rule ought to be embodied in the law of the land. The power to vary or limit the operation of that rule should be given to those whose particular position makes it inapplicable in their case, but the few and not the many should be compelled to provide by positive arrangement against possible injustice.[10]

It is important to note that the author of this attack on the common law did not advocate the control of such property by the wife herself; the argument was that the safeguards accorded on an individual basis in the Court of Chancery ought to be extended to all wives, that the property ought to be placed 'out of the reach of her husband or his creditors,' under the care of a trustee. Such provisions would reinforce rather than undermine the traditional family. As the editors of the *Upper Canada Law Journal* asserted in 1857, reform would strengthen the family by eliminating 'gross instances of injustice – it might be said oppression,'[11] and thereby ensuring to the wife her financial security and the enjoyment of her separate and proper domestic sphere. Criticisms of the harsh provisions of the common law in the popular press and by the legal community would suggest that the editors of the *Upper Canada Law Journal* were correct in their assertion that in Upper Canada there was 'certainly a feeling, which day by day gains strength, that the law as to married women is not as it ought to be, and must be amended.'[12]

This perception that 'the law ... is not as it ought to be' seems to have been particularly strong amongst women themselves. It was the 'ladies of the province' who took the lead in promoting reform. The first petition for amendment of the law was submitted in the legislative session of 1852-3 by 'Anne Macdonald and other ladies, for an Act to secure to Married Women certain rights of property in certain cases, now unprovided for by law.'[13] Although the petition was virtually ignored at this time, from this inauspicious beginning in 1852 would develop an intense lobbying campaign. Although less vocal and less well-known than their American and British counterparts,[14] the women who lobbied the assembly and the council for amelioration of the married women's property law played an important role in the passage of the act of 1859. More important, this campaign was the first organized effort of Upper Canadian women to improve their own position in society. A second petition by Anne Macdonald and other ladies, about which no details are extant, was submitted in the session of 1854–5.[15] And in 1856 Elizabeth Hawley and others delivered a petition requesting a '[married women's property] act similar to the one in New York.'[16]

The petitioning campaign of the province's women reached a crescendo in 1857. The timing of the intensification of the campaign was very likely connected to a knowledge of the contemporary petitioning efforts of the Law Amendment Society and the Married Women's Property Committee in Great Britain. On 19 January 1857 the *Globe* published excerpts from a petition submitted by 'Elizabeth Dunlop and others' to 'render the property of Married Women free from the control of the husband.' The arguments presented in this petition reflect both a liberal revulsion at the fact that by marriage 'a woman is instantly deprived of all civil rights,' and a concerted effort to emphasize the 'acknowledged grievances' that would allow the petition to be viewed with favour by Parliament.[17] The petitioners lamented the 'absolute power' vested in husbands with regard to the property brought to marriage or earned by the labour of their wives, and argued that this power 'occasion[ed] manifold evils becoming daily more apparent.' Their emphasis on the particular problems this created for poor women, for whom marriage settlements were not an option, would have elicited the chivalric sympathy of many legislators: 'More unequivocal is the injury sustained by women of the lower classes for whom no [marriage settlements] can be made ... She may work from morning to night to see the produce of her labour wasted in a tavern.' It was essential that the law be changed so that 'entering the state of marriage, [wives] shall no longer pass from freedom to the condition of a slave, whose earnings belong wholly to the master.' Such a call for change could be viewed with considerable favour because the two reforms the women specifically demanded involved the protection of a wife's inheritance and her earnings from the husband and his creditors. There was widespread agreement in the legal community and in the population at large that common law provisions for wives with regard to such property were archaic:

Your petitioners, therefore, humbly pray that an Act may be passed making the personal property of the wife previous to marriage free from the control of her husband, and that she may be able to hold separate property by law, as she now may in equity; that a woman marrying without any previous marriage settlement may have a right to her property and also her earnings.[18]

The petition itself is no longer extant, and it is impossible to know who signed and supported it or their reasons for doing so; unfortunately, we are afforded only tantalizing glimpses of the demands made by women.[19]

Dunlop's petition was only one of several presented during the 1857 session. On 16 March of that year a petition 'from 1300 married women in Western Canada, praying that their property rights might be protected' was presented in the Legislative Council.[20] This was a very significant number of signatures, and a petition of this magnitude could not have been achieved without some level of organization amongst women; it suggests that a considerable, if informal, reform network existed in the colony. Again, on 6 May 1857, 'among the petitions presented was one ... from many married women and old maids praying that a law might be passed to protect the property of other married women.'[21] Moreover, no fewer than eleven municipalities also submitted petitions supporting reform of the law of married women and property.[22]

Pressure from women was supplemented by ferment from within the legal community. The mid-nineteenth century was characterized by wide-ranging legal reform in North America, the United Kingdom, and continental Europe, a fact that advanced the cause of transformation of the law of married women and property.[23] Two issues in the legal reform debate – codification and the fusion of law and equity – provided considerable fuel for proponents of marital property law reform.

The mid-nineteenth century was the great era of legal codification in Europe. Closer to home, codification was in process both in Lower Canada and in the state of New York. The possibility that codification might also serve Upper Canadian needs was at least considered by the legal community during this decade. Its supporters argued in the *Upper Canada Law Journal* that 'the state of complication in which our laws have become latterly involved, forms the principal motive of other states to rid themselves of an influence [British precedent] which is found to be more burdensome than beneficial.'[24] While a full codification of the common law was ultimately deemed impracticable if not impossible, the confusion that characterized both procedure and pleading in mid-nineteenth-century Upper Canadian courts was lamented in the legal community: 'It is, indeed, full time that the Legislature of this country was awakened to a sense of the important duty of promulgating the law in an intelligible and accessible form, a duty second only to that of providing laws sound and efficient in substance.'[25] Attempts in this direction had been made throughout the 1840s and 1850s; the Judicature Act of 1849 reorganized and simplified the court system and procedure, and the statutes were consolidated during the 1850s.[26] It only made sense that during this process of consolidation specific issues, problems, and anomalies in the common law should be eliminated. However, the commissioners appointed 'to examine, revise, consolidate, and classify the public general statutes of Upper Canada'[27] were given limited powers that did not include the power to amend the law. Therefore, the editors of the *Upper Canada Law Journal* argued, it was the responsibility of the legislature to reform specific laws that were perceived as archaic or inappropriate for the Upper Canadian community.[28] Married women's rights of property were thought to be one such area of law.

The other great issue that absorbed the legal community throughout the 1850s and beyond was the possibility of the fusion of law and equity. The principles enforced in Chancery were believed to be essential for justice, yet the existence of two systems of law that were intended to complement, but in fact often contradicted, one another provided an excellent example of the need for general legal reform, simplification, and perhaps even codification. As the *Upper Canada Law Journal* asserted in 1858, the contradictions between law and equity made a mockery of the alleged superiority of English justice:

Law in general involves a command, enjoining what is right, and prohibiting what is wrong. It is the exercise of the sovereign will, which ought always to accord with the dictates of justice. By reason of its universality, we are told, Law may operate injustly [*sic*] in particular cases. To prevent injustice in such cases, we are told, Equity interferes. The difficulty is to prevent Law, which is designed for good and to apply in all cases, from itself doing wrong in some cases ...

Equity is now administered by rules, as well understood as any rules of law. In a word, equity is law. If then, equity is law, why should there be one class of judges to dispense equity, and another class to dispense law?[29]

In New York, codification had involved the elimination of a distinct Court of Chancery and the absorption of equitable principles into the common law.[30] In Nova Scotia, equity and law were merged in 1855 and the separate Court of Chancery abolished.[31] In Great Britain, the Law Amendment Society had also recommended the fusion of law and equity.[32] Comments from the *Upper Canada Law Journal* make it clear that local lawyers were not only aware of the existence of the Law Amendment Society, but applauded its purpose and recommendations:

The declared object of the association is to promote, by discussion and otherwise, the careful and cautious improvement of the law of England in all its branches; to point out to the Legislature and the public the defects in the legal system; and to suggest appropriate remedies ... We cannot say too much in praise of such an association.[33]

Married women's property law provided an example of the contradictions between the common law and Chancery; these contradictions illustrated why reform of Chancery was necessary and simultaneously why reform could not simply translate into abolition without the creation of considerable injustice. The call for the fusion of law and equity, therefore, provided convincing evidence for proponents of the transformation of the law of married women and their property. One need not have been a supporter of 'woman's rights' to recognize that the inequality of remedies available to married women under the common law and equity left poor women unprotected and that, as one advocate of reform asserted in the Legislative Council of Upper Canada in 1857, the 'present law was a law for the rich, for those who understood the making of marriage settlements. It was not a law for the poor.'[34] In the light of the propensity of reformers and legislators to assume that abusive and irresponsible behaviour were largely working-class problems, the discrepancy between law and equity imposed an obligation on men of wealth, standing, and power to provide chivalric protection for poor and vulnerable women.

The contrast between equitable and common law provisions was exacerbated and made more visible by the economic instability that characterized the 1850s. Depression provided an essential backdrop for reform that would shield a portion of family property, for all families and not simply the rich, from seizure by creditors.[35] Crop failures, land and railway speculation, and world economic dislocation had created, by 1857, a full-fledged financial crisis in Upper Canada. On the same day on which the Married Women's Property Act was passed in 1859, a measure that eliminated imprisonment for debt also received assent.[36] Business failures were frequent in these years and discontent with the laws of bankruptcy and insolvency was widespread. The editors of the Upper Canada Law Journal argued that the failure of the legislature to enact modern bankruptcy legislation undermined the growth of the colony:

A law of bankruptcy we want ... We do not advocate the indiscriminate release from debt of all who are unable to meet their obligations. We do not propose to encourage mad speculation and insane extravagance. We do not desire to abet refined robbery or gentlemanly swindling. But we do advocate an abatement of that ferocious trait of our laws which makes a debtor, however honest, however well-meaning, the slave of his creditor. It is a characteristic of our laws wholly at variance with the genuine and true spirit of English liberty ... The trader who, untainted with fraud, and free from the charge of recklessness, is unable to meet his engagements but willing to assign all his assets to pay his debts, should be discharged in respect of future acquired property.[37]

Even without a new bankruptcy law, a married women's property act would achieve certain of these objectives by placing a proportion of family property outside the reach of creditors. This measure, therefore, could be seen not only as an attempt to correct an injustice perpetrated against defenceless married women, but as a measure for family relief and protection. Although direct connection was not explictly drawn in the 1850s between married women's property law reform and benefits that might accrue to husbands, in his later treatise on wives and property George Holmested argued that these potential benefits were well understood by legislators and were central to the passage of the act of 1859:

It is doubtful whether the recent legislative emancipation of the property of married women from marital control is altogether due to a disinterested desire on the part of men to do justice to the weaker sex. Man is at best a selfish animal, and it is to be feared that, even in this apparently disinterested legislation, he has had an eye to the casual advantages which may accrue to his own sex from its adoption ...[38]

Protection for the property of wives would provide support for the family itself by ensuring its economic viability in times of crisis.

For all of these reasons, it is not surprising that married women's property law was the subject of legislative debate on numerous occasions throughout the 1850s. The first bill on this subject was introduced in the Legislative Assembly in 1850; this bill, presented before much pressure for reform seems to have developed in the province, was probably a result of the passage of marital property reforms in New York State in 1848. On 15 June 1850, the Hamilton *Spectator* reported that

Mr. Flint, the member for Hastings, has introduced a Bill 'to provide for the protection of married women in the enjoyment of their own properties.' The principal provisions are, that women now married, and women marrying hereafter, shall possess any property they own, beyond the control of the husband, and it shall not be liable for his debts; that married women may acquire property and dispose of it; and that contracts in contemplation of marriage shall be valid.[39]

Billa Flint, ostensibly a reformer, was a 'loose fish' in Parliament, a man known for adherence to principle, whatever the dictates of party. A founder of the Canadian Temperance League and a devout Methodist, Flint's own father had been an alcoholic whose habits had interfered with the support of his family.[40] Flint may have had this experience in mind when he drew an explicit connection between married women's property law reform and the problems faced by families in a volatile economic climate:

He considered it but just that the female should not be made to suffer for the extravagance or reckless prodigality of her partner ... In ninety out of one hundred cases of improvidence, the women and children were the sufferers.[41]

The time, however, was not yet ripe for such a measure, and although the editors of the *Spectator* declared themselves 'as anxious as Mr. Flint may be to see women protected in their just rights,' they decried the bill as likely to produce an inducement to fraud.[42] This proposal for reform was much more liberal than many that followed, for Flint advocated not only the protection of the wife's assets but also the granting to the wife herself of the right to dispose of such property. Interestingly, he manipulated the stereotype that wives were more honest and moral than their husbands to defend this position. Because of these characteristics, he asserted, it would benefit husbands to allow their wives to handle family financial affairs: 'The law as he desired it would afford still greater guarantee to the creditor, by placing the property under the control of the women, where it would be much safer, and give greater security to him, than if the husband was left at liberty to squander it. He thought the gentlemen would be safer in the hands of the ladies, than the ladies with the gentlemen.'[43] Apparently at least a small proportion of the population was willing to accept this comparatively radical view of women's rights, as the Hamilton *Journal* hailed Flint's bill as 'the greatest hit of the season.'[44] While Flint may have had limited popular support, he did not present petitions to strengthen his argument for reform, and the subject was brought before the house again only in 1852–3. A bill based on the first of the petitions presented by the women of the province was read once in this session, but its second reading was postponed for three months, effectively making its passage impossible.[45]

Despite further petitions, the next mention of married women's property law reform did not come until 1856. In this session, however, the subject for the first time received serious legislative consideration. A bill

'to secure to Married Women certain separate rights of property,' introduced in the Legislative Council by William Morris, a Conservative,
passed in that House, and was duly referred to a select committee of the
Legislative Assembly.[46] William Hamilton Merritt, another, somewhat
erratic, Conservative,[47] and the member who had introduced the unsuccessful bill of 1852–3, brought the report of the committee to the House
on 19 June 1856:

Mr. WILSON advocated the measure as necessary for the protection of married
women and their children, and not unjust to creditors, as due notice of the new
legislation would be given. He believed it would be most acceptable to the people
at large, and no complaint of its operation had been made in New York where the
same law had been passed.

Mr. FREEMAN was opposed to the Bill. Under the present law the wife was entitled to maintenance out of the estate of her husband, according to the sphere in
which he moved, and he was responsible for all the debts of her contracting, however foolish, and at his death she received one third of his real estate. If this Bill
was passed she would retain all these privileges, being entitled to maintenance by
her husband while at the same time she would keep the control of her own property, and could dispose of it to her kin or otherwise as she pleased.[48]

The bill did not pass, in large part because Attorney General John A. Macdonald opposed it.

   After the failure of this bill, and as the petitioning campaign of the colony's women reached its height, debate in both the council and the
assembly intensified.[49] In 1857 three bills regarding married women's
property were prepared, but only one of these reached discussion. Bills
introduced by Morris and Merritt, long supporters of reform, were both
discontinued in order to give the full attention of the Legislative Assembly to a bill introduced by Malcolm Cameron 'to protect the property and
rights of married women.'[50]

   Although Cameron's bill is no longer extant, excerpts from it were
printed in the Globe on 17 March 1857. The editors of the Globe praised
Cameron as 'a lawyer of much experience, admitted on all sides to stand
in the front ranks of his profession,' and endorsed the bill as 'well-
drawn.' Cameron had a large and active legal practice in Sarnia–
Lambton, where he specialized in equity. Like Merritt and Morris, he was
a political maverick, an erratic reformer whose volatility prevented him
from working continuously with any government faction.[51] Like Billa
Flint, he was, first and foremost, a temperance man, and it is likely that he

perceived the expansion of married women's rights to property as necessary to protect women from drunken, abusive husbands who might
'reduce [them] to beggary.'[52] Like other reformers, he erroneously
assumed that working-class men were most likely to be irresponsible,
drunken, and abusive, and that more 'enlightened' men were therefore
obliged to act *in loco parentis* to protect the interests of defenceless
women. The *Globe* reported the central provisions of his bill:

1. From and after the passing of this Act, every woman who shall already have
   married or shall hereafter marry without any contract or settlement, shall and
   may, notwithstanding her coverture, have, hold and enjoy all her personal
   property whether belonging to her before marriage, and also all her personal
   earnings and any acquisitions therefrom, free from the debts, obligations, control and disposition of her husband without her consent, in as full and ample a
   manner as if she continued sole and unmarried, any law, usage or custom to
   the contrary notwithstanding;

2. The real estate of a married woman shall not, during her life, be subject to execution on any judgment against her husband, on account of any interest he
   may have acquired in such real estate as tenant by the curtesy ...

5. Every married woman shall and may make any devise or bequest of her separate property, real or personal, or of any rights therein, whether such property
   be acquired before or after marriage, in the same manner as if she were sole
   and unmarried; provided that such devise be executed in the presence of two
   or more witnesses, neither of whom shall be her husband, and that her husband shall not be deprived by such devise or bequest of any right which he
   may have acquired as tenant by the curtesy.[53]

Cameron showed considerable concern that the wife might be coerced by
her husband and forced by him to alienate or devise her property against
her own interest.

   In their description of Cameron's argument, the editors of the Hamilton *Spectator* emphasized his concern for women married to irresponsible
men. Despite their hostility towards the nascent 'woman's rights movement' in the United States, the editors shared Cameron's sympathy for
abused wives and expressed a willingness to support limited remedial
legislation:

He alluded to the hardships at present experienced by married women, in being
liable to be reduced to begging by their husbands wasting their property, even

when accumulated after separation by their own industry. He alluded to the wide differences of the position of married women in law and equity.[54]

Reformers and conservatives could agree that the protection afforded married women under the common law was inadequate and that the glaring contrasts between law and equity must be eliminated. As Cameron put it, to the general approval of the House,

Not only as regards the higher but also in the lower classes of society the present law was exceedingly unjust. Among the poorer classes, for instance, everyone in large cities must have felt the misery resulting from the conduct of one who passed from careful industry and sobriety into dissipation and wretchedness, reducing the unfortunate partner of his affections, as well as her children, to misery. In these cases, where the wife is honest and industrious, and desires to protect the children from their father's extravagance, she may be able, after a time, to use her earnings so as to enable her to live in comfort, yet the moment her pittance is such to enable her to do so, her husband can step in, take away all her honest earnings, and dissipate them without the slightest hesitation.[55]

As Cameron also asserted, despite the obvious advantages of equity, only a small minority of wealthy women actually executed marriage settlements; those without separate estates were as vulnerable as their poorer sisters. A bad husband could, upon the death of his wife, dispose absolutely of her personal property, 'even to the prejudice of her children, or against any other views she may have had.'[56] Cameron drew the attention of legislators and the public to reform elsewhere, and asserted that 'he had conversed with the members of the Law Amendment Society in England, and had profited by their views on the question.'[57] Moreover, he argued, 'in every state of the Union, except two, a similar law to that which he advocated was in force and a protection had been thrown over the property of married women.'[58]

Although Attorney General John A. Macdonald argued that 'in several respects he thought the Hon. member's Bill went further than prudence would dictate,'[59] the bill was referred to a select committee for discussion. It was reported and passed with amendments, although the amendments themselves are not extant, on 22 May 1857.[60] Because this measure was received so late in the session by the Legislative Council, however, it did not reach discussion in that House and did not become law.[61]

In this context, it is not surprising that newspaper debate regarding married women's rights to property reached a crescendo in 1856–7. It was by this time widely acknowledged that reform was both necessary and inevitable, and what remained to be determined was the specific shape that amendments to the law might take. Lawyers, legislators, judges, and to some degree the general public in Upper Canada seem to have been aware of contemporary transformations within legal systems elsewhere; they evinced an open-mindedness with regard to the possibility of importing reforms and ideas not only from other common law jurisdictions but also from the civil law of Quebec and Europe.[62] These jurisdictions provided varied examples of ways in which the law of property might be altered to better protect the needs of married women. The legislators borrowed selectively from the other jurisdictions, adapting their ideas to fit the perceived needs of the Upper Canadian community.

In Upper Canada it was believed that the civil law provided better protection for married women than did the common law, and that amendments to the law were, as the editors of the *Globe* asserted in 1856, 'rendered unnecessary in Lower Canada by the more equitable provisions of the French law prevailing in that section of the Province.'[63] In contrast to the derision that common law lawyers would heap upon civil law doctrine by the end of the nineteenth century, the editors of the *Upper Canada Law Journal* declared themselves 'quite prepared to admit that some improvements might be drawn from the civil law, which would remove such evils as might be found in the principles of the Common Law.'[64]

The civil law of France was pointed to as providing better protection for the wages of married women. In Upper Canada a husband had an absolute claim on all wages earned by his wife, even if she lived apart from him because of his cruelty or neglect; as the *Globe* lamented in 1857, 'she may be separated from her husband, who may be living with a mistress, no matter, the law gives what she has to him ... A married woman cannot legally claim her own earnings, her salary is her husband's and he could compel a second payment and treat the first as void if paid to the wife without his consent.'[65] In France, by contrast, the editors of the *Upper Canada Law Journal* asserted, 'a wife, when engaged in any branch of commerce, as keeping a shop, has entire protection against the husband's interference with her gains – she is termed Marchande publique, and must have her husband's consent to set up trade; but, that consent once given, she has the same power of trading, and of contracting debts, as if she were a feme sole.' Although such protection did not apply when a woman was working with her husband in a joint business, even when working with her spouse, 'the judges ... receive[d] the wife's complaints when her earnings were interfered with ... and [gave] her a summary redress.' Such an amendment to the common law, or 'the importation of some such law, or some such judicial practice,'[66] could provide judges and magistrates with the means to prevent the worst cases of male abuse of marital economic privilege. The editors were particularly favourable to such a reform because it had the merit of providing protection to individual women in exceptional cases without making exceptional cases the basis of general legislation; protection orders for wages were only given to married women in France under the specific direction of the bench, under conditions that paralleled those accepted in Upper Canadian alimony suits.

Examples of reform from common law jurisdictions were also carefully considered. It was well known that 'ameliorations have obtained in the principal States of the Union.'[67] In New York State, for example, in 1848 all women had been granted the right to hold property which they brought to marriage, or inherited by gift or devise, separate from the control of their husbands and without liability for their husbands' debts.[68] The petition submitted by women to the Legislative Council in 1856 had made specific reference to this act as a model upon which Upper Canadian reform might be based. It is clear, however, that legislators in Upper Canada were not entirely comfortable with the provisions of the 1848 New York act; the wording of the New York statute implied the right of the wife to dispose of her property without the consent of her husband, a possibility which Upper Canadian legislators sought specifically to preclude.[69]

The agitation in Britain for a married women's property act and the passage of the Matrimonial Causes Act of 1857 were also closely followed by the Upper Canadian press and by the legal community.[70] The Law Amendment Society in England advocated a thoroughgoing reformation of the law regarding married women and property. A liberal law analogous to the New York act of 1848, Sir Erskine Perry's 'Bill to Amend the Law with Respect to the Property of Married Women,' was defeated in 1857.[71] Despite the determined efforts of a small number of vocal and committed feminists, English legislators chose to limit the scope of reform so as to deal only with those cases in which injustice against married women was most glaring; the Matrimonial Causes Act of 1857 allowed separated women and wives deserted by their husbands to apply to police magistrates for 'an Order to protect any Money or Property she may acquire by her own lawful Industry, and any Property which she may become possessed of, after such Desertion, against her Husband or his Creditors.'[72] The legislation did not establish the concept of a statutory separate estate for all married women, thereby leaving all inherited property, except that held under marriage settlements in the Court of Chancery, under the complete control and disposition of husbands.[73] The Matrimonial Causes Act was considered by Upper Canadian legislators, but was rejected as an inadequate remedy for the legitimate grievances married women faced in the province. In particular, statutory provisions for married women's separate property were perceived as necessary in Upper Canada, while such might not be the case in England: as one member of the Legislative Assembly argued, 'In England, generally speaking, there were always made marriage settlements, and provisions for wife and children. Such things were not common in Canada – the rule being quite the opposite to what it is in England.'[74] The Matrimonial Causes Act was also inadequate because protection orders were only to be issued upon judicial separation or when husbands had deserted their wives for a period of at least two years. These provisions did relieve some of the worst cases of injustice, but grievances remained. Many examples of drunken, cruel, adulterous, or lazy husbands could be found, and under this act the wives of such men had no remedy.

Cameron's bill was closely followed by the press and was evaluated against this background of reforms elsewhere. Despite a widespread acknowledgment that the grievances of married women were real, his specific proposals were deemed too radical by most commentators; few, however, were opposed to some limited reform. As the editors of the *Upper Canada Law Journal* admitted, it was clearly not productive of justice that a woman 'equal before marriage, becomes legally an inferior.' This journal, the voice of the legal community, had been, with the *Globe*, a consistent critic of the present state of the law; yet the editors were adamant that strict limitations be placed on the extent of reform: 'The violent remedies proposed in the present day [particularly in America] would be worse than the alleged disease.' While eager to 'remove such evils as may be found in the principles of the Common Law,' the editors urged proponents of reform to 'reason fairly, without resorting to the clap-trap of the Bloomer School.'[75] According to them, Cameron's bill was 'going too far as an experiment' and would have given women excessive powers:

It deals with a subject upon which legislation is required; but we scarcely think it furnishes the legislation necessary. The difficulty of at all mastering the law of husband and wife has in England, until recently, deterred her most experienced and most gifted jurists. It is a delicate, and it may be unsafe, thing to enact that husband and wife shall no longer be one but two persons. The dependence of the wife upon the husband has long been recognized as a guarantee of connubial felicity. The absolute dependence may in some cases work hardship. Why then not proceed by making provision for exceptional cases instead of making exceptional cases the basis of general legislation.[76]

Ultimately, it was this view of reform that would triumph.

It was not only lawyers who drew these distinctions between excessive demands and legitimate grievances, between providing relief in exceptional cases and undermining the husband's just authority. Even the Toronto *Globe*, the most consistent advocate of reform, was careful to distinguish between the need to better protect wives and the excessive demands of 'strong-minded women,' demands which the editors did not support: 'The absurd demands of a small party of strong-minded women in the neighboring Republic, for equality of political rights as well as those relating to persons and property, will never make much headway in Canada.' In contrast, the Married Women's Property Committee in England, closely associated with the Law Amendment Society, was viewed with favour: 'The movement in England has assumed a more reasonable, and at the same time a more practical and practicable shape. The distinguished ladies who have petitioned Parliament for a reform of the law in that country have very properly limited their demands to a remedy for acknowledged grievances.' Because the women in Canada were making similarly moderate and 'reasonable' demands, the *Globe* gave the petitioning campaign its unqualified support.[77]

Despite a widespread fear of allowing reform to go 'beyond what prudence would dictate,' it is interesting to note that one anonymous individual, in an open letter to the *Globe*, suggested a much more far-reaching solution to the problems faced by married women. He or she argued that all women should be able to control and dispose of their 'widow's thirds,' or dower, during their husbands' lifetimes. The author argued that 'those favoured ones who have got good husbands' would find such powers of control unnecessary, but that if such a rule were implemented 'thousands ... would affix their gratitude,' although many of these very women were 'afraid' to make any demands for improvements in married women's property rights because of the possible reaction of domineering husbands. It is not surprising, however, that such a model of reform was not adopted. This right to a one-third claim during the marriage would have seriously interfered with the husband's common law ability to manage family property. Indirectly, the letter-writer also asserted that women's domestic labour entitled them to an inalienable share in family property at all times during marriage. Such a vision of marriage as an economic partnership was incongruous with the cult of domesticity and the doctrine of separate spheres, and even the more liberal act of 1884 would not include such provisions.[78]

In this context of mounting public discussion and pressure, Cameron's bill was reintroduced in the Legislative Council in 1858. The debates that are extant reveal little if any opposition to the measure in the upper House. The bill was advocated as a measure that would protect innocent and defenceless married women of the lower classes, and much emphasis was placed on the stereotype of the irresponsible, drunken, workingman husband: 'Cases of a very harsh nature, not far from the parliament buildings, had occurred, arising from the dissipation of the property of married women by dissolute husbands.'[79] Although the bill was passed by the council on 30 April 1858, it was not considered by the Legislative Assembly, most likely because the government was completely deadlocked.[80]

Pressure for reform, however, did not abate, and accordingly the measure was once again introduced in the Legislative Council at the opening of the 1859 session. The bill was introduced on 1 February, read for a second time without debate on 11 February, and passed on 18 February.[81] If it had not previously been clear to Macdonald and other opponents of reform in the Legislative Assembly that pressure for such a measure would continue until some form of protective act was passed, it was now patently obvious. On 18 March the bill was introduced in the Legislative Assembly,[82] and on 11 April, on the motion of Cameron, the House went into Committee to consider it.[83] Considerable opposition to the bill was expressed by Mowat[84] and by Attorney General John A. Macdonald who, despite party differences, joined forces to ensure the amendment of the bill to exclude its most liberal clauses:

Mr. MOWAT proposed to amend the first clause by striking out the words 'personal earnings' and inserting the words 'all property acquired by her by inheritance, demise, bequest as next of kin of an intestate, or any other way after marriage.'

Mr. MERRITT preferred leaving the Bill as it stood.

The amendment was carried.

Attorney General MACDONALD said the clause as it originally stood was calculated to increase the number of bachelors in the Province. It certainly put the husband at the mercy of the wife – a position which was not desirable. The happiness of married life much depended on there being a community of interest and community of property. [Hear, hear and laughter]

Mr. BROWN ... thought a committee of bachelors would be able to weigh the facts dispassionately. The creation of separate monied interests between married people was not desirable. It was calculated to raise differences where – as an honourable friend next to him suggested – all should be sweet as sugar and honey. [Laughter] Only fancy a rich wife domineering over a poor husband.[85]

Despite the sarcasm and levity of Brown[86] and the attorney general, support for the bill was widespread. On 25 April the bill was recommitted, on the motion of Mowat, 'for the purpose of introducing some amendments he had drafted, in which the Attorney General West concurred.'[87] When recommitted, the bill received the assent of the House and, upon reconsideration and the assent of the Legislative Council, became law. As passed, the legislation was clearly protective in intent.

The Married Women's Property Act of 1859 began by providing that

[e]very woman, who has married since the Fourth day of May, one thousand eight hundred and fifty-nine, or who marries after this Act takes effect, without any marriage contract or settlement, shall and may, notwithstanding her coverture, have, hold and enjoy all her real and personal property, whether belonging to her before marriage, or acquired by her by inheritance, devise, bequest or gift, or as next of kin to an intestate or in any other way after marriage, free from the debts and obligations of her husband, and from his control or disposition without her consent, in as full and ample a manner as if she continued sole and unmarried, any law, usage or custom to the contrary notwithstanding.[88]

This clause did not give married women the right to dispose of such property without the consent of their husbands, a right that limited the practical usefulness of the measure for needy wives; a deserted or abused wife could hold her property but not alienate or encumber it to provide an income for her day-to-day maintenance. This limitation was made very clear by the inclusion of the proviso that 'no conveyance or other act of a wife in respect of her real estate shall deprive her husband of any estate he may become entitled to as tenant by the curtesy.'[89] This clause gave all women married after 1859 a statutory separate estate analogous to those upheld in the Court of Chancery. Any real property was protected for the wife and could not be dissipated. The husband served as automatic trustee, as the court could not select third parties to serve in this capacity; he could manage her property, but was precluded from alienating or disposing of it, at least in theory. He also served as trustee over her personal property – money and chattels – and this act did not make clear to what degree, if any, the wife had powers of disposition or control over such goods. Unlike under marriage settlements, therefore, this legislation did not guarantee women with separate property an independent income or the means to escape from brutal spouses. Because the chancellors had been successful in the enforcement of such settlements, this act was seen as a reasonable democratization of the law. In practice, however, and not surprisingly in view of the experience of Mary Torrance, the unfortunate woman whose husband had absconded with her settled property, the fact that the husband became the automatic trustee for his wife's separate property was the central weakness of this section of the legislation. The failure to provide women with an allowance out of the profits obtained by way of their property also limited the ability of women to benefit from their property; they were dependent upon the consent of their husbands to use any money or chattels to buy luxuries for themselves in a functional marriage, to go into business for themselves, or to ensure their own survival in the case of separation.

Mowat and Macdonald's amendments were even more damaging to the section of the Act that dealt with the separate earnings of the wife. While Cameron had advocated giving all wives control over their earnings, it was ultimately enacted that 'no married woman shall be entitled to her earnings during coverture without an order of protection under the provisions hereinafter contained.'[90] Protection orders were to be granted at the discretion of the magistrate under the following conditions:

Any married woman having a decree for alimony against her husband, or any married woman who lives apart from her husband, having been obliged to leave him for cruelty or other cause, which by law justifies her leaving him, and renders him liable for her support, or any married woman whose husband is a lunatic with or without lucid intervals, or any married woman whose husband is undergoing sentence of imprisonment in the Provincial Penitentiary, or in any gaol for a criminal offense, or any married woman whose husband from habitual drunkenness, profligacy or other cause, neglects and refuses to provide for her support, and that of his family, or any married woman whose husband has never been in this Province, or any married woman who is deserted or abandoned by her husband, may obtain an order of protection entitling her, notwithstanding her coverture, to have and enjoy all her earnings and those of her minor children, and any acquisitions therefrom, free from the debts and obligations of her husband, and from his control or disposition, and without his consent, in as full and ample a manner as if she continued sole and unmarried, any law, usage or custom to the contrary notwithstanding.[91]

The use of the phrase 'without his consent' is revealing. When a husband was clearly irresponsible or absent, it was acknowledged that a wife required the power of using, not merely holding, her property, or else it would be impossible for her to ensure her own support and that of dependent children. It was considered unnecessary, however, to give all women control over their earnings; it is striking that no parallel mechanism was created to allow women control over the rents and profits from land in cases in which husbands were irresponsible, abusive, or profligate. Despite these limitations, legislators were attempting to avoid the mistakes of English legislation, which granted control of earnings only to women who were legally separated or had been deserted for at least two years. In Upper Canada, protection orders were made available to all women who would be deemed deserving of alimony and therefore to a much larger number than were protected under the English Matrimonial Causes Act.[92] It is instructive to note that procedures and remedies in alimony cases were also confirmed and clarified in 1859, perhaps – in a manner parallel to events in Britain surrounding the Matrimonial Causes Act – as an alternative to providing wives with control over their earnings.[93] The legislation of 1859, like the model in Chancery upon which it was based, was dependent on judicial discretion for its successful operation.

The Act of 1859 attempted to eliminate the problems faced by women married to abusive, irresponsible men, while simultaneously preserving family unity and the authority of the husband. Ultimately, legislators created a unique law that reflected the particular concerns and beliefs of Upper Canadians and the established precedent of the local Court of Chancery. The Act did not challenge traditional conceptions of the family, and legislators were more concerned with forcing men to behave in a responsible manner than with expanding 'women's rights.' Legislators, like the chancellors, were willing to uphold a woman's 'rights as a wife ... to [her husband's] company and to his respect ... and to a comfortable and convenient home.'[94] These rights of women within the separate domestic sphere were, as one woman argued in an open letter to the Sarnia *Observer* in 1857, believed to have been 'given to her at creation, and not many are disposed to deny them.'[95] The act of 1859 was intended to protect women from the power of abusive and irresponsible husbands, to ensure their rights as loving helpmates within a still hierarchical family. It was only in this context that remedial legislation could be passed, and it was because the legislation was explicitly protective that its objectives were applauded by the general population. The act received the support of reformers and conservatives alike, and, despite its limitations, represented the first quasi-feminist legislative victory for Upper Canadian women. It was particularly welcomed by the 'ladies' of the province. As the editors of the Barrie *Northern Advance* asserted in their review of the legislative accomplishments of the 1859 session, the act was widely believed to be 'a righteous one, [which] deserves to be made the law of the land.'[96]

5

'The Difference between Women's Rights and Women's Wrongs': The Acts of 1872 and 1873

The Married Women's Property Act, 1872, was much more controversial than its predecessor of 1859. The Hamilton *Spectator*, for example, decried the new Act as 'an act so extraordinary in its provisions that we hasten to give a summary of it for the benefit of our numerous readers – especially the married [presumably male] ones.' The editors proceeded to exaggerate the liberating potential of the legislation and concluded their attack with a deliberate attempt to link this legislation to the 'extreme' demands of the 'woman's rights' movement of the United States:

Who will say, after this, that women have not equal rights in Ontario? Oh, Woodhull, Claflin! Cease your clatter. Come to the land of the free. Shake off from your sandals the dust of the Republic; unite your voices in obtaining for the ladies of Ontario the right to thrash their husbands, free love and female suffrage, and, among women, blessed indeed will be the mothers, wives, daughters and sweethearts of the free and independents of this enlightened Province.[1]

Such arguments, however, were based upon a faulty reading of the Act. The Married Women's Property Act of 1872 was remedial and improved upon the practical relief afforded to wives under the act of 1859. It removed the necessity of protection orders, gave all women the right to hold their earnings separate from the control of their husbands, and granted wives powers of disposal over their personal property, rights that were essential to the enjoyment of money and chattels. The 1873

Married Women's Real Estate Act both confirmed that the act of 1872 had not granted wives dispositive powers over their real estate and provided a mechanism by which deserted and abused wives could be granted such rights in order to use land – and, more important, profits from the sale of land – to ensure their day-to-day maintenance. The two acts were based upon a continuing belief that it was unnecessary and unwise, except in cases of neglect and irresponsibility on the part of the husband, to separate the interests of husband and wife, 'two parties who,' in the words of the *Globe*, 'are in ordinary cases – to all intents and purposes – one.'[2] For this reason, the husband retained his role as trustee over his wife's separate property. The *Globe's* language illustrates that while property law reform began the process of deconstructing the legal fiction of marital unity, it did little to change the ideal of marital unity, and wifely subordination, as a social construct.

Reform was necessary in the 1870s because the limitations of the act of 1859, particularly its failure to include a woman's earnings as part of her statutory separate estate and to allow wives to dispose of their money and chattels, were recognized in and beyond the legal community. As the *Globe* asserted in 1869, the act of 1859 had provided married women with very limited practical relief:

In these days when the rights of women of all classes are so persistently discussed, it is very natural that the condition of married women should come in for a share of attention. These have other and more formidable wrongs to complain of than not being allowed to vote at Municipal or Parliamentary elections, or take their places as representatives in Her Majesty's 'faithful Commons.' The condition in which they [married women] have been held in Britain for centuries, has in fact been very injurious, and has had its origin in the fact that the wife was regarded as her husband's slave. She can hold no property of her own, and her husband may compel her to work for her own support and that of her children, and then come in and appropriate to his own use the fruits of her labours. He can maltreat and desert her, and then, when, by her own industry, she has made a home for herself, he can appropriate everything, occupy her house, if it is her own, may sell it, and go off again, and leave her utterly destitute. She can occupy no house in her own name into which her husband cannot legally force his way, and can inherit or earn no property which he cannot seize. Among the better classes some relief is secured by marriage settlements; and among the humbler a 'protection order' from a magistrate affords a limited degree of much needed safety in certain cases. The latter, however, is very limited at present in its application.[3]

While this description of the law was deliberately exaggerated, as the editors of this paper were well aware that the wife's separate estate was now statutorily recognized and protected and that the husband therefore had no claim on any house or property that his wife had inherited, the husband could still force his way into a home which his wife had purchased from her own earnings, unless she had a magistrate's protection order. Moreover, even when the wife had inherited property her ability to use such property for her own benefit and protection was limited since she did not have powers of alienation, even over money and chattels, and such goods could easily be seized and squandered by ruthless husbands. As the editors further argued in 1870, while it was considered morally wrong for a husband to waste the property which his wife had earned by her own labour, he still had a legal right to behave in such an irresponsible manner: 'No man has a right to pauperize himself and his family ... the sooner a good many of them understand that they have not a right to do what they like with their own property or that of their wives, so much the better.'[4] The fact that the editors made specific reference to working men in this discussion is suggestive of the class bias that underlay marital property reform; in the minds of reformers, if the drunken, irresponsible behaviour of working-class men could not always be controlled, its damaging impact on children and wives could at least be limited. The *Local Courts and Municipal Gazette* was explicit in its call for remedial legislation: 'The remedy is to be found in that which we have again and again advocated, namely, the abolition of the control of the husband over the property of his wife.'[5]

While law editors and journalists intermittently decried the state of the law, the women of the province, in contrast to the 1850s, seem to have played little direct role in the passage of remedial legislation in 1872 and 1873, perhaps because middle- and upper-class women were much more likely to have inherited property than wages, and such property was already protected under the legislation of 1859. Even without such specific pressure, however, the stirrings of the nascent 'woman movement' in the province, and the example of more radical female agitation south of the border, imposed an obligation upon the legislature to better meet the needs of women. The Toronto *Daily Mail* asserted happily that the woman movement was not yet well established in Ontario:

The women of this country have no claim to be considered strong-minded. Thank Heaven for it. While their sterner sisters in other lands disturb the public tranquillity by efforts to upset a social system which dates from Eden, they are content to stay at home and cultivate the domestic arts. They are not ambitious to issue from the home and wrangle in the courts of law. They do not insist upon their right to aid the cause of science by assisting at the dissection of medical subjects. They do not harass the community with public lectures. They blush at the mere mention of Bloomers. In their most playful moods they do not, as a rule, smoke cigarettes, or ride velocipedes, or shoot inconstant lovers. We doubt if our ladies would consent to meddle with a 'Contagious Diseases' movement, and it would be difficult to find the ferocity of a petroleuse among the poorer sort.[6]

While the woman movement was not as strong in Ontario in the early 1870s as it was in the United States or Great Britain, there was, none the less, growing knowledge of and interest in woman's rights. As early as 1855 the American Lucy Stone had spoken to enthusiastic and receptive audiences in Toronto;[7] and the founding of the first Canadian branches of the Women's Christian Temperance Union in 1873 and of the suffrage organization, the Toronto Women's Literary Club, in 1876 suggest that this was a period of growing political awareness for Ontario women.[8] While no explicit connection was drawn in the papers or the legislature between property law reform and a desire to head off any tendency of the province's women to greater organization and demands, it was recognized that a failure to eliminate legitimate female grievances would encourage moderate women to make more radical demands for political equality. Even the conservative *Daily Mail* acknowledged this possibility:

But when we consider that men have always been the law-makers, the suspicion of their having secured to themselves an undue portion of the powers and privileges of social life may possibly be well-founded, and, if not, the suspicion may be pardoned, seeing it is so easy and natural for law-makers to frame laws in favour of themselves.[9]

In this context, despite the failure of women to mount a petitioning campaign, the legislature acted to eliminate acknowledged grievances and to reassure women that their needs and concerns would be protected by an all-male Parliament.

As in the 1850s, pressure for legal reform, and in particular for the fusion of law and equity, also contributed to the readiness of the legislature to re-examine married women's property law. As the editors of the *Canadian Law Times* argued in 1872, the continued existence of two contradictory systems of law made a mockery of assertions of the superiority of English justice and created numerous practical hardships for litigants.[10] It is not surprising that this subject aroused the attention of the law journal. It is, however, indicative of a popular discontent with the state of the law that similar complaints were voiced in the Toronto *Daily Telegraph*: 'It is very strange if British law, which is said to be the perfection of reason, cannot be administered except by two courts acting on two different and often antagonistic principles.' The Court of Chancery had 'sprung out of the great moral ideas of veracity and justice – it has been expanded in our national life – it has been developed and applied with wisdom to the requirements of the infinite variety of human concerns.' These principles, the editors continued, must be introduced into the common law itself:

If the machinery of the common law courts is too narrow to do substantial justice to all parties, can it not be extended and made more powerful so that in each case every point may be reached, every right enforced and every wrong remedied, without adding to the first wrong an additional one in the shape of an inequitable decision?[11]

In England, the Law and Equity Commission was studying the possibility of the fusion of these courts; its investigations were followed with interest in Ontario.[12]

In Ontario there was much support for fusion, but considerable fear existed that proceeding too quickly on this issue, particularly if fusion did not take place in England, would deprive the courts of the benefit of British precedent. The Toronto *Globe*, while applauding the general purpose of fusion, expressed a fear that, 'supposing the courts should be amalgamated, our court could not adopt the decisions of the courts of England unless these courts were amalgamated like our own.'[13] In 1873, in response to these concerns, Oliver Mowat introduced and passed a compromise measure that provided for the partial fusion of law and equity. The Administration of Justice Act decreed that 'the courts of law and equity shall be, as far as possible, auxiliary to one another respectively, for the more speedy, convenient and inexpensive administration of justice.'[14]

The Administration of Justice Act set the stage for the eventual complete fusion of the two courts, a fusion that would raise the question of whether English or Upper Canadian Chancery precedents regarding married women's property would be adopted in the amalgamated common law of Ontario. In the interim, however, no such dilemma faced the legislature; the complete separation of the property interests of husband and wife, possible under marriage settlements in the English Court of Chancery, was explicitly rejected by legislators who showed a consistent preference for the more limited, unique precedents set in Upper Canada. What was necessary, in the eyes of legislators and the public at large, was some 'medium measure,'[15] which would better protect the property and security of needy wives without creating a complete separation of the interests of spouses, a measure that would eliminate wrongs perpetrated against defenceless women without granting wives excessive rights and independence. The fear that legislation might go too far and undermine family unity and masculine authority remained pervasive, despite the widespread understanding of the limitations of the act of 1859.[16] Even the *Globe*, the most consistent advocate of reform, argued that to grant women powers of management and disposition over their separate estates would only 'abate one great inequity by inaugurating another still more intolerable.'[17] Advocates of reform were eager to distinguish between the remedies they proposed, which, they argued, would eliminate legitimate female grievances, and the excessive demands of 'strong-minded' women. This distinction drawn in the legislature and in popular debate between the 'rights' and 'wrongs' of women was central to the passage of the Married Women's Property Act of 1872.

In their search for such a 'medium measure,' legislators looked to the example provided by the English Married Women's Property Act of 1870, itself an interim measure that preceded the fusion of law and equity. In April 1868, a married women's property bill that had been drafted by Richard Pankhurst of the Social Science Association was introduced in the British House of Commons.[18] The preamble to the bill stated that the 'law of property and contract, with respect to married women, is unjust in principle, and presses with particular severity upon the poorer classes of the community.'[19] The central provisions of the bill would have given married women full control over their separate estates, including the right to enter into contracts and to alienate their property.[20] The wages of all married women, not just those who had been issued protection orders under the Matrimonial Causes Act, were to be held as the wife's separate property.[21] The bill was not passed in 1868 because, introduced late in the session, it died in committee.[22] Concerns raised about this bill during debate, however, are revealing. Legislators expressed a 'chivalric' fear that women, no matter what laws might be enacted, were unable to resist their husbands' physical power and powers of persuasion. In the context of such a view of marital relations, protection and independence were, as the editors of the *Solicitor's Journal* argued, contradictory and irreconcilable: 'Would not ninety-nine women out of a hundred ... put their fortunes into their husband's hands to do what he liked with and is not that the very evil which settlements were meant to avert?'[23] Changes such as those proposed by Pankhurst, the editors continued, would 'revolution-ise the position of married women in England as regards property,' but it was not clear to these men that such a revolution in property rights would protect women or serve their interests within the family. These concerns were shared in Ontario, at least within the legal community, as is illustrated by the reproduction of this article in the *Local Courts and Municipal Gazette*.

In 1869 Pankhurst's bill was reintroduced and passed in the House of Commons, but reached the House of Lords too late in the session for it to be discussed. In 1870 two bills with regard to married women's property, Pankhurst's bill and a much more conservative measure, were introduced in the Commons. The alternative bill, as Lee Holcombe has argued, 'embodied suggestions made earlier in the Commons that married women could be best protected not by giving them the same property rights as unmarried women but by two other means: by applying to all married women the equitable principle of a married women's separate property held in trust, and by extending to more women the protection-order system instituted by the Divorce Act of 1857.'[24] The object of this bill was to make all husbands the automatic trustees of their wives' sepa-rate estates; as such, they would be obliged by law to use the property to the benefit of their wives and would be prevented from alienating it or disposing of it, but wives themselves were explicitly to be denied any control over their statutory separate property.[25] Although this alternative measure was defeated in the House of Commons by a vote of 208 to 46 and the more liberal measure passed, many of the limitations on women's control over their property recommended in this bill were insisted upon by the House of Lords. Despite these amendments, the Commons passed the revised bill.[26]

The Married Women's Property Act of 1870 was condemned by the original proponents of reform as 'a legislative abortion', a 'feeble compro-mise,' and 'so badly drawn, so faulty and so absurd in many of its details as to be unintelligible.'[27] The central provisions of the Act allowed a mar-ried woman to hold her earnings separate from the control of her hus-band without the necessity of a protection order, to hold money acquired by inheritance during marriage not exceeding the value of two hundred pounds, and stocks and bonds held in her own name as her separate estate.[28] This property was protected from being squandered or abused by the husband, but wives were not given dispositive powers over their statutory separate estates.

The English act met with considerable approval in Ontario, and more than any other factor encouraged the passage of the act of 1872. It was believed that the English act, as amended by the House of Lords, provided a model upon which reform could safely be based. In the years preceding the act of 1872, while newspapers and legal periodicals had occasionally lamented the problems that remained under the act of 1859, no attention had been given to the possibility of reform in the legislature. In 1872, however, in the wake of the passage of the English act, a bill was quickly introduced and passed by Blake's Liberal government.

Adam Crooks, Attorney-General in the Blake government and in his own time a well-known reformer and a lawyer with extensive experience in Chancery,[29] emphasized the protective purpose of the bill when he moved its second reading:

> He pointed out that a previous Act had given married women the right to all property which she held at the time of coverture, or which subsequently became hers, so that the principle of the Bill now under consideration was no new one ... He had framed this Bill while on the other side of the House, and had since examined the Act passed in relation to the subject by the Imperial Parliament, in 1870, and he found a number of the clauses identical in their scope with those of this Bill.[30]

Crooks stressed the fact that the legislation was based upon English precedent, and presented it as an extension and clarification of the rights already granted to wives by the act of 1859. Wives were given the right to alienate and dispose of the personal property they already held under the act of 1859; the right to use money and chattels, it was acknowledged, was integral to the right to enjoy them. Moreover, this made statutory separate estates correspond more exactly to separate estates in Chancery, which almost invariably provided wives with powers of disposition with regard to any income derived from real property, thereby allowing them some scope for personal purchases and for independent survival when husbands proved reckless or abusive. The necessity of protection orders was also removed, and wages were hereafter to be considered part of the wife's separate estate. Premier Blake himself argued in favour of the bill, asserting that it did not challenge the natural order of the family, but was intended to provide wives with protection against wrongs committed by men:

> Mr. LAUDER said this was a Woman's Rights Bill and he did not see why the Attorney General did not go farther and give women the right to vote and to hold office. [Hear, hear]

Mr. CORBY suggested that the Attorney General should insert a clause allowing a woman to give three days notice of an action for divorce. [Laughter]

Mr. BLAKE My hon. friend does not see the difference between women's rights and women's wrongs.[31]

Although the bill was mocked by a few backbenchers and condemned by the Conservative opposition, it received assent on 2 March 1872.

The most far-reaching change introduced in 1872 was the inclusion of the wages of married women as part of the statutory separate estate. This was consistent with a popular and legislative belief that it was working-class wives who were most grievously injured by the provisions of the common law and that the operation of protection orders under the act of 1859 was 'very limited at present.'[32] The new act read:

All the wages and personal earnings of a married woman, and any acquisitions therefrom, and all proceeds or profits from any occupation or trade which she carries on separately from her husband or derived from any literary, artistic or scientific skill, and all investments of such wages, earnings, moneys or property shall hereafter be held and enjoyed by such married woman, and disposed of without her husband's consent, as fully as if she were a feme sole; and no order of protection shall hereafter become necessary in respect of any such earnings or acquisitions.[33]

This granted the wife the explicit right to dispose of her personal property – her money and chattels – 'without her husband's consent.'

The act was confusing, however, because such rights of disposition were not clearly granted with respect to real estate. Under section 1 of the act, the right of married women to hold their real estate separate from the control of their husbands was reiterated from the act of 1859, but the extent to which a wife would be able to control this property herself was not made clear. This section read:

After the passing of this Act, the real estate of any married woman, which is owned by her at the time of her marriage or acquired by her in any manner during her coverture, and the rents, issues and profits thereof respectively, shall without prejudice and subject to the trusts of any settlement affecting the same, be held and enjoyed by her for her separate use, free from any estate or claim of her husband during her lifetime, or as tenant by the curtesy, and her receipts alone shall be a discharge for any rents, issues and profits; and any married woman shall be liable on any contract made by her respecting her real estate, as if she were a feme sole.[34]

Although this section purported to make a married woman liable on her own contracts, and such liability implied a right to alienate the lands with respect to which a contract might be made, the right to alienate real property was not explicitly given, as it was with personal property.

Reactions to the new act were mixed. The *Globe* was characteristically supportive of legislation that, in its view, would protect the interests of women married to irresponsible or abusive men: the measures 'seem to us to give married women a very fair amount of protection.'[35] The Toronto *Daily Mail*, perhaps because it was a Tory-sponsored paper and because reform had been enacted by a new Liberal government, responded to the passage of the Act with great hostility: 'As to married women it may be questioned whether our Legislature, in substituting for the ancient spirit of the Common Law new theories of the wife's independence of the husband, has not overstepped the limits of prudence and endangered the harmony of wedded life.' Under the common law, 'it may be stated generally that all her lands and chattels pass on her marriage to her husband for their joint lives. The maintenance and protection afforded by the husband are considered sufficient compensation for such surrender by the wife.' Such an argument, however, ignored the fact that this legislation was intended to protect women whose husbands failed to maintain and support them; opposition to the act was based on a false perception that it had unequivocally granted women full powers of control and disposition over their separate estates, including their real estate:

By the Married Women's Property Act of last session, it is provided that all the real and personal property of a married woman, unless affected by a settlement, shall be held by her as separate estate ...

But the subsequent sections of the Act give wives in Ontario powers which they never ask for, which they would be better off for not possessing, and which, if they exercise, put an end to domestic happiness. The married woman may now carry on business on her own responsibility and for her own advantage; she may hold stocks and vote as a stock-holder; she may deposit in her own name in the bank, and 'check-out'; she may insure the life of her husband for her own benefit and that of her children; she may institute lawsuits and defend them apart from her husband; she can make contracts rendering herself alone liable. Such are the reckless laws with which the Reformers of Ontario inaugurate their reign. In gratitude for these, the first principles of revolution, the 'strong-minded' matron of a future day may teach her infants to lisp the name of Crooks.

Even in this attack, however, these critics of the act admitted the necessity of protecting wives from the coercive power of husbands: 'There is one case, that where a woman is linked in wedlock to a cruel or profligate husband, in which she and her property should be rescued from the control which the Common Law gives to the husband.' Despite this admission, the editors attempted to discredit reform by exaggerating the differences between provincial legislation and the English act of 1870. Part of this attack, it is clear, was political in motivation: 'We have hinted above at some of the dangers which attend the Attorney-General's maiden effort in legislation. We have now only to hope that the good sense of the married women of Ontario will neutralize the Quixotic zeal of Mr. Crooks.'[36] By playing upon deep-seated fears of disruption of the social order, the editors hoped to undermine the government. It is suggestive of the social climate which shaped reform that such an attack could be considered potentially damaging.

The act, however, had not granted wives the dispositive powers over their property which the editors of the Daily Mail and other conservative papers feared would be disruptive of domestic harmony. This fact was clearly proved in 1873. The act of 1872 had explicitly granted wives dispositive powers over their separate personal property and had made wives liable on contract, and therefore, if given a broad reading, could have been interpreted in the courts as having granted women some powers of control over their separate real estate. Contradictory decisions with regard to the dispositive power of wives were recorded in 1872.[37] In response to these decisions, legislators specifically ruled out a liberal interpretation of the act by the passage, in 1873, of An Act to facilitate the conveyance of Real Estate by Married Women.[38] During the debate on this legislation, Crooks himself denied that the act of 1872 had ever been intended to grant wives dispositive powers over their separate real property:

Mr. BETHUNE moved the second reading of a Bill to enable married women to convey their estates. The Bill, the hon. gentleman explained, was for the purpose of enabling married women to convey their estates in their own right in the same manner as before marriage, without the concurrence or consent of their husbands. The legislation of former years was followed up by the Act introduced by the Attorney-General of this Province last session, by which she was enabled to deal with her property as if she were unmarried. Lately, however, a difficulty had arisen as to whether it was competent for a married woman within the meaning of the statute, to convey property without the consent of her husband. He proposed merely to remedy a slip in the Bill of the last session and he could not see how this important point could have been missed ...

Mr. CROOKS said that the Act of last year did not intend to provide any machinery for the conveyance of property by a married woman, but it was now proposed to establish a mode of conveyance ...[39]

The Married Women's Real Estate Act, which received assent on the 29 of March 1873, confirmed that no conveyance of real estate by a married woman would be deemed 'to be valid or effectual unless the husband is a party to and executes the deed.'[40] The act of 1872 had granted wives explicit dispositive powers over their separate personal property, powers that were not revoked by this act because it was recognized that such property would otherwise be useless. While most wives were now explictly denied dispositive powers over their land, the act of 1873 simultaneously reflected a recognition that wives in the most desperate of marriages did require control over their separate real estate in order to use this property for their own protection and to support themselves and their children. To protect women in such cases, the act granted wives dispositive powers over their separate real estate, at the discretion of the bench, on conditions that paralleled those accepted in both alimony cases and under protection orders for wages under the old act of 1859:

If a husband be, in consequence of being a lunatic, idiot or of unsound mind, or be, from any other cause, incapable of executing a deed, or if his residence be not known, or he be in prison, or be living apart from his wife by mutual consent, or if there be, in the opinion of the judge, any other cause for so doing, a judge may, by an order to be made by him, in a summary way, upon the application of the wife, and upon such evidence as to him shall seem meet, and either *ex parte*, or upon such notice to the husband as he may deem requisite, dispense with the concurrence of the husband in any case in which his concurrence is required by this Act or otherwise; and all acts, deeds, disclaimers, surrenders or powers of attorney done, executed or made by the wife, in pursuance of such order, in regard to her real estate shall be done, executed or made by her in the same manner as if she were a feme sole, and when so done, executed or made by her shall be as good and valid as they would have been if the husband had become a party to and executed the same.[41]

In all other cases, however, women were denied the right to alienate their real property, although the act of 1872 had explicitly granted wives full rights of disposition over their personal property – their money, chattels, and wages. The Married Women's Real Estate Act was, like the act of 1872, a remedial measure intended for women's protection, not their emancipation. At the same time, however, the two acts, by granting dispositive powers to wives, albeit in a halting and contradictory fashion, allowed some women scope to participate actively in the burgeoning economy of the province.

There were voices of dissent raised against the limitations imposed upon married women's dispositive capacity. Most importantly, in what was clearly a defensive attempt to influence the interpretation of the act of 1873, Richard Thomas Walkem, in his treatise on the new laws regarding married women and their property, minimized the limitations on disposition that had been affirmed by the Married Women's Real Estate Act. He asserted that 'in view of the powers indirectly conferred on married women by the Act 35 Vict., c. 16 [1872] with respect to their real estate, and assuming that these powers are not affected by the new Act,' the requirement for the husband's concurrence in the conveyance of the wife's real estate was only 'an empty concession to the prejudices of those who did not approve of the principle on which the Statute 35 Vict., c. 16, was founded.'[42] Walkem had to admit that dispositive powers, if any, had only been 'indirectly granted' by the act of 1872. His assumption that these powers were 'not affected by the new act' and his assertion that the provisions of the act of 1873 could be 'regarded only as an empty concession to the prejudices' of a conservative minority were ill-founded. The act of 1873 had deliberately been framed to eliminate the confusion that had arisen out of the act of 1872. Walkem's treatise has to be understood as a piece of propaganda, as his description of how the law ought to work. Walkem was unusual in his liberal assertion that it was the right of the wife to control her own property; his warning that without granting full dispositive powers over their separate estates the act gave women 'peculiar facilities for the commission of frauds'[43] went unheeded by the legislature throughout the 1870s. Not surprisingly, however, the contradictory powers of disposition granted under the acts of 1872 and 1873 ensured that the law remained unclear both to lay people and to lawyers. In this context, neither married women nor their creditors could adequately protect themselves.

6

'Many Frauds Not Previously Practicable': Creditors and the Acts of 1859 and 1872

In 1883 John Dynan claimed that Thomas Walls had fraudulently conveyed property to his wife and co-defendant, Catherine. Dynan, a merchant, had a judgment against Walls, an auctioneer, for $13,926, but had been unable to make good on this claim. Subsequent to the judgment, Walls had sold his businesses in Montreal and Toronto with a net gain of over $20,000, an enormous sum of money for this period. He then transferred all the cash to the ownership of his wife. Thomas Walls fled to the United States, remaining out of the jurisdiction until Dynan dropped his suit, but his wife stayed in Montreal the entire time, living with their children in the home purchased in her name with this property. Ultimately Dynan's business proved unable to withstand the losses sustained in this case.[1]

Before the passage of the acts of 1859, 1872, and 1873, Thomas and Catherine would have been unable to flout the law so blatantly. Relations between creditors and families had been straightforward under the common law; the husband was the legal owner of all family property, and although the wife might pledge credit and enter into binding contracts, she could do so only as an agent of her husband. Profits from family businesses and wages earned by the husband, the wife, and all minor members of the household belonged at law exclusively to the husband. Although entire families might abscond or refuse to pay their debts, the legal position of a creditor was clear; as one critic of the new laws observed, 'before the statutes to which we refer were enacted, the rights of husbands and wives ... were pretty generally understood, not only by the legal profession whose business it was to comprehend them, but by the community at large.'[2]

Reform, however, created enormous confusion, with the result that 'neither one class nor the other can be said to understand how the law stands.'[3] Much of this confusion stemmed from the fact that the husband served as trustee over what was ostensibly his wife's property. It was frequently unclear who owned property being used by a family and who, if anyone, had the right to alienate or dispose of land, chattels, or money. This confusion, of course, did not transform societal mores, but it did allow increased scope for fraud amongst couples who were predisposed towards dishonesty. It also dramatically transformed the way in which creditors needed to interact with married clients in order to protect their own interests. Under the common law the husband was liable for all family debts, but after the passage of the acts of 1859, 1872, and 1973 creditors had to be much more specific about who assumed liability for a debt and about the ownership of property with regard to which such debts were contracted.

Ironically, given the protective intent of the statutes, the vast majority of cases litigated under the married women's property acts involved not disputes between husband and wife, but fraud on the part of couples. Mounting evidence of such behaviour served as an inducement to liberalize married women's rights over their property so that women in such cases could be held liable under contract.[4] Armour J stated in 1881 that

the practical results of ... [the acts] have been particularly disastrous to creditors. There are hundreds, I might say thousands, of cases throughout Ontario in which the husband has contrived that the wife shall own everything; she is wealthy, he is worthless; his creditors are set at defiance because his wife owns the property; her creditors are set at defiance because...her property is not of that particular quality of separate estate which will permit them to have remedy against it.[5]

As he also lamented in dissent, 'the course and tendency of judicial decision in this country has been and is in favour of the married woman and against her creditors.' This, he asserted, was in contrast to other common law jurisdictions: 'In England it has been and is against the married woman and in favour of her creditors.'[6] Unfortunately, he did not elaborate on any reasons for this difference in statutory interpretation. Ironically from the perspective of women's rights, but not surprisingly in this context, it was often creditors, not married women, who argued for a broad interpretation of the statutes. Haunted by the possibility that an innocent wife might be defrauded by her husband or by scheming third parties, few judges in the years immediately following reform seem to have considered the possibility that a wife herself might be unscrupulous. The volume and variety of fraud litigation under these acts, however, ultimately convinced many that assumptions regarding women's innocence and lack of business acumen were erroneous.

While still proclaiming that the intent of the law was to protect defenceless women, therefore, judges slowly accepted the reality of female economic agency. By the late 1870s it was widely argued on the bench and in the business community 'that many frauds, not previously practicable, may be committed under colour of th[ese] statute[s].'[7] Perhaps not surprisingly, a number of cases in which injustice to creditors was particularly glaring appear in the law reports; such cases were reported because of the growing belief in the legal community that further reform of the law of married women and property was necessary to provide creditors with a 'remedy at law' against 'the intelligent married woman.'[8]

Since the husband, as trustee under the acts of 1859, 1872 and 1873, managed all family property but owned only some of it, confusion plagued relations between married couples and their creditors. When wives inherited property or earned income from work outside the home, their relationships with creditors were subject to three central problems: the wife had limited and contradictory powers of contract; the separate business of the wife was not clearly defined; and the husband, as trustee over all his wife's statutory separate estate, could misrepresent himself to the community as the owner of such property, thereby fraudulently obtaining credit. The most frequent problem that creditors faced, however, involved the creation of separate estate by the transfer of property from husband to wife; couples 'contrived that the wife shall own everything,'[9] and without joint ownership creditors were left without redress. In many of these cases, despite the judicial emphasis on the 'intelligent married woman,'[10] evidence suggests that husbands were still managing property independently of their wives, but were manipulating the wife's right of ownership for their own benefit (and often that of the family as a whole).

Under the Married Women's Property Act of 1859, married women were denied any contractual power. In a community long accustomed to the common law and, unlike England, with apparently little experience in dealing with settled property, the concept that someone could own property, but not dissipate it, was anomalous, and caused confusion and hardship for creditors. These problems are well illustrated in *Wright v Garden and Wife*, a case decided in 1869 in the Court of Queen's Bench. Elizabeth Garden owned separate estate consisting of a large lot and a house. She had entered into an agreement with the plaintiff to make $1,000 worth of improvements to the house. The plaintiff completed the contract, but she refused to pay him for his labour, pleading coverture. The central question to be determined in this case was whether or not the act of 1859 had given married women the right to contract debts with reference to their separate property: 'either expressly or by implication of law, [a wife could contract] a debt for the improvement of that property without the consent of her husband ... though such improvements may enable her to enjoy such property in a more full and ample manner than she could have done had they not been made.'[11]

The liability of the wife could not be upheld because her right over her real estate was a *jus protegendi*, not a *jus disponendi*, a right of enjoyment not of disposition. Richards CJ was concerned lest the wife be defrauded of her property. Although it seems likely in this case that the Gardens were acting in collusion to avoid the payment of a legitimate debt, it was also possible that Mrs Garden had been forced, whether through violence or by more gentle means of persuasion, to enter into the contract against her will, whatever story she might tell in court. Moreover, the husband could not be proceeded against because as trustee over his wife's separate estate he also was denied dispositive powers over it, despite his rights of management and control. The interests of the individual married woman were well served in this case. Clearly, however, the act of 1859 had created a species of property that was unattachable. Whatever property a married woman might hold in her own name, whether land, chattels, or money, a contract with respect to such property could not be enforced at law.

The problems that creditors faced under the act of 1859 would not have been insurmountable; once creditors learned that separate property was completely inalienable, such cases should have become obsolete. However, the position of creditors was further complicated, not clarified, by the acts of 1872 and 1873, which made wives partially liable on contract. This partial liability increased the scope for fraud. While under the act of 1859 women simply could not make binding contracts, except as agents or representatives of their husbands and with regard to their husbands' property, after 1872 they could be held liable on contract, but only with regard to certain types of property, under very limited conditions. By section 9 of the act of 1872 it was enacted that 'any married woman may be sued or proceeded against separately from her husband in respect of any of her separate debts, engagements, contracts or torts as if she were unmarried.'[12] However, married women were denied dispositive powers over their real property under the Married Women's Real Estate Act of 1873. A wife, therefore, could be held liable only to the extent of her separate personal property, her money and chattels, and such property was notoriously easy to transfer. This made it a simple matter for couples to avoid payment of their debts. The theoretical liability created by the act of 1872 was meaningless to many creditors, for it did not provide effective recourse against dishonest couples; while prosecution of a married woman was now possible, the barriers to collection of a legitimate debt remained formidable. As Patterson JA explained in 1876, the plaintiff had to prove:

1. Possession of Separate Estate at the time of the contract or when the liability accrued.

2. The contract or debt.

3. The possession of the same Separate Estate at the time of the judgment because it was the realizing out of the estate of the charge created thereon by the contract or debt.[13]

Once a debt was contracted, a wife could dispose of the separate property to which reference was made in the contract and purchase lands or chattels that could not be held liable under the original agreement. Creditors not well versed in the specifics of the law might fail to ensure that the contract contained sufficient reference to the separate estate to be enforceable. They might also make the mistake of entering into a contract on the basis of the ownership of real estate that could not be sold in execution under any circumstances. As Armour J held in 1881, the restrictions placed upon a married woman's liability on contract created an impossible situation for creditors who sold goods or rendered services to married women:

This resolution still further proves how illusory the remedy at law would be, for the intelligent married woman would take care that the property with reference to which she might be supposed to have contracted, would not wait to be charged with a judgment, and in virtue of it she would probably be entitled to plead in bar of action that she had parted with it, if she had done so before the action.[14]

A case heard in the Court of Queen's Bench in 1876 made the potential for fraud inherent in the acts of 1872 and 1873 clear to the legal community. Rosamund Stripp, who had been married in 1874 and owned separate estate, gave a promissory note, with her husband, in return for the forbearance by the creditors of her husband's debts. When the promissory note came due, Rosamund pleaded coverture and refused to pay; her husband declared himself destitute. This was a clear case of attempted fraud, and the court was loath to allow the protection of the act to be used for such a purpose. It was held that the property was her separate estate and that the notes 'were made by her respecting her said separate estate, and while the same, and the rents, issues and profits thereof were held and enjoyed by the defendant.'[15] To allow Rosamund to avoid her debt would set a dangerous precedent for all creditors:

It may be said that the effect of our Act of 1859, Consol. Stat. U.C. ch. 73 was, as it were, to create a marriage settlement for women married without a settlement, so as to protect their weakness against their husband's power, and their property against the husband's control. This is perfectly true. But the legislature by the Act of 1872, 35 Vic. ch. 16, having given to married women power to contract under certain conditions stated in the Act, the power to contract within these conditions is just as absolute as the power of any man. While the legislature has seen fit to confer the power, it is not for the Courts to limit the responsibilities arising from its exercise.[16]

It was a relatively simple matter for the judge to reach a decision in this case because Rosamund's income from her separate real property was sufficient to cover the debt; separate personal property was attachable under the legislation and her land did not have to be sold in order for the debt to be made good. Sale of the land was precluded by the Married Women's Real Estate Act of 1873, and had Rosamund's income been insufficient to cover the debt, her creditor would have been left without remedy. But personal property was now liable and, as Harrison CJ asserted, the 'right to act and bind her estate ... [would now carry] ... with it the right to act unwisely, and to her own injury, if she so wills.'[17]

The limitations on the wife's right and liability on contract also created serious problems when married women engaged in business. No confusion with regard to the ownership and management of family farms and businesses had existed under the common law, since all earnings and property became vested in the husband and he was liable for all family debts and contracts, both personal and with regard to any business in which his wife and children might labour. The act of 1859 was intended to insulate the earnings and businesses of women from abusive husbands, but made only limited changes to the common law; married women could hold and control their separate earnings only after having obtained a protection order from the local magistrate. Such orders were to be issued upon the presentation of evidence that the husband was drunken, irresponsible, absent, or abusive. In all other circumstances a woman's wages and income from a separate business were still considered the property of her husband and were therefore liable for his debts. This provision did not create any new or insurmountable complications for creditors. When a wife had obtained a protection order she was liable for all debts that she might contract with regard to her separate business, and her earnings could be attached if she failed to pay a personal debt for rent or other common necessaries. Without a protection order, redress was still possible against her husband, who remained the legal owner of her separate business even if he played no role in its day-to-day operation.

Foulds v Courtlett confirmed this interpretation of the act of 1859. For several years the defendant and his wife had operated a shop. The husband managed a confectionery business, while his wife ran a fancy-goods store. She had always given orders for her own goods, but he had paid for them. In 1862 the defendant gave up his business, but the wife continued to operate her store. The couple also continued to cohabitate. In 1869 she ordered goods for which her husband subsequently refused to pay. The plaintiff sued for this money.[18] Hagarty J rendered judgment in favour of the plaintiff and stated that:

I entertain a very strong opinion that where a husband knowingly permits his wife, who is cohabiting with him, to carry on a business of buying and selling in a shop in which he is frequently seen, that such business is to be considered to be his business, and that in absence of notice to the contrary from him, all persons dealing in the shop, or supplying goods to it, are dealing not with a person under a known disability like a wife, but directly with him, and that his authority to her will be presumed.

The fact of his coming forward and swearing that he did not buy the goods, or authorize her to pledge his credit, or that he did not interfere with the business, though cognizant from day to day of all that she was doing, cannot in my judgment free him from liability.[19]

The creditor could not obtain judgment against a married woman who did not have a protection order, and to deny him redress against the husband as well would not only be unjust to the creditor but would render it impossible for any married woman to conduct business. The husband, while living with his wife, clearly participated in the profits from the business and could not be allowed to deny his liability with regard to them. This case did not involve the protection of a married woman. This distinction was made clear by Hagarty J, who asserted that 'it would no doubt invest this case with a very different character if the parties lived separately' and that the property must be considered to be his 'so far as third persons were concerned.'[20]

Under the act of 1872, however, the position of creditors with regard to married women and their separate businesses and employment became much less clear-cut. By that act the necessity of a protection order was dispensed with, and all wages from employment outside the home and profits from separate businesses became the separate property of the wife. The act did not, however, explicitly outline the conditions under which a woman would be deemed to be employed in a separate business in which she, rather than her husband, would be entitled to profits and be liable on debts. When a husband and wife worked together, for example, to whom did the business, and the profits from it, belong? In such situations did both husband and wife retain the right to pledge credit for each other under the common law doctrine of agency? How would complicated legal rules regarding business partnerships be applied to married couples? Could wives, even when they worked in businesses on their own account, be equal players in the marketplace when they were denied full liability on contract?

These unresolved questions left married women who wanted to operate businesses in an unenviable position. Since a wife could be held liable under a contract only when she owned separate estate, women without such property, who needed to work to support themselves and their children, faced considerable obstacles in obtaining credit. This problem was recognized and lamented by Wilson J:

If the woman have no capital or separate estate, as is the case with many who go into business, so that there is no fund or assets of any kind for her creditors to look to for payment, unless the goods then bought are to be considered as the fund upon which the faith of the sales were to be made to her, a fund diminishing day by day as her business goes on until it disappears and is represented by goods purchased from others, or it may be by only a number of bad or doubtful debts, or perhaps by nothing, and the creditors are debarred from establishing a personal claim against the woman which will be binding upon her subsequently acquired property – if, in fact, the business of the married woman can be carried on only under such disadvantages, and if her creditors are to be hand-bound in that manner – will it be possible for the married woman to carry on business as it must be carried on, and as it is carried on by those in trade or business? Or will any one credit her with such a risk against him of ever being paid?[21]

As Wilson also recognized, such unresolved problems left considerable scope for fraud: 'She is successful – abundantly able to pay, only not willing. When he proceeds against her her defence is that as she had nothing when she got the money he has nothing to resort to for payment, and it is therefore unreasonable for him to expect payment.'[22]

The dishonesty with which judges could be confronted is well illustrated in *Meakin v Samson et al.*, a case that came before the court in 1878. The plaintiff's husband had become insolvent in the course of his business dealings. Certain suppliers, knowing of his insolvency and of his inability to continue in the business, had provided stock for a new venture, taking the wife's note in payment, despite the fact that she did not own any separate estate. She allowed her husband to carry on the business, giving him power of attorney and allegedly a salary of ten dollars a week. The husband, his wife, and their children continued to live together. Goods supplied to her had been seized by judgment creditors of her husband, and she entered suit to reclaim them.[23]

In his summation, Hagarty J concluded that the business 'was substantially the same old business, both in character and management, as that carried on by the husband before the insolvency.'[24] The wife knew nothing of the business, and in this context it could not be deemed her separate business exempt from liability for her husband's debts. Moreover, she admittedly did not own any separate estate. Therefore, she could not enter into a contract to purchase the goods for the store. Although she had promised to pay for these goods, such a promise was not enforceable at law. The goods, Hagarty J held, 'follow the rule of the common law and become the property of the husband.'[25] Most important, to deny her liability would be to enforce a substantial injustice against creditors:

In construing these statutes we are bound to consider the object apparently in the view of the Legislature, the wrong or injury designed to be redressed, and the remedies therefor provided ...

I understand the main objects to be the full protection of any personal property

(I need not speak of realty) of a married woman from her husband's creditors to ensure her enjoyment of them for use and support.

I also understand the object of protecting her and giving her full liberty in any business carried on by her for her own support, or that of her family, or even her husband.

But I think it must be really and truly her separate trade or business, not resting on the observance of a few empty forms, very transparently veiling the plain reality. I cannot believe that the Legislature intended to legalize an attempt like the present to evade the plain requirements of the law.[26]

If such an interpretation of the statute were to be upheld, it would undermine the insolvency laws: 'He can carry on the business precisely as before, enjoying the great advantage of having all the new stock exempt from all his old creditors' claims. He can thus have the actual benefit of a discharge in insolvency without having to conform to the legal conditions on which such discharge can lawfully be obtained, and possibly still enjoy the fruits of the evil conduct or the secreted assets which prevented his discharge.'[27] This case did not involve the protection of a married woman from coercion by her husband, and the interests of legitimate creditors must, under such conditions, be safeguarded or else confusion and disorder would reign in the business community.

Such decisions created precedents that had unfortunate consequences for married women whose husbands were irresponsible. Without full liability on contract, wives had a limited ability to conduct businesses; judges, not surprisingly, asserted that a business was only a separate business under the statute if the husband expressly removed himself from its operation. Any business in which husband and wife laboured together would be considered the property of the husband, and the profits and liabilities of the business would follow the rules of the common law. The reasoning behind such decisions was made clear by Harrison J in his ruling in *Harrison v Douglas*. William Harrison, a farmer, was in financial difficulties, and his creditors claimed the right to seize his farm assets. In contesting this claim, his wife argued that the farm belonged to her and that her husband merely acted as her agent. Harrison J ruled for the creditors, concluding that 'attempts, however ingenious, to convert the wife of a farmer into the husbandsman and the husband into her mere servant, agent or manager, so as to enable him to live on the farm, work the farm, derive his support from it, and do so in defiance of his creditors, are not to be encouraged.'[28] Although the judge may have been correct in suspecting that the Harrisons were attempting to use the legislation to shield property from the rightful claims of creditors, the important theme to emerge from this decision was that a woman could not be conceived of as operating a farm as her separate business because a farm could not, as Harrison J put it, be successful without the expertise of a man: 'If the occupation or trade be such that a wife cannot carry it on without her husband's active cooperation or agency it is not easy to discover in what sense it can honestly be called an occupation or trade, carried on by her separate from her husband.'[29] Such a ruling, while potentially ruinous for women whose husbands squandered the joint earnings of a family business, was entirely consistent with the image of the wife as helpmate, occupied solely in her separate domestic sphere, and with the common law assumption that a husband would manage all family property because he was ultimately responsible for family maintenance and support. While it was undoubtedly true that a wife would have had difficulty running a farm without a husband, or at without least hired hands, this fact did not lead logically or necessarily to the assumption that because a husband worked on a farm, it belonged to him. Moreover, no parallel acknowledgment was made in law of the fact that a husband could not run a successful farm without the labour and expertise of his wife.

A much more frequent problem for creditors under the act of 1859 and those of 1872 and 1873 was determining who was the legal owner of property being managed by the husband. As trustee, the husband could fraudulently present himself to the community and to potential creditors as the outright owner of his wife's property and thereby incur liabilities with respect to it; if the wife could then prove that the property was part of her statutory separate estate, the creditor would be denied redress. The case of Mercie Jane Mitchell provides an example of such misrepresentation. Mercie Jane had been married in 1859 and had inherited land from her father since her marriage. Her husband had been employed for the plaintiffs as a commercial traveller and had been arrested by them on charges of embezzlement and forgery. They insisted on security for his debt, and he fraudulently misrepresented to them that he owned the land in question. When they realized that the property was the rightful estate of Mrs Mitchell, they threatened to lay further charges against her husband if she did not assign her property as collateral for his debts. Without any opportunity to consult her lawyers, and although she had not been party to the fraud and was not indebted to the plaintiffs, Mrs Mitchell mortgaged her lands. She claimed that she had done so 'solely in consequence of the duress and coercion brought to bear against me by the said plaintiffs,' and 'would never have signed the mortgage had my husband not been under arrest.' Mrs Mitchell had, as the plaintiffs admitted, been 'unfortunate in her choice of husband,' but the property was hers and the court could not allow either a dishonest husband or unscrupulous creditors to coerce a wife into forfeiting the security that her inheritance had been intended to provide. Moreover, any contract with Mrs Mitchell was unenforceable at law because she did not have dispositive powers over her separate estate under the act of 1859.[30] In this case Mrs Mitchell's need for protection was clear. However, such precedents had potentially disastrous consequences for creditors when couples acted in collusion.

This problem was not remedied by the act of 1872, since the husband remained the trustee of his wife's estate. The ease with which married couples continued to avoid their legitimate contractual debts by this simple misrepresentation is well illustrated in *Wagner v Jefferson*. Maria Louisa Jefferson owned real estate that she had inherited from her family. Her husband had employed the plaintiff to build on her land. When the debt came due, the husband claimed that he owned no property out of which it could be paid and that he 'never told the plaintiff for whom he was acting, and that all accounts were rendered in his, the husband's, own name.'[31] Maria Louisa Jefferson pleaded coverture and argued that her husband had entered into the debt without her knowledge or permission, thereby interfering with her right to 'have, hold and enjoy the property' by making it liable upon contracts of which she did not approve.

The court denied the creditor relief. Harrison CJ asserted that 'while I am desirous, if possible, to sustain the recovery against the defendant, I am unable [to].'[32] Maria Louisa Jefferson was undeniably the owner of a separate estate, but the debt had been contracted by her husband, not by her, and to enforce such a judgment would be to set a precedent that would undermine the protective intent of the legislation by giving husbands an unrestricted right not only to manage, but to alienate, their wives' separate property. While it was entirely possible, and in this case very probable, that Maria Louisa was acting in collusion with her husband, the legislative imperative to protect her property from dissipation by him could not be ignored; to grant the creditor relief would have been equivalent to returning wives to their absolute powerlessness under the common law. As Harrison CJ held in his summation, 'the plaintiff on the facts proved in this case is without remedy, save as against the husband. If he be worth nothing, the remedy is valueless. But this is a matter which ought to have been ascertained by the plaintiff before he delivered the materials on his credit. Not having done so, the plaintiff must submit to the consequences of his own neglect.'[33] Although by checking title to land

and inquiring more fully into questions of ownership regarding family property creditors could clearly protect themselves better than this plaintiff had done, couples could deliberately lie about property ownership, even when directly questioned by creditors, and non-land forms of property were notoriously easy to transfer from one owner to another without the need of legal documents. In this context, the dangers that such rulings created for creditors are obvious.

The concern to protect married women from the possible despotic powers of their husbands was central to the ruling in *Wagner v Jefferson*. The protective mandate of the court was emphasized by Wilson J, who disagreed with the court's restrictive insistence on the ownership of a separate estate and a contract specifically to bind it, yet concurred in this judgment. The contract could not be enforced, he insisted, because Maria Louisa herself had not been party to it; the husband might be guilty of fraud against his wife, the very circumstance the statutes were intended to prevent:

If she has borrowed money or bought goods, and refuses to pay her creditor, why should he not have judgment against her, and make it available as in any other case so soon as his debtor is in the possession of property? And why, also, if she is going to abscond should she not be arrested?

If the defendant had personally contracted in this case or had contracted a separate debt in the language of the statute, I should have held her liable, so far as I am concerned, whether she had a personal estate or not, or had contracted in respect of it or not. But the facts shew here that the wife did not contract a separate debt.[34]

This judgment confirmed the worst fears of creditors that the statutes protected not needy wives, but fraudulent transactions and dishonest couples.

Not only could husbands fraudulently misrepresent themselves as the outright owners of their wives' separate property, but they could create separate property for their wives; they could transfer their own earnings and accumulated property to their wives to avoid their legitimate debts. Because the wife could now hold property in her own right, gifts from husband to wife involved a legal transfer of title. Under the common law, gifts between husband and wife had been impossible; the husband could not make a valid gift to his wife because legally she was not a person. In equity, gifts between husband and wife were possible, but confusion over ownership of property was generally avoided by written marriage settlements and post-nuptial agreements. Under the act of 1859 gifts were not required to be registered.[35] A husband, at any time during a marriage, but particularly if he knew himself to be in financial difficulties, could transfer property to his wife and thereby render his land, goods, and chattels unattachable. While land had to be transferred by written instrument, a prudent husband could make such a transfer before falling into insolvency; personal property could legally be transferred by oral agreement, agreements that were almost impossible to disprove when husbands and wives acted in collusion.

A further issue that complicated matters for creditors was the equitable doctrine of resulting trust. Under normal circumstances, property transferred from one individual to another was presumed to be held by the second party only as trustee; thus creditors could still attach such property because legal title remained with the original owner. When a transfer was made from a husband to his wife, however, the assumption of trusteeship was ignored and title was held to have been legally transferred. This provision was based on the belief, long established in the Court of Chancery, that it was within a husband's rights to make a settlement upon his wife for her future security. In practice, however, the presumption of gift ensured that in cases of attempted fraud the onus was on creditors to disprove couples' claims. The act of 1872 attempted to limit the potential for abuse inherent in the right of gift, and under section 7 it was enacted that 'nothing herein contained in reference to moneys deposited, or investments by any married woman shall, as against the creditors of the husband, give validity to any deposit or investment of moneys of the husband made in fraud of such creditors, and any moneys so deposited or invested may be followed as if this Act had not passed.'[36] This provision was vague and difficult to enforce, however, since the plaintiff had to prove that the transaction had deliberately been made 'in fraud of creditors.'

A plaintiff seeking to set aside a conveyance from husband to wife as fraudulent and void against creditors had to prove not only that the conveyance had denied the creditor redress, but that this had been the purpose of the conveyance. Legal fraud could not be committed without intent; if a husband had been solvent at the time of the conveyance, whatever his financial fortunes might be thereafter, the settlement upon his wife would be deemed valid. Moreover, it had to be proved that the wife herself was party to the fraud. Particularly in cases in which the settlement was a post-nuptial one, the wife stood in a position in which collusion with her husband was clearly possible, and her knowledge of his business affairs could easily have been extensive; however, the popular doctrine of separate spheres could be used by unscrupulous couples to disclaim any fraudulent intent on the part of the wife. One wife's assertion that 'I leave the business matters entirely to him'[37] illustrates the way in which a belief in women's exclusion from the world of business could be exploited by scheming couples.

Fraud was easily perpetrated by couples who were knowledgeable regarding the technicalities and loopholes of the law. For example, in 1870 Richard Dunbar sought to have a conveyance from George McKinnell to Julia McKinnell, his wife, declared fraudulent and void. He had a judgment against George for $404; the debt had been incurred on the basis of the husband's assertions that he owned lands that could serve as security for the debt. By the time at which the debt was incurred, however, the lands had been conveyed to Julia. She claimed that the property had been purchased with money she had inherited during the marriage and that the deed had been taken in her husband's name because she was 'ignorant at that time of the fact as I now understand the law to be that a married woman could hold lands in her own name.' When she learned about the married women's property acts, she insisted that the land be conveyed to her. Moreover, she claimed that at the time of the conveyance her husband had not been indebted. It appears, however, that he had fraudulently obtained loans on the basis of his claims of ownership and had deliberately encumbered the land, secure in the knowledge that his wife's real property could not be liquidated. He then fled to the United States, leaving Dunbar without redress, and the case was dropped when Dunbar recognized that prosecution would be fruitless.[38]

Although the doctrine of gift was easily and frequently abused by dishonest couples, the protective role of the court was important. It is not difficult to understand why judges were reticent to disallow such gifts except when wives could clearly be proved to have themselves entertained fraudulent intent. For women, marriage was, above all else, an economic bargain that ensured future security, and many wives would have refused proposals of marriage without a transfer of property that would guarantee material comfort even in the case of speculation or bankruptcy on the part of the husband. In this context, to deny the wife such security retroactively would be unjust.

In a case that illustrates this theme, Elizabeth Allen, a widow, sought to impeach a conveyance from Samuel Brodie to his wife, Sarah. The defendant had leased a flour and feed store from the plaintiff in 1875. In 1876, the defendant being in default of payment, the plaintiff had obtained judgment against him in County Court. Samuel owned no property, however, and Elizabeth had been unable to obtain any satisfaction on her claim. In 1872 the defendant had inherited considerable sums of money from his mother and, according to the plaintiff, 'being of a venturesome and speculative disposition conceived the fraudulent design of securing the said money in such a way as to defeat, hinder and delay any subsequent creditors.' The money was deposited absolutely as the separate estate of his wife but, according to the plaintiff, 'in reality as a secret trust for his benefit and subject to his order and control, and the said Sarah Brodie accepted the said trust and agreed to assist her husband in his fraudulent design.' Elizabeth claimed that because of debts at the time of the inheritance Samuel Brodie 'was not competent to make such a gift or settlement to the prejudice of future creditors.'

In her answer Sarah Brodie asserted that, to her knowledge, the defendant had not been indebted at the time of the settlement. The debt to the plaintiff had not been incurred until three years after this time. Sarah had never 'sought to conceal from any person that the property in question was my own separate property, but on the contrary it was always well and publicly known.' If the plaintiff had been unaware of this fact, it was due to her own negligence. In managing this property, she claimed, her husband had not acted under any 'secret trust for his benefit,' but in accordance with the provisions of the act of 1872, which denied wives the right to manage such property themselves. Samuel Brodie confirmed this information and asserted that the settlement had been made as 'a permanent provision for her and the children.' His inability to pay the plaintiff was solely due to business losses incurred on the leased property itself, losses for which his wife was in no way liable. The plaintiff's bill was dismissed. Samuel Brodie was unlucky in business, but his attempt to ensure the security of his family had been within his means at the time of the settlement.[39]

Not all cases, however, were equally clear-cut, and the protective intent of such decisions had potentially disastrous implications for creditors, as John Dynan learned in his dealings with Thomas Walls. The protective intent of the acts of 1859, 1872, and 1873 proved difficult to reconcile with the needs of the business community. These reforms created an anomalous form of property that caused peculiar problems for creditors who chose to deal with married women. Legislators had limited women's contractual ability and retained husbands as trustees to prevent husbands from coercing their wives into squandering separate property. As trustees, husbands could misrepresent themselves as owners of their wives' property or transfer their own property to their wives to evade legitimate debts. Without any requirement that separate property be registered, questions of proof of ownership were endemic. Without joint ownership, couples had little difficulty acting as partners in fraud. In the vast majority of cases litigated under these acts, couples used the new right of the wife to own property as a means of insulating land and chattels from seizure by legitimate creditors; some wives colluded with husbands and were active, dishonest agents in the marketplace. Ironically, these limitations imposed upon women's rights of management of their property undermined the protective intent of the legislation by denying wives the means to conduct businesses in their own names, for their own support and the support of their children. The ambiguity inherent in the legislation and the position of the husband as trustee over the separate property of his wife also allowed dishonest husbands to commit fraud against unsuspecting wives.

'But How Are You to Exempt It from His Control?': Abuse of Trust by Husbands

Emily Smart lived in Waubashene, but owned land in York County that she had inherited from her father. Emily had been married in 1870 and, from early in her marriage, had been physically abused by her husband. In 1882 she had him bound over to keep the peace, but to no avail. In 1883 they parted by mutual consent. They had six children, five of whom were living with Emily. After the separation, Emily laboured intermittently as a domestic helper; but, not surprisingly, with five young children, she had insufficient income to ensure her family's support. Her husband, meanwhile, as trustee over her separate property, continued to collect the profits due to her from the estate and mortgaged the land for his own benefit. He also advertised that he would not be responsible for any debts she might accumulate and refused to pay her bills for board and lodging. In 1883, under the terms of the Married Women's Real Estate Act, she petitioned to have her husband relieved of his rights as trustee over her separate property and to enable her to mortgage or sell the lands to obtain cash to pay the debts she had accumulated since leaving him.[1] Her petition was granted. Her case, however, underscores the vulnerability of women under the acts of 1859, 1872, and 1873; her husband had greatly encumbered her property with debt and had substantially reduced her potential income from the estate. Emily had rights of control and management over what was ostensibly her own property only at the pleasure of the court.

Despite the success of the Chancery model upon which remedial legislation was based, these acts failed to achieve their central objective – the protection of all married women from the coercive power of abusive and irresponsible husbands. Of course, for some wives access to wages and to inherited property allowed a modicum of security and a means of escape from abusive relationships or the opportunity for participation in the market economy. Recourse to the court also provided public affirmation that women's demands for decent treatment within marriage were legitimate. Despite this, the husband's position as trustee allowed him powers of management and control which most well-drawn settlements in the Court of Chancery had explicitly avoided by placing the property in the hands of a trustee who was not the husband. The separate property that belonged to a wife under statute was not explicitly enumerated in any written marriage settlement, a fact that created new problems of proof of ownership. In the Court of Chancery written documents clearly set out the powers of the trustee and provided mechanisms for removing irresponsible trustees. Under legislation, however, the powers of the trustee were not clearly defined or limited, and until 1873 no mechanism existed by which a negligent or abusive husband could be removed from his position as trustee. Judges used their powers of discretion to aid women whenever possible, even granting particularly needy wives rights that were ostensibly denied under legislation; but unreported cases reveal that frequently such sympathy was of little practical value to married women, since husbands with *de facto* control over property could abuse their powers as trustees with impunity. Ultimately, judicial recognition that a significant number of husbands could not be trusted to manage their wives' property honestly encouraged the abolition of the husband's powers as trustee in 1884.[2]

Under the acts of 1859, 1872, and 1873 wives were denied powers of disposition and management over their separate property because it was believed that to give women such powers would be to provide husbands with a new means of squandering their wives' property. The editors of the *Local Courts and Municipal Gazette* outlined this fear in 1868: 'That the wife's property should be exempted from the husband's debts is highly desirable, but how are you to exempt it from his control? We fear that it is beyond the power, even of parliament, to do that.' If wives had control over their property themselves, vicious husbands, it was feared, would beat their wives and force them to part with the property against their will and best interest. Moreover, given the belief that it was the duty of the wife to obey her husband and to look to him for financial support and guidance, it was assumed that most wives would voluntarily put their property at their husbands' disposal. Even loving husbands, therefore, would be enabled inadvertently to squander their wives' property unless legislative limitations were placed on the use to which separate property could be put.

Stereotypes about women's lack of business knowledge and acumen, exploited by unscrupulous couples in fraud cases, also contributed to a hesitance to grant wives dispositive powers over their separate property. Legislation was perceived as necessary only to protect wives in exceptional circumstances, and most legislators and judges still believed, despite their fear of the potential coercive power of husbands, that in the majority of cases the husband was the person best able to take care of the interests of his wife. In a decision rendered in 1869, Gwynne J. alluded to a fear that the wife, because of her lack of business experience, might make improvident use of her estate or be defrauded of it by a third party if the husband were denied all voice in the management of his wife's property:

I fear that the result may be to deprive her of the benefit of his advice and protection, while relieving her property from his obligations and control, and may expose her to the contrivances of designing persons, who may persuade her to make bargains and dispositions of her property highly prejudicial to the joint interests of herself and her husband.[4]

It is ironic that the legislation under discussion had been passed to prevent wives from being defrauded or coerced by unscrupulous husbands who might also be 'designing persons.' The inherent contradiction between the belief in the husband as the natural guardian of the family and the fear of his potential use of coercion meant that legislative change was halting, ambiguous and of limited practical value to women. Although the acts of 1872 and 1873 improved upon that of 1859, all three were inherently limited by the failure to eliminate the role of the husband as trustee over the estate belonging to his wife.

Under the Married Women's Property Act of 1859, all wives were granted the right to hold their separate real estate and personal property against the claims of their husbands and their husbands' creditors; husbands served as trustees over such estates, and both husband and wife were denied dispositive power over the wife's land, money, and chattels. These provisions created confusion and failed to alleviate the hardships faced by many wives. An unreported case from Brant County, heard in 1871, illustrates both the use of judicial discretion to extend the protection afforded by the act and the inability of judges to protect women adequately when husbands deliberately abused their powers as trustees. Margaret Philips filed a petition for alimony and for a restraining order to prevent her husband from interfering with her separate estate. Although her husband, as trustee, had no power of disposal over her property, her estate consisted largely of chattels and money and her signature was not required for the sale or disposition of any of this property. She had fled their home because of her husband's incessant violence, but she had been unable to take all her goods with her. Since her departure, he had threatened to sell her separate property and to abscond. She asserted that the bill for alimony would be unnecessary were she to be granted control over her separate property, the value of which was evidently sufficient for her support. She also sarcastically dismissed the possibility that her husband would ever pay any alimony that might be awarded by the court. She pleaded that without the use and control of her separate property, she would either starve to death or be forced to return to the husband who put her life in constant danger. In her petition, Margaret sought

an order of the Honourable Court restraining and prohibiting the Defendant from selling, making away with or disposing of the goods and chattels of the Plaintiff in the possession of the Defendant at the Township of Ancaster in the County of Wentworth referred to in the pleadings or wherever else the said goods and chattels may now be and also restraining and prohibiting the Defendant from taking the control and possession of the goods and chattels of the Plaintiff in her possession in the Township of Burford referred to in the pleadings in this cause and from selling or in any way disposing of said goods and chattels or any part or parts thereof and that the custody of all such goods and chattels may be ordered to be given to the Plaintiff forthwith.

Margaret's solicitor argued that she was 'entitled to the enjoyment of her property' under the Married Women's Property Act of 1859 and that her husband had deliberately and maliciously denied her this rightful enjoyment. Margaret's petition was granted, despite the fact that the legislation of 1859 had not provided any mechanism for removing the husband from his position as trustee. Although Margaret thereby received legal sanction to retain her property against her husband's claims, she was unable to collect the items that she had left behind in Ancaster. The goods had been sold by her husband, who subsequently denied that the property had ever belonged to his wife.[5] Judicial discretion, while a marked improvement over the common law, provided only a partial solution to Margaret's problems; she would not live out her life in abject poverty as Hannah Snider had, but her ability to support herself had been greatly reduced by her husband's misappropriation of her property.

Margaret's lack of control over her separate property was problematic in another way also. Under the Married Women's Property Act of 1859 she did not have the right to alienate even money and chattels, and she could not, in theory, purchase food and other necessaries for herself with her separate estate. This problem did not go unnoticed on the bench. In 1868, Mowat J protested against the limitations on *jus disponendi* with regard to personal property.[6] Although he acknowledged that the statute of 1859 had failed to differentiate between real and personal property, and had explicitly denied women the right to dispose of their real property without the consent of their husbands, he asserted that 'money and many other descriptions of personal property cannot be enjoyed at all without being disposed of, and to require the consent of the husband to the disposition by the wife of any of her personal property would ... be to make her subject to his control, which is what the statute says shall not be.'[7] Moreover, if the purpose of the act was to democratize Chancery practice, then dispositive rights over the income from real estate and over chattels and money must be established, since well-drawn settlements in Chancery always provided wives with an income, and thereby with the ability to live separately from abusive spouses. Wilson J also argued that to deny women the right to control their personal property 'practically nullifies the beneficial purpose of the statute.'[8] Both Mowat and Wilson agreed with the protective intent of legislation: 'If the wife could not by suit protect her separate estate or earnings from and against her husband's wrongful appropriation of them, her separate estate or any order for protection would be a farce. It is against him and his acts that the protection is needed.'[9]

Case law illustrates that Mowat and Wilson were correct in their assertion that the act of 1859 did not provide wives with 'the protection [that was] needed.' For this reason, the Married Women's Property Act of 1872 expanded wives' powers of control over their separate property; all wives were granted the right to dispose of their personal property – their money, their chattels, and the wages which by this act were included in their separate estate – without the consent of their husbands. Although this right of alienation was still withheld with regard to a woman's real estate, the right of disposal over personal property was intended to ensure that abandoned and abused wives would be able to use their wages and inherited cash to support themselves. This right had been granted hesitatingly, and only because of the acknowledged hardships which unfortunate wives, such as Margaret Philips, faced. Legislators and judges sought to protect vulnerable wives, but they did not want to give all wives rights that would, they believed, imperil marital unity and wifely subordination. In this context, judicial discretion could also work against wives who attempted to use these dispositive powers not to protect themselves from abusive husbands, but to leave marriages that were merely unhappy.

This possibility is made clear in *McGuire v McGuire*. The wife sought to reclaim the separate property that was in the possession of her estranged husband; on the surface, therefore, the case was very similar to *Philips v Philips*. Here, however, the wife had left her husband without reasons that would have made her eligible for alimony. In the language of the court, she had left without just cause, however miserable her marriage might be. Gwynne J held that

[a]s affecting chattels of this description [movable goods], brought by the wife into the marriage, and in virtue of the marriage placed in the control and possession of the husband for the mutual use, convenience and enjoyment of both husband and wife during the marriage, [the Act] secures to the wife the enjoyment of them free from his debts and obligations, and from his control or disposition without her consent: that is to say, it divests the husband of his common law rights, but leaves the chattels so placed in his possession there, as they were placed, as it were, in his hands as a trustee under the statutory marriage settlement for the purpose of which the property was placed in his hands, namely for the mutual use, convenience and enjoyment of both husband and wife during the marriage; but it gives to the wife no power of taking these goods out of the possession of the trustee and disposing of them at her pleasure, so as to destroy and defeat the trust purposes for which they came into and were placed in the husband's possession. No act of hers could make him a tort feasor for keeping and appropriating the goods, as far as in him lay, for the trust purposes under which he may be said to have received them ... There is no occasion for an action to recover property already in its proper place and custody; there is no need for an action to protect and secure property already under the protection and security of the duly appointed trustee, who has done no act in breach of his trust.[10]

McGuire, the defendant in this case, insisted that his wife could have the proper use of her goods 'by fulfilling her marriage vow and returning to live with him.'[11] Despite the fact that the act of 1872 had ostensibly granted wives the right to dispose of their separate personal property, Gwynne J denied Mrs McGuire relief. Such rights of control and disposition were only necessary, he asserted, when a husband failed to use his wife's separate property for 'the mutual ... convenience and enjoyment of both husband and wife.' He expressed considerable concern that should the wife's right to reclaim such property be enforced, it would set a precedent productive of conflict in many marriages. It was not desirable that a married woman might have 'a right to treat her husband as a trespasser whenever he, although in the house in which they live together, intermeddles with any property which was her separate property before marriage' and to 'prosecute [him] as a trespasser if he continues in her house after having received orders from her to leave it.'[12] It was the duty of the wife to live with and obey her husband in all but the most exceptional circumstances. Mrs McGuire was not allowed to reclaim her property because, 'when the wife leaves her husband [at least in cases in which she leaves without legal reason], it is she who violates the marriage contract, which was the consideration of the husband assuming the trust in respect of those goods.'[13] Mr McGuire had not been proved an incompetent or irresponsible trustee or husband.

McGuire v McGuire, despite the rarity of cases in which wives' petitions were denied, is important. Unlike *Philips v Philips*, it was reported not because it was representative, but because it illustrated circumstances in which women would not be eligible for relief. It also proves that judicial discretion, which was usually used to protect abused and abandoned wives, could be invoked to limit the scope of legislation when judges believed that women were using the statutes in a manner that implied a rejection of wifely subordination. It is instructive to note that cases such as that of Margaret Philips, in which 'husbands violate[d] the marriage contract,' were much more common. These cases, in which wives were granted relief, were not reported, because when a husband could be proved guilty of abuse, desertion, or misappropriation of property, the right of women to protection was not questioned.

The act of 1872 was limited by more than the problem of judicial discretion. It allowed women rights of disposition only over their personal property. For this reason, Mrs McGuire could try to reclaim only her money and chattels. Rights of disposition of land were not granted under this legislation. It was recognized, however, that this limitation created hardship in some cases, since abused and abandoned wives who owned only land might need to sell such property in order to obtain cash and goods necessary for their day-to-day survival. Under the 1873 Act to facilitate the conveyance of Real Estate by Married Women, a wife could apply to the local magistrate for permission to dispose of her separate real estate without the concurrence of her husband, thereby effectively bringing his trusteeship over her land to an end. Such orders were to be granted only in limited circumstances to wives who would otherwise have been eligible for alimony in the Court of Chancery.[14] In other words, the legislature explicitly made the distinction with regard to land, which judges had enforced with regard to money and chattels, by their discretionary decisions in cases such as *Philips v Philips* and *McGuire v McGuire*; wives had a recognized right to protection against mistreatment, not a right to independence.

Not surprisingly, when wives could provide evidence of misbehaviour on the part of their husbands, judges showed no hesitation in revoking trusteeship under the provisions of the act of 1873. A complete accounting of all the protection orders issued under this mandate is impossible, as the records for most counties are no longer extant; however, a minimum of 125 such orders were issued in Huron and York Counties between 1873 and 1884.[15] Every petition in this sample was granted; yet not a single case dealing with the Married Women's Real Estate Act appears in the published reports, because such cases were uncontroversial. Judges were sympathetic to the plight of these women who, without control over the property that was legally theirs, would have been left without the means of supporting themselves and their children. These decisions did not challenge the husband's authority within the family; husbands in these cases were either absent or abusive, and had therefore forfeited their positions as heads of households.[16]

The need to provide married women with the means of supporting themselves was patently obvious when husbands deserted, leaving their wives in legal limbo. As married women such wives could not convey their own property to support themselves; they were simultaneously denied the right of spousal support assumed by the common law because their guardians and providers had absconded. Of eighty-seven cases in which the reasons for the petition to convey real property were given, fifty-two women had been deserted and left without any means of support except the separate real estate which they could hold but not dispose of or control.[17] One such wife, Emily Harris, petitioned for a protection order in 1882. She wished to sell a lot in Victoria County and use the proceeds to support herself and her small child. She had been deserted by her husband in 1878: 'He has left me without assigning any reason whatsoever. I have no knowledge as to where he now is. I have not heard from

him since he left me in July 1878, and I have no reason to expect him to
return.' No provision had been made for her, and without the money that
could be realized from the sale of her lands she would soon be destitute.
Not surprisingly, her petition was granted; not only did judges sympa-
thize with such women, but it made economic sense to ensure that they
would not become a public liability.[18]

Abused wives also received sympathy. For example, in the first protection order to be issued by the York County Court in 1873, Martha
Gilmour, who had married the defendant in 1858, charged that her husband had been abusive from early in their marriage and had finally
deserted her, leaving her to support their six children by her own labour:

The said Gilmour began to abuse and maltreat me soon after our marriage and he
continued to do so until he left me ... He slapped me in the face the first Sunday
after we were married and he frequently beat me afterwards, up to the day he left
me, when he threw me headlong out of bed. Sometimes he slapped me with his
hand; sometimes he struck me with his clenched fist; sometimes he kicked me
with his foot; and sometimes he struck me with a stick or whatever he might hap-
pen to have in his hand.

She asserted that she had always acted 'as a good and faithful wife to my
husband, and never did anything to justify his misconduct or abuse of
me.' When confronted about his behaviour 'he would promise to forbear
in future and say that it was from love that he beat me; but at other times
he told me that it would be the happiest moment of his life when he saw
my breath leave my body.' She had refrained from telling her neighbours
and family about his abuse because of shame and fear, and the facts had
only recently come to the attention of her parents when her husband had
beaten her so noisily that a neighbour had intervened, 'whereupon one of
my daughters told her the facts.' The decision of the magistrate would not
have been difficult in this case; not only did children and neighbours cor-
roborate Martha's tales of woe, but her husband addressed the court to
'acknowledge that I have been unkind.' Although he claimed to seek forgiveness and reconciliation, the court left the possibility of resumed
cohabitation a private matter. In the light of Charles Gilmour's admitted
abuse, his desire to live with his wife was of less concern to the court than
her right to live in peace, free from his molestation.[19] This case was typi-
cal of those that would follow, and judges recognized that women in abusive relationships required rights of alienation and disposition over their
real property to ensure their day-to-day survival.

That judges were willing to use judicial discretion to protect unfortunate wives – and at times to grant women rights explicitly denied under legislation – is clearly demonstrated in a case that came before the Norfolk County Court in 1878. Mary Goodwin had been married in New York in 1840 and had moved to Canada in 1873 with her husband and their children. The family had purchased property with money Mary had earned from her separate business as a hotel-keeper in New York.[20] In the last few years her husband had become increasingly intemperate, and she argued that he 'interferes with and squanders your complainant's property in spite of remonstrances from her and her sons on her behalf.' Unlike the majority of women who petitioned the court for protection, Mary was still living with her husband and, despite his intemperance, wished 'to continue in her duties as a wife':

He wishes to treat the property as his own and does not use the place as a reasonable man should. If he did I would not object. I take these proceedings for his own good as well as mine. I love him too much to do anything to injure him. I wish to keep a home for him.

Mary's request for a restraining order against her husband was granted despite the fact that technically she did not qualify for such an order under the act of 1873; her husband was not physically abusive, nor had he abandoned her, and the act made no provision for depriving a husband of his rights as trustee during cohabitation. The court, however, was sympathetic to Mary's plight and ignored the limits of legislation to support her efforts to protect her property from inappropriate use by a drunken husband. Mary presented herself as a duly subordinate and loving wife, but this case reveals more about what was deemed proper behaviour for husbands than for wives. While under the law Mary's husband had committed no marital offence, the judges clearly believed his behaviour to be reprehensible; they overstepped their authority in order to ensure that her property would not be squandered.[21] Such use of judicial discretion was consistent with the practice of the Court of Chancery in alimony cases and with popular beliefs about the roles and responsibilities of spouses within marriage. It is important to note, however, that judicial discretion and the expansion of women's rights over their property remained dependent not on the desires of the wife, but on proof that the husband was unwilling or unable to perform his marital duties.

This emphasis on male behaviour is also illustrated in *Webster v Webster*. Eliza Ann Webster applied for an injunction to prevent her husband from continuing in his collection of the rents from her separate property. She had been turned out of the family home; her husband refused to support her, and had threatened that he would continue to collect the rents at her expense. The next instalment on the rent was coming due, and Eliza Ann claimed that her husband had no right to these lands, that 'on the contrary I am the proper person to receive the said rents.' In his defence Albert Webster acknowledged that the property was legitimately the separate property of his wife, from whom he had been separated for only three weeks. He argued that all proceeds from the farm, whether worked or rented, 'went into the common fund and [were] used together with other monies to support the family.' He agreed not to disrupt her collection of the rents 'while the plaintiff is living apart from me,' but argued that he was not obliged to account for money 'received while we were living together,' as during their cohabitation he had only exercised his legal right to manage the property for the mutual benefit of all family members. The court issued the injunction requested to ensure that Eliza Ann's enjoyment of her property would not be disrupted, but agreed with her husband that no accounting of the use of the money during their cohabitation was necessary. This case illustrates the line that judges drew between granting women independent control of their property and providing relief for women whose husbands were irresponsible. As long as Albert Webster lived with and supported his wife in an appropriate manner, her property was his to manage, although not to dispose of, in the way that he deemed proper. Although ultimately Eliza Ann was granted relief, she was lucky that her husband had not encumbered her property before the injunction could be enforced.[22]

Rose McKeown was not so fortunate. Both judicial discretion and the vulnerability created by the position of the husband as trustee are clearly illustrated in *McKeown v McKeown*. Patrick and Rose McKeown had been married in 1865 without a marriage settlement and at the time of the marriage Rose McKeown had owned no separate property. Patrick McKeown claimed that he had earned considerable sums of money that had been deposited in a bank and used in 1870 to purchase land. The deed for this land, although purchased with his money, had been taken in the name of his wife, he claimed, 'on the understanding, intention and agreement that she would hold the said lands and premises as a Trustee for the plaintiff and that the same should be within his order and deposition in as full and ample a manner as if the conveyance thereof had been taken in his own name.'[23] On this understanding, he had erected buildings on the property. He asserted that his wife was now a drunkard and that although she had never before claimed any interest in the lands except as a trustee, she was now threatening to sell or mortgage the lands for her own benefit. (Of course, under the act of 1872 Rose did not have any right to alienate her separate lands without his consent.) He sought to have the property returned not only to his control and management, but to his outright ownership.

In her statement of defence, Rose McKeown argued that her husband had given her gifts of large sums of money, which she had subsequently used in the purchase of the property, and that 'if any of the Plaintiff's moneys were used in the purchase of the said properties – which the Defendant does not admit – the same were intended as an advancement to the Defendant, and were voluntary payments.' In other words, Rose denied her husband's assertion that the property was held by her only as trustee, and argued instead that absolute title had been transferred as a gift. She invoked the rebuttable equitable presumption, so problematic for creditors, that in cases of transfers of property from husband to wife, property is assumed to have been given as an outright and irrevocable gift. In theory, therefore, this was a straightforward case in which either husband or wife would be granted absolute title to the lands in question, estopping any further claim by the contending party. The evidence was sufficient to overturn the presumption of gift, but any decision favouring Patrick raised the possibility that Rose would be left destitute. It was clear that the McKeown marriage was in trouble, and the court did not want to leave Rose without support. Rose McKeown was ordered to convey the lands to her husband. A mortgage for $4,000 in her favour was to be secured at the rate of interest of 6 per cent per annum. This mortgage was in lieu of dower, and was not to be payable to her until her husband's death, except in the case that Patrick should refuse to live with her and support and maintain her, in the words of the presiding judge, 'as a husband should.' The court did not have the right to grant what was in effect an agreement in advance of separation, and the judges had clearly rendered an anomalous decision. They sidestepped the problem raised by the presumption of gift and, while returning title to Patrick, asserted that he was obliged to use the property for the support and maintenance of his wife. The mortgage settlement, however, despite its creativity, did not solve Rose's problems. Rose and Patrick continued to live apart. Patrick not only failed to pay the money due under the settlement, but also, when his wife attempted to force him to support her by moving into one of his rental properties, 'through his bailiffs, agents and servants took and carried away and disposed of to his own use and benefit' her separate goods and chattels worth $1,400. Rose then sued Patrick for alimony, but dropped this suit before it could come to hearing.[24]

The powers husbands held as trustees were very wide, and although judges responded to the abused and abandoned women who sought their protection with consistent sympathy, the acts of 1859, 1872, and 1873 failed to protect all needy wives. The powers necessary to control separate real estate were only granted by a court order; personal goods, although technically alienable by the wife after 1872, were often managed by the husband and could easily be seized and squandered by him. In the minds of judges and legislators, however, it was better to leave such cases dependent upon judicial discretion than to provide all wives with powers that might allow them to abandon the responsibilities and obligations of marriage. The court, as surrogate patriarch, reserved unto itself the right to determine which women were and were not deserving of relief. Without the means of controlling their own property, women could not use their land and chattels for their own support and protection, and husbands could easily appropriate their wives' property and abscond. Evidence from petitions in suits for alimony underscores the inability even of sympathetic judges to provide protection for the separate property of married women when husbands were deliberately dishonest.

For example, Catherine McArthur had been awarded alimony on the basis of cruelty in 1864. On the urging of her husband, she agreed to accept a lump settlement from him in lieu of alimony; he conveyed one hundred acres of land to her for her separate use, and she released him of all claims for maintenance for herself and their children. In 1865, promising that he had reformed, he convinced her to allow him to return to their home on the understanding that this cohabitation would not invalidate their agreement. Shortly thereafter, his abuse and drunkenness recommenced and Catherine insisted that he leave. Her husband, having found himself in financial difficulties, applied successfully for a writ of ejectment in the Court of Common Pleas, arguing that by their cohabitation the deed between them was null and void. Catherine managed to have this judgment overruled by the chancellors. James McArthur argued that he had been reluctant to sign the deed and had done so only under the promise that he would return and live with her and manage the property. The chancellors rejected this defence as nonsensical. To accept such terms would have made the agreement invalid from the outset. In a last-ditch attempt to discredit the testimony of his wife, McArthur also argued that she 'behaved herself in a demeaning manner ... and I could no longer with due respect to myself continue to live with her.' This line of attack, however, was also unsuccessful. Catherine produced several witnesses, including the brother of the defendant, to attest to the fact that the defendant was 'a worthless and drunken person' who would squander the property and leave his wife and children destitute. Catherine was lucky; she had insisted on keeping accounts of the separate property throughout the cohabitation, their original agreement was in writing, and she had de facto control of the property.[25] Women who had been more trusting of their spouses, who were less well advised in the technicalities of the law, or who had seen their property confiscated by conniving or violent spouses found recovering their separate property to be a difficult if not impossible task. Alimony cases provide considerable evidence illustrating this problem; fifty-three of the wives who sought alimony reported that their husbands had absconded with what was ostensibly their separate property.

Ann Eliza Wage complained that her husband had deserted her and had taken with him her separate property – some furniture, silver plate, and money.[26] Nancy Munro had lent her entire separate estate – $500 in cash – to her husband to assist in his business; upon their separation he refused to repay or compensate her.[27] Margaret Locke, who had fled her home because of her husband's abusive behaviour, had inherited a farm worth over $1000 from her father; her husband had sold the property without her permission and appropriated the gains for his personal use.[28] Rose Johnston had been unable to prevent her husband, who was living in open adultery with a fourteen-year-old concubine, from selling the home that had been purchased with her separate earnings; the proceeds were used to support his mistress, with whom he then fled the jurisdiction.[29] Daniel Sullivan, whose wife had left him because of his 'excessive use of ardent spirits' and because he was 'very violent and abusive,' admitted that he retained property that his wife had brought to their marriage. He argued, however, that he was 'entitled to the possession thereof and retain them in my dwelling during the plaintiff's lifetime.' His wife, Isabella Sullivan, asserted that 'your complainant never had, while living with the defendant, free or reasonable liberty of thought or action, but on the contrary she has been controlled and fettered by the defendant, and treated more as a slave than as a wife, and the plaintiff submits that she was not bound to live with the defendant and be treated that way.' Although the court concurred and granted her alimony, her husband refused to pay the sums ordered and squandered his wife's separate estate. Ultimately, Isabella Sullivan returned to her abusive husband because, without any family to help her in her time of need, she had no means of even feeding herself.[30]Without power to control the property to which they held title, wives could not protect themselves from abuse or use their property to support themselves, and they could not prevent violent and scheming husbands from absconding with property or squandering it on mistresses and booze.

The acts of 1859, 1872, and 1873, by retaining the husband as trustee over his wife's separate property, failed to insulate the wife's property from the husband, although it was acknowledged that it was 'against him and his acts that the protection [was] needed.'[31] Chancery precedent, which was democratized under these acts, did not work in the absence of written agreements outlining the extent of separate property and the powers that a trustee would hold over it. Most important, in Chancery prudent families had not chosen husbands to serve as trustees under marriage settlements. Without these protections, it was ultimately realized, wives married to abusive men needed powers of control over property if they were to be able to use their land, money, and chattels for their own support; husbands could not – at least in a significant proportion of cases – be trusted to manage their wives' property honestly. Judicial recognition of this fact encouraged the abolition of the husband's powers as trustee in 1884.

8

'A Thing of Shreds and Patches':
The Act of 1884

It must be confessed that there are few branches of law which are involved in more doubt than that embraced in the modern statute law relating to married women. Before the statutes to which we refer were enacted, the rights of husbands and wives ... were pretty generally understood, not only by the legal profession whose business it was to comprehend them, but also by the community at large. But the result of the legislation to which we refer is that neither one class nor the other can be said to understand how the law stands.[1]

The acts of 1859, 1872, and 1873 had failed. The position of the husband as trustee over his wife's separate property left him with significant scope for coercion and created an inducement to fraud. A return to the harsh conditions wives had faced under the common law was clearly unacceptable, and members of the bench and the legal profession increasingly asserted that the only way to ensure creditors adequate remedy against married women, and wives the means for self-protection, was to grant all married women unequivocal dispositive powers over all separate property.

The failure of the acts of 1872 and 1873 was obvious to the bench, but legislators required political justification for further remedial action. Liberalization of married women's property law was possible in the 1880s, therefore, because of the changing political pressures in the decade. First, the legislature was under increased scrutiny by women and was forced to consider the myriad demands of the woman question. Second, mounting pressure for the fusion of law and equity had come to fruition in Britain in 1873 and 1875 and in Ontario in 1881. As a logical conclusion to this, in 1882 the English Parliament passed a Married Women's Property Act based upon the most liberal precedents in Chancery. Ontario faced a choice between adopting English legislation and thereby the Chancery precedent, or losing the benefit of English decisions altogether. In this context, the passage of the liberal Act of 1884 is not surprising. The Married Women's Property Act of 1884 granted wives rights of control and disposition that had been denied under earlier remedial acts and eliminated the role of the husband as trustee.

Within the legal community, it was recognized that the acts of 1872 and 1873 had not succeeded in eliminating the problems that had emerged under earlier legislation. The anomalous position of married women's separate property had created an inducement to fraud; wives were ostensibly liable on contract, but their real property could not be liquidated. One contributor to the *Canadian Law Times* complimented Justice Armour for his attempt, in *Clarke v Creighton*, in which a married woman had deliberately manipulated the statute of 1872 to avoid the payment of a legitimate debt, to 'grapple fairly with the difficulty ... of the question of liability of married women under the Ontario Act of 1872 ... and to drag creditors out of the slough of despond into which they have strayed.' He also expressed the hope that Armour's comments in this case might 'have the effect of arousing the attention, not only of jurists, but of legislators, to the anomalies to which the decisions of the Courts have given rise.' The author ended his article with an explicit plea for legislative clarification: 'It might be more satisfactory if some clear-headed member of the Legislature would take the matter up and carry through an Act which would be incapable of misconstruction.'[2]

More important, as one writer in the *Canadian Law Times* asserted in 1881, without rights of control over their property, wives were afforded inadequate means of protecting their separate estates: 'The writer recollects having heard the learned Judge say during the course of an argument upon a married woman's case, that if she could not personally contract, there would arise many cases of hardship, where the husband refused to support her.'[3]

If a woman could not contract with respect to her real property, or alienate it, of what use was such property for her own support? Confusion about the distinction between the powers of disposition granted to wives over their real and personal property and the position of the husband as trustee for his wife's separate estate undermined the act's protective intent. If, as the editors of the *Canadian Law Times* urged their readers, traders were to be wary of credit transactions with married women and 'in future, deal with married women for ready money only,'[4] abused and abandoned wives would be denied the protection that the acts purportedly provided.

This call for legislative clarification was echoed in the *Canadian Law Times* in 1883 in an extended analysis of the problems that had arisen under the acts of 1872 and 1873. The author of this article, George Holmested, was a vociferous advocate of further reform; he argued that 'the result of the present state of the law in Ontario is simply to enable married women to commit frauds with impunity, provided they can get anyone foolish enough to deal with them.'[5] Under the legislation as passed, it was unclear to whom control of the wife's property rightfully belonged; husbands were denied the right of disposition, but this power had not been vested in the wife herself, at least with respect to real property. Such a situation was fraught with risks for creditors, 'for it is clear that there is nothing to prevent a married woman from entering into a contract upon the faith of having separate estate sufficient to answer it, and immediately afterwards disposing of the whole of it, with the satisfaction of knowing that both herself individually and any property that she may afterwards acquire will be free from liability for the debt so incurred.'[6] More important, the acts had failed in their central objective – the protection of married women. The contradictory aims that had inspired reform – the desire to maintain the husband's position as head of the household while simultaneously protecting the wife from his potential abuse – had led to bad law. Holmested was unequivocal in his assertion that 'it is obviously necessary that [the law of married women and property] be amended'.[7]

Despite recognition of the limitations of the acts of 1872 and 1873 in the legal community, legislators would have been hesitant to enact further reform had more practical pressures not coincided with judicial and legal calls for clarification of the law. The legislature received impetus for reform from the growing strength of the woman movement in Ontario. By the 1880s this movement had become well established and could no longer be ignored as irrelevant or as an example of the excesses of American democracy. Internationally, one of the most prominent issues within the woman movement was law reform, particularly property law reform.[8] In Canada, the Literary Club discarded its euphemistic name in 1883 and became the Canadian Woman Suffrage Association. During this decade, enormous increases in membership in reform organizations such as the Women's Christian Temperance Union and the Young Women's Christian Association gave notice that women were emerging into the public sphere.[9] In this context of heightened awareness and activity, individual women began to argue that it was insufficient for the law to attempt to protect women in exceptional circumstances; all women needed legal rights, including the franchise, which paralleled those of men.

As one indignant author argued in an open letter to the Toronto *World*, many marriages were less than ideal and, even when husbands were flawless, disasters could befall families. Ensconced in their domestic sphere and excluded from the decision-making processes of government and business because of definitions of femininity that stressed dependence and fragility, women were unprepared to protect and care for themselves:

Put a woman in a home, let her realize all the happy lot that [some] consider her only true sphere. Give her enough money for all the fair demands of her family; let her husband be the excellent man he is assumed to be, free from any vice of temper or morality; let them both realize to its fullest degree all that is necessary to the welfare of the home-life, shut the mother up in the home interests alone, let her firmly believe that the married woman is the only true woman, and let death or disaster intervene and where are all your theories of womanliness? Accustomed to 'obey' her husband, to look to his judgment in all matters of moment, to his action in all business affairs, to his choice for religious and political views, and to him as guardian of her interests and those of her children, what will she do when she finds herself penniless, unguarded, without direction spiritual or mental, a 'clinging vine' torn roughly from the stem to which she had attached herself ...[10]

Because she wished to assert that rights were necessary for all wives, the writer did not emphasize the harsh realities faced by women whose husbands were not 'free from any vice of temper or morality', the women for whose protection the acts of 1859, 1872 and 1873 had been intended. She argued instead that all women, even those whose husbands were loving and attentive, could be faced with circumstances that would require them to enter the masculine sphere of business and the world outside the home. Instead of helping women, the law made self-protection more difficult. At a minimum, women needed to be educated to protect themselves and to be able to defend their own interests; the acts of 1872 and 1873 had not served this purpose adequately.

As the same writer argued in a second letter that formed part of an extended debate waged in the *World* in 1883–4,[11] the needs of women had not been met or protected by an all-male Parliament. This provided irrefutable evidence of why the franchise was necessary:

[Some are] shocked at the idea of women having to think about politics and say we pay our male relations a poor compliment when we cannot trust them to vote for us. But the serious business of the world is not done in compliments, and if men were so anxious to do perfectly right by women we should have equal pay for equal labour and have no need for the married women's property acts and other protections that have to come between us and the other sex.[12]

In comparison to demands for the franchise, property law reform seemed relatively harmless. While for obvious reasons this connection was not drawn explicitly, it is entirely conceivable that the demands of the 'woman movement' encouraged the consideration of property law reform; if the men of Parliament could prove themselves 'anxious to do perfectly right by women,' perhaps the issue of female suffrage could be entirely avoided.[13]

The fusion of law and equity was also a necessary prerequisite for the liberalization of married women's property law. The passage of the Judicature Act of 1881 represented the culmination of a movement towards amalgamation that had been gathering momentum for two decades. As Premier Mowat, the author of the Administration of Justice Act of 1873, acknowledged, it had never been considered a permanent or complete solution to the problems that plagued the legal system:

A uniform system of pleading and practice was not adopted in the Administration of Justice Act of 1873 for various reasons. That such a system would be adopted in England was certain, though it was doubtful, when, and it was desirable that we should have the benefit of the discussions and legislation that would take place on the subject there.[14]

Fusion was completed in England in 1873 and 1875; ultimately, this made fusion in Ontario inevitable. As Mowat argued when introducing the Judicature Act in 1880, 'the only question was when the change should be made.' Having had four years to watch the 'working of the English system,' he argued that 'he would not be justified in further delaying the adoption of that system, with such modifications and improvements as might be necessary for this country.'[15] Despite long-term agitation for the fusion of law and equity, the introduction of this bill by Mowat seems to have been unexpected, No committee had been formed to determine the specifics of reform, and the bill was not proceeded with. Reintroduced in 1881, however, it passed with little opposition.[16]

The Judicature Act was a complicated piece of legislation that completely reorganized the court system. Most important, the principles and procedures of equity were to take precedence in cases of conflict between the common law and Chancery. Fusion established a legal context that created considerable potential for confusion and conflict in cases involving married women's separate property. Lee Holcombe has argued that in England the fusion of law and equity ensured that 'with time, inevitably, by judicial decisions, the old common law rules that gave a married women's property to her husband would be superseded by the equitable rules that recognized a married women's separate property.'[17] In Ontario, however, a liberal interpretation of Chancery rules did not necessarily follow from fusion. Since marriage settlements had been much more conservative in Upper Canada, the possibility remained that women's rights over their separate property would not be expanded. The necessity of choosing between Upper Canadian and English Chancery precedent became obvious in 1882 with the passage of the English Married Women's Property Act, under which the most liberal Chancery precedents were explicitly applied to all statutory separate property. Not surprisingly, the passage of this Act was followed with considerable interest by provincial newspapers.

In England, much discontent had been expressed by women with the 'abortive' act of 1870; throughout the 1870s the Married Women's Property Committee remained vigilant, and several bills on the subject were presented to Parliament.[18] Ultimately, however, it was not this feminist pressure that ensured the passage of the liberal act of 1882. The women gained the support of Lord Selborne, the lord chancellor. Selborne was conservative-minded and had opposed the Married Women's Property Act of 1870 as 'not conducive to domestic peace and harmony.'[19] He had been a leading figure in the completion of the fusion of law and equity, however, and, as Holcombe has argued, 'doubtless he now viewed reform of the married women's property law as merely a logical consequence of the much broader legal reform which had already been enacted under his leadership.'[20]

The English Married Women's Property Act of 1882 'bestowed an equitable marriage settlement upon every married woman who did not have one.' Every married woman in England became entitled to hold all 'real and personal property,' whether acquired before or after marriage, as her separate estate. More importantly, she would be 'capable of acquiring, holding, and disposing by will or otherwise of any real or personal property as her separate property, in the same manner as if she were a feme sole, without the intervention of any trustee' and of 'entering into and rendering herself liable in respect of and to the extent of her separate property on any contract, and of suing and being sued.'[21] This act democratized the most liberal precedents of the English Court of Chancery and granted married women clear dispositive powers over their real and personal separate property. However, it also maintained the equitable distinction between the proprietary liability of a married woman and the personal liability of all other debtors. Such distinctions were based upon a traditional view of marriage in which personal liability of the wife was unthinkable; if she were to be jailed, the husband would be denied his right of consortium, his marital right to his wife's company and sexual services.[22] The right of families to opt out of the common law system by the use of marriage settlements was preserved. As Vivienne Ullrich has argued, 'it was felt at the time that settlements with restraints on anticipation would still be used by wealthy people in order to protect a woman's capital from dissipation by her husband.'[23] Considerable concern remained that wives would be unable to oppose the physical and persuasive power of abusive husbands. Most important, separate property was of limited value in practical terms because the wife did not acquire any title in the property accumulated during marriage; most women were housewives who did not earn large wages or inherit separate property, and they remained economically dependent upon their husbands. The act 'did not adequately or justly deal with the social realities of the position of married women. [It was], however, consistent with other social and legal attitudes of the period which emphasized the equality of persons before the law without regard for differing material circumstances.'[24] It was on this model that the Ontario Married Women's Property Act of 1884 was based; therefore, while the act of 1884 was liberal in comparison to its predecessors, it was by no means egalitarian in intent.

Despite the obvious failure of the acts of 1872 and 1873, amendment of the law in Ontario seems to have been considered only in the wake of English reform. Two bills 'to amend the Married Women's Property Act' were introduced in the 1882–3 session, but in both cases the order for the second reading was discharged.[25] During the 1884 session, the married women's bill was passed with almost no debate. Mowat argued in defense of the Act that it corresponded 'very nearly with the English Act,

144 Married Women and Property Law in Victorian Ontario

the object being to have the benefit of the English decisions.'[26] Despite the fact that in order to 'have the benefit of English decisions' English Chancery precedent would have to be adopted – meaning that the conservative, local model of separate property would have to be overturned – the passage of the act seems to have excited little controversy. In contrast, an act passed during this same session, which allowed municipalities to grant unmarried women the local franchise, gave rise to significant debate. This debate illustrates the fact that the passage of the Married Women's Property Act, 1884, was not the result of any widespread acceptance of the equality of the sexes.[27]

The act provided that 'a married woman shall ... be capable of acquiring, holding and disposing by will or otherwise, of any real or personal property as her separate property, in the same manner as if she were a feme sole, without the intervention of any trustee.'[28] Married women were explicitly made liable upon contract:

(2) A married woman shall be capable of entering into and rendering herself liable in respect of and to the extent of her separate property on any contract, and of suing and being sued, either in contract or in tort, or otherwise, in all respects as if she were a feme sole, and her husband need not be joined with her as plaintiff or defendant, or be made a party to any action or other legal proceeding brought by or taken against her; and any damages or costs recovered by her in any such action or proceeding shall be her separate property; and any damages or costs recovered against her in any such action or proceeding shall be payable out of her separate property and not otherwise.

(3) Every contract entered into by a married woman shall be deemed to be a contract entered into by her with respect to and to bind her separate property, unless the contrary be shewn.

(4) Every contract entered into by a married woman with respect to and to bind her separate property, shall bind not only the separate property which she is possessed of or entitled to at the date of the contract, but also all separate property which she may thereafter acquire.[29]

When a married woman reneged on a contract, therefore, her land could thereafter be liquidated.[30]

Legislators were concerned that dishonest husbands might try to defraud their wives of their separate property; by section 15 of the act wives were provided with the means to apply to the High Court of Justice or the County Court 'in any question between husband and wife as to the title to or possession of property.' In such cases the judge was given wide discretionary powers to 'make such an order with the respect of the property in dispute, and as to the costs of and consequent on the application, as he thinks fit.'[31] Decisions under this section of the act, based on judicial discretion, were analogous to the protection orders for wages and real property that had been granted under the acts of 1859 and 1873, respectively, and were intended to provide judges with the means necessary to protect wives when husbands were abusive or despotic.

Moreover, even this liberal act retained a parallel provision to those earlier protection orders. By section 18 (1) of this Act it was established that:

Any married woman having a decree for alimony against her husband, or any married woman who lives apart from her husband, having been obliged to leave him from cruelty or other cause which by law justifies her leaving him and renders him liable for her support, or any married woman whose husband is a lunatic with or without lucid intervals, or any married woman whose husband is undergoing sentence of imprisonment in the Provincial Penitentiary or in any gaol for a criminal offence, or any married woman whose husband from habitual drunkenness, profligacy, or other cause, neglects and refuses to provide for her support and that of his family, or any married woman whose husband has never been in this Province, or any married woman who is deserted or abandoned by her husband, may obtain an order of protection entitling her, notwithstanding her coverture, to have and enjoy all the earnings of her minor children, and any acquisitions therefrom, free from the debts and obligations of her husband, and from his control or dispositions, and without his consent, in as full and ample a manner as if she continued sole and unmarried.[32]

This provision was intended to aid desperate women in providing support for their families,[33] but it was not deemed necessary, under normal circumstances, to grant wives any extended control over either children or their potential earning power, both of which remained paternal property.

As this last provision clearly illustrates, the act of 1884, despite its more liberal terms, was not intended to place wives on an equal footing with their husbands. Wives and their separate property were not made liable for the maintenance of the family, and the liability of a wife on her separate contract remained proprietary, not personal. Such limitations reveal the continuing assumption of marital unity, of the husband's responsibility for family maintenance and guidance, and of wifely subordination and obedience. Moreover, while the wife could apply to the court for an order to reclaim her separate property if it was misappropriated by her husband, decisions in such cases were dependent upon judicial discretion and the perception that the wife was an aggrieved and innocent spouse. The wife did not have any claim on family property accumulated during the marriage by the joint labour of spouses. The act granted those women with inheritances or separate incomes most of the privileges and few of the responsibilities of property ownership; it did not provide much protection for the average housewife, who neither earned significant wages nor inherited sufficient property for self-support. While the act was an important theoretical advancement over the common law, and while it explicitly acknowledged that husband and wife were separate people with potentially different interests, it was of little practical value to many women who remained economically dependent on their husbands and therefore trapped if relationships became abusive.

As George Holmested would later argue in his 1905 treatise on married women's property law, the law 'persistently regards the female as the weaker vessel and the subject for special protection by the law against both herself and her husband.'[34] In his view, these 'special contrivances' ensured that the act of 1884 had failed to eliminate the problems that had arisen for married women and their creditors under earlier legislation. Holmested argued that wives' special status under the law denied the fundamental equality of husband and wife and was therefore morally, legally, and socially indefensible:

The common law, whereby the rights and property of a wife were so largely vested in her husband during coverture, was indefensible ...

It must be apparent that the special contrivances that the law has sanctioned, assumedly for the protection of married women, are equally indefensible. If it is admitted that women should be on an equal footing with men as regards their rights of property, on the ground of the equality of the sexes, it seems to follow that those laws which have been devised for the special protection of married women ought to be abolished. They cannot be supported on the ground that women are weak and liable to be imposed upon, or unaccustomed to business, or have need to be protected against their own improvidence; because all these may be equally said of some men, and yet no law is specially provided to meet their case; neither can it be said that the fact that they are liable to be the victims of their husbands' extravagance is any sufficient reason for surrounding them, or their property, with special safeguards; because some men are equally liable to be the victims of their wives' extravagance and yet no special law is considered necessary to protect them.[35]

Holmested correctly decried the Married Women's Property Act, 1884, as 'a thing of shreds and patches, combined together in a crude and ill-digested form and extremely difficult to unravel.'[36] He failed to recognize, however, that in the eyes of most legislators, judges, lawyers, and ordinary citizens, the married women's property acts had not been the result of any belief in 'the equality of the sexes.' On the contrary, 'the special protection of married women' had been perceived as necessary precisely because the sexes were not thought to be equal, and because, despite a growing belief in the spiritual and intellectual equality of husband and wife and the centrality of companionship to the marital relationship, husbands, it was believed, would always be physically and economically the stronger party in marriage; wives, therefore, required special safeguards against coercion. Reform, as Goldwin Smith recognized and lamented in a scathing critique of the demands of the 'woman movement,' was 'inspired by a mistrust of [the husband]'.[37]

While the physical power differential between husbands and wives clearly could not have been eliminated by legislative fiat, the economic power of the husband could have been mitigated by granting wives a claim on family property. Such an innovation, however, was unthinkable in the context of nineteenth-century beliefs about marriage and the respective roles of husbands and wives; despite his liberality, not even Holmested recommended it. Without such reform, the legislation of 1884 provided inadequate protection for both married women and their creditors. The act of 1884 eliminated the most glaring injustices evident under the legislation of 1859, 1872, and 1873 by depriving the husband of his role as trustee over his wife's estate; no longer could husbands simply misrepresent themselves as the owners of their wives' property and commit fraud or abscond. However, couples could still avoid paying their debts by transfering property from a liable to a non-liable spouse; more important, most wives did not own significant amounts of separate property and were therefore denied the means to escape from abusive partners. The act of 1884 provided women with formal legal equality but ignored the 'social realities of the position of married women';[38] this contradiction ensured that the act would not meet women's needs. Ironically, it also served to mute further criticism of the law of married women and their property since, with regard to property ownership, 'the equality of the sexes' had ostensibly been achieved.[39]

9

'Lending Aid or Encouragement to Fraudulent and Dishonest Practices': Wives and Their Creditors after 1884

Despite its comparative liberality, the act of 1884 did not solve all the problems creditors faced when dealing with married women. Less than a decade after the passage of the act, this fact was recognized both within and outside the legal profession. As one woman argued in an open letter to *The Week* in 1891, the new law was publicly perceived as an inducement to fraudulent behaviour:

The fact that almost in every sheriff's and bailiff's office in the Province there are numerous unsatisfied writs of fi fa against men whose wives are in business or in possession of ample means which they would never have possessed, if it had not been first acquired by the husband, is a very significant fact. A man will take a building or other contract and obtain expensive credit, apparently being in possession of property, but when his creditors take steps to realize, the man owns nothing, his wife owns everything ... If the tendency of the new law is in the direction of lending aid or encouragement to fraudulent and dishonest practices, or of lowering the standard of commercial morality, it is the clear duty of the legislature by amendment to apply such checks and safe-guards as will counteract that tendency.[1]

Such fears were neither unfounded nor misgonynistic. Inspired by similar concerns, the editors of the *Canadian Law Times* explicitly called for legislative reform:

This law must be placed on such an intelligible basis that the lay mind can compass it. By slow gradations, with the help of Equity, married women have advanced from a stage at which they could by no possibility charge themselves or their property to a stage at which they can charge their separate estate, but by such devious, or rather uncertain methods, that the law is much more easily evaded or mistaken than fulfilled or understood.[2]

This call, however, went unheeded because the act of 1884 had eliminated the most glaring inequities that had emerged under earlier legislation. Under this legislation, wives who owned separate property were made explicitly liable on contract and the husband was removed from his position as trustee. This did not, however, prevent problems of misrepresentation of ownership of family property. Not only could the husband transfer property to his wife but now she, with new dispositive powers over her estate, could transfer goods to her husband to avoid her own legitimate debts. Although creditors learned to deal more warily with married couples, and to ensure that both spouses signed legal documents and assumed liability for debts, the law would have been more easily 'fulfilled and understood' had automatic joint liability of husband and wife been instituted. Joint ownership and liability, however, were unthinkable in the context of the nineteenth century, as they implied the economic equality of husband and wife. This was problematic for creditors, however, because it denied the social reality of marriage as a form of economic partnership.

Under the act of 1884 the contractual capacity of married women was expanded and clarified. A wife could now render herself liable on any contract in respect of and to the extent of her separate estate. All contracts by married women were deemed to have been entered into respecting any separate estate, including land, which a wife owned at the time of contracting the debt and any property that she might thereafter acquire. For creditors, this represented a significant improvement over the act of 1872. As Robertson J held in 1892:

The result of this is that with respect to contract the plaintiff has now to prove:
1. The contract or debt.

2. The possession of separate property at the time of the contract.
   He need not prove its existence at the time of the judgment as under the old law, because the statute declares that she intends to charge future acquired property unless the contrary is shown.[3]

While creditors had been able to prosecute married women under the acts of 1872 and 1873, the act of 1884 made the collection of such debts much more likely. For example, a woman could no longer enter into a contract and then sell the personal property that was liable, buying land or new chattels that were not chargeable; all property, present and future, was attachable.

This expanded liability was affirmed in *Moore v Jackson*, a case that involved extensive litigation and numerous appeals and was finally resolved by the Supreme Court of Canada. Edward Moore first sued Jane Jackson for $4,262 at the Toronto Assizes in November of 1888. She had given promissory notes for over $12,000 to him as security for her son and his business associate. These notes were accepted by the plaintiff as collateral for the son's debt on the condition that Jane Jackson not alienate her real estate until the notes had been paid in full:

Edward Moore

Dear Sir – I hold four hundred acres of land which is worth thirty-three thousand dollars, and is all in my own name and right.

... I pledge myself solemnly to do nothing to affect my interest in said lands, either by deed or mortgage, until said notes are paid to you in full.[4]

Upon being given notice by her son that his business was about to fail and that payment of the notes by him would be impossible, Jane Jackson conveyed this property to her daughter. The plaintiff claimed that the conveyance was entered into for the purpose of 'defeating, delaying and hindering the plaintiff' in the recovery of his claim. Jane Jackson argued that as a married woman she had no authority to contract with regard to lands in which her husband held an interest by virtue of curtesy. In this claim she contradicted herself, as she had encumbered the property and had conveyed it to her daughter despite her supposed disability. She knew, however, that if the court accepted her plea all transactions would be deemed invalid and the property would not be lost to the creditors. In the examination conducted by the court it became clear that Jane Jackson was deliberately attempting to evade what she knew to be legitimate debts:

Q: But you thought that he might have some claim against you, didn't you?

A: Yes.

Q: Why did you not think of paying Mr. Moore before you gave the property to your daughter?

A: (Refusal to respond) ...

Q: Then you have nothing left at all?

A: My husband keeps me.

Q: And if anything happened to your husband you would be without means.

A: Yes.

Q: Dependent on your daughter.[5]

The daughter tried to justify her mother's actions by asserting that Jane Jackson was an old woman with a poor memory. She also argued that she had taken the conveyance in order to relieve her mother of the burden of responsibility for her property: 'I think when a woman of her age is too much troubled it shortens her life.'[6] Boyd J was distrustful of this attempt to evade responsibility on the basis of weakness due to age and gender and rendered judgment in favour of the plaintiff: 'It seems to me that this writing is sufficient to indicate all that the statute requires. The parties were dealing on the faith of this being such estate as could be laid hold of by the creditors, and it is doing no injustice to give it this fair and reasonable meaning.'[7]

This judgment was appealed by Jane Jackson; in 1889 Boyd's ruling was overturned in the Ontario Court of Appeal on a technicality, and the complainant was granted the right to a new trial. In September 1890 the case was once again heard at the Toronto Assizes. Considerable additional facts were brought to light in this trial. Jane Jackson had been married in 1869. In 1879 and 1882 she had acquired lands in Etobicoke that she held under the terms of the Married Women's Property Act of 1872; in 1887 she had acquired further lands in Parkdale that she held under the terms of the act of 1884. In his decision Armour J ruled that the Parkdale lands were subject to the claims of the plaintiff, but that the lands in Etobicoke, because of the interest by way of curtesy held by Mr Jackson under the act of 1872, were not property over which Mrs Jackson had any right of disposition.[8] Since the Etobicoke lands were of much greater value than the Parkdale lands, this judgment left the plaintiff without full compensation.

The plaintiff then entered a motion to have this decision varied and the Etobicoke lands declared liable for the debt. Jane Jackson also moved to have the judgment set aside on the basis that 'she had never contracted or assumed to contract with regard to her separate estate.'[9] Of course, she could not 'assume to contract' except with separate property, and this was a thinly veiled attempt to avoid her legitimate debt. Street J determined that at the time of making the notes in 1886 she owned a separate estate, the lands in Etobicoke, with which she had a statutory right to contract. She did not have such a right under the act of 1872, which gave women only the right to hold their real property, not to dispose of it without the consent of their husbands. By section 22 of the act of 1884, however, the necessity of the husband joining in the conveyance of any separate real estate had been eliminated:

The position of Mrs. Jackson appears, therefore, so far as the lands in Etobicoke are concerned, to have been at the time she conveyed them to her daughter, Mrs. Graydon, that she could not convey them free from her husband's right to enjoy them after her death as tenant by the curtesy without his concurrence, but that subject to this right of her husband's, accruing only in case he survived her, she dying seized intestate, she had the same absolute right that she would have had, had she been unmarried, to hold, enjoy, lease, convey or devise the freehold and inheritance without his consent and without interruption on his part – the right to hold free from her husband's debts and control having arisen under the Act of 1872 and the right to convey under sec. 22 of the Act of 1884.[10]

Despite her husband's claims for curtesy, the Etobicoke lands were 'liable to be seized and sold for the satisfaction of the plaintiff's claim.'[11] The conveyance to her daughter was set aside as fraudulent and void as against creditors, and judgment was rendered for the plaintiff.

This judgment was once again reversed by the Court of Appeal, and the plaintiff appealed to the Supreme Court of Canada in 1893. In the Supreme Court, Strong CJC held that not to consider Mrs Jackson liable on the notes would be to make a mockery of the obvious intention of the legislature in granting wives dispositive powers over their separate property. Of equal importance, such a decision would seriously endanger the rights of creditors:

Can any rational meaning be attributed to such a statute other than this, that a creditor was to be at liberty not only to sue and proceed against a married woman upon her separate contract, but also having so sued and proceeded against her and having obtained a judgment, he was to have the execution of that judgment out of her separate property? Surely it was not meant to mock at creditors by telling them they might sue and recover judgment, but that such a judgment was to be barren and fruitless ... If there is such a thing as a necessary implication we must have recourse to it here and hold that this right thus conferred to sue and proceed against a married woman upon her separate contracts as if she was sole and unmarried implies that the judgment thus recovered was to be satisfied. Then if it was to be satisfied, satisfied out of what? What could be available to satisfy it except the judgment debtor's separate property. It must follow that the intention was to confer upon creditors the right to sue and proceed against and enforce payment out of the statutory separate property of the debtor, or otherwise the clause would be wholly illusory.[12]

The decision of the Ontario Court of Appeal was overruled, and Moore was granted judgment against all of Jane Jackson's separate property. Strong's decision reflected a belief that the act of 1884 had been passed to solve the problems that had arisen under the act of 1872, under which many judgments against married women had been 'barren and fruitless.' This decision established unequivocally the right of a wife to contract with regard to her separate estate, including land, without the consent or interference of her husband, and the right of her creditors to obtain judgment out of any and all separate estate that a debtor wife possessed. It confirmed that the special categories of property established in 1859 and 1872 had been retroactively abolished and that all wives had equal rights over their separate property.

In most cases the enlargement of the wife's contractual rights granted by the act of 1884 and confirmed by *Moore v Jackson* served creditors well. Problems remained, however, since the liability of the wife was proprietary, not personal. The possession of property was essential to the ability of a married woman – though not of a man – to make a contract; as the editors of the *Canadian Law Times* lamented in 1888, 'that the power to become liable or rather to make a contract, should depend on the possession of property is manifestly unfair to those who cannot ascertain the capacity of those with whom they are treating.'[13] This also ensured, of course, that married women faced greater obstacles in obtaining credit than did men or unmarried women. Moreover, although a married woman could no longer deny her contractual capacity if she owned separate property, the question of agency continued to complicate cases regarding a married woman and her contracts. The wife could still act as agent for her husband, purchasing necessaries under his authority, and couples were sometimes deliberately ambiguous as to who owned property with reference to which a contract was made. In the context of the traditional belief that it was the husband's responsibility to support his wife and family, the court refused to make a woman liable for household goods unless she entered into a contract specifically with regard to her separate estate. As Hagarty CJQB concluded, there was 'no legal implication resulting from a woman ... ordering household goods, other than that she is doing so on her husband's credit and authority.'[14] As well, although the husband no longer served as trustee for his wife's separate property, he did have the right to act as her agent. Husbands, therefore, could claim to own property that belonged to their wives; if creditors had not investigated title thoroughly, they could be defrauded of their rights. Eliminating the role of the husband as trustee did not prevent misrepresentation with regard to the ownership of family property, and in fact increased the ways in which property could be transferred between spouses. Over 130 cases of attempted fraud found in the unreported court documents illustrate the myriad ways in which dishonest couples manipulated the statutes.

Even without rights of trusteeship, it was a simple matter for husbands to lie to creditors, to claim that they owned property that in fact belonged to their wives, and thereby to obtain goods by deceit. For example, in 1892 the Hamilton Lumber Co. sued Jane and F.F. Appleton in the court of Common Pleas for $1,040.38 due for lumber that had been used by F.F. Appleton in the construction of buildings on properties in Hamilton owned by his wife and co-defendant. F.F. Appleton had never informed the plaintiffs that the property belonged to his wife and had always, the plaintiffs claimed, 'promised to pay, and represented to the President of [the] Company, J. Hearst, that he would do so once money from Provident and Loan [$1,000] came due.'

In her defence Jane Appleton pleaded coverture and argued that her husband had acted without her consent: 'I never at any time authorized my husband or any other person to purchase lumber or any other materials or goods from the plaintiffs.' She claimed not to have been aware of the purchases until the commencement of proceedings against her, and argued that she 'never at any time had any dealings with said plaintiffs.' Her husband, not surprisingly, also asserted that the materials had been obtained 'without the knowledge or consent of my co-defendant.' The court rejected this plea. The judges distrusted Jane Appleton's claim that she was unaware of her husband's business affairs. The construction site was very close to the Appleton's home, and the court thought it inconceivable that she was unaware that construction was taking place. In this context it was her responsibility to deny her husband the right to act as her agent and to stop the proceedings herself by direct contact with the plaintiffs. The court also regarded F.F. Appleton's fraudulent presenta-

tion to the company that he was owner of the lands as evidence of his dishonesty. The Appletons were ordered to pay the amount demanded by
the plaintiffs into the court within two days.[15]

Husbands also conveyed property to their wives in the hope that
they could thus evade legitimate debts. Many wives in Ontario were 'in
possession of ample means which they would never have possessed if it
had not first been acquired by the husband.'[16] For example, in 1892,
Michael Piggott, a contractor, charged that Samuel Medley, a stone-
cutter, had fraudulently conveyed all his property to his wife in order
to avoid the payment of his just debts. Piggott had recovered judgment
against the defendant in Chancery for $1,015.43, but the judgment
remained unsatisfied as the defendant owned no property out of which
it could be made good. Four months after the judgment, the defendant
had conveyed two lots in Hamilton to his wife. According to the plaintiff, the deed was 'made with intent to defraud, defeat, hinder and
delay.' The defendants also failed to respond to the plaintiff's statement
of claim, a tacit admission of guilt. Not surprisingly, the case was
decided against them, although by this time the lots had been sold and
the couple had absconded.[17]

In cases such as those of Jane and F.F. Appleton and Samuel Medley
it is unclear to what degree wives were themselves participants in fraudulent transactions; wives might simply have left their property to be
managed by husbands who subsequently dealt with such property dishonestly. More interesting from a feminist perspective are cases in
which wives themselves were active agents, manipulating new statutory rights to their own advantage. In one such case James Boustead
had been named as assignee of the effects of one Mr Culverwell for the
benefit of his creditors. Before this time Culverwell had carried on an
unspecified business in Toronto, but upon the realization that he would
soon be insolvent he had used all the assets of his business to purchase
lands in the name of his wife. Boustead claimed that at the time of the
conveyance the wife was 'well aware of the fact ... that her husband was
totally insolvent.' She had publicly stated her intention of selling the
lands and the rents and profits from the estate were being used to support the wife, the insolvent, and their children.

Under examination, Ella Culverwell admitted that at the time of her
marriage she had owned no separate estate. During the marriage, however, she claimed to have inherited money from her father, although she
could not produce a will to prove this fact. She asserted that her husband
had borrowed money from her throughout their marriage and that she

had finally insisted that land be purchased in her name to provide her and the children with security. At the time at which the properties were purchased, 'as far as I knew he was in good circumstances.' Despite Ella's manipulation of traditional assumptions about the role of wives within the family, the court rejected her claim that she knew nothing of her husband's business transactions; the husband and his partner had been on bad terms for several months and the litigation between them, which had led to the husband's insolvency, was common knowledge. Even if she had lent her husband money, the debt to the creditors had been incurred before the time at which money was lent by Ella; therefore, to compensate her in advance of the declaration of insolvency was illegal. The conveyance to Ella Culverwell from her husband was declared to be fraudulent and void as against creditors.[18]

Although in the Culverwell case the court was able to protect the interests of creditors, this was not always possible. Liens could be placed upon land, although the court, as in alimony cases, seems to have issued liens only irregularly. Movable property was even more difficult to reclaim; couples could easily abscond with money and chattels, leaving their creditors without redress. Evidence from three cases involving Clemson and Lida VanWormer suggests that some couples made extensive and unscrupulous use of the statutes, misrepresenting who owned family property and transferring such ownership whenever necessary to avoid responsibility for their debts.

Clemson VanWormer was a successful merchant and his wife owned separate estate. In 1888 John Kay, a salesman, sued Lida VanWormer for $525.77. She had purchased rugs and other household materials and, the plaintiff argued, 'the goods were purchased from the plaintiff by the defendant for herself and on her own behalf and were charged to her account.' Because she owned separate estate and because of the expansion of married women's liability on contract under the act of 1884, Kay believed that he had protected his interests by entering directly into a contract with Lida VanWormer. The defendant, however, used the common law concept of agency to disclaim any responsibility for this debt: 'The claim of the plaintiff herein is for goods sold and delivered by the plaintiff to my husband, the said Clemson VanWormer. The actual purchase of the said goods was made by me, but was made for my husband and upon my husband's credit.' Lida VanWormer claimed that because the goods so furnished were 'household necessaries' it was her husband's legal responsibility to provide her with such goods, irrespective of her ownership of any separate property. Although she was an astute businesswoman, Lida VanWormer emphasized the traditional ideal of the wife as a dependent partner in marriage in the hope that she could avoid responsibility for her debt. She also claimed that at the time of the purchases she 'was possessed of no separate estate whatsoever other than my own clothing and personal effects.' She neglected to mention, however, that her 'personal effects' included jewellery worth over $7,000, a not inconsiderable sum of money and certainly an amount more than sufficient to cover her debt to the plaintiff. Moreover, according to the plaintiff, Lida's husband had explicitly told him to 'look to his wife for terms and payment.' No decision is extant for this case, but further suits against Clemson and Lida VanWormer suggest that this unwitting salesman was unlikely to have recovered his debt.[19]

Later in 1888 Lida and Clemson were again in court. In this case Clemson had given the plaintiff a promissory note for $2,500 on the representation 'that he was worth the sum of about $80,000 and that he had liabilities not exceeding $24,000.' At the time, Lida owned separate estate consisting of a home on College Street in Toronto, furniture, chattels and jewellery. She also owned a hotel, and shortly before the commencement of this action Clemson had mortgaged it for $51,000 on the pretence that the property was his own. When proceedings were commenced against her husband, Lida sold her hotel and absconded to the United States with all of the cash from the mortgage on her property, with $50,000 from the sale of this same hotel, and with all her chattels and jewellery. Her husband was detained under writs, but she returned with sufficient cash to pay the first instalment on some of his debts and thereby secured his release from jail. Further payments, however, were not forthcoming, and the plaintiff sought a speedy judgment before Lida could abscond:

I believe that the said Lida VanWormer has in her possession ample means to satisfy the amount of the note sued upon in this action but that if speedy judgment be not obtained herein that she will leave the city of Toronto and the Province of Ontario in order to prevent recovering the judgment and collecting the amount due by her to the plaintiff, and in order to defeat her creditors in the payment of their just claims against her.

Lida and Clemson may have managed to abscond, they may have paid the debt, judgment may have been rendered only against the husband, or the plaintiff may have abandoned his suit; it is impossible to say which, since no further documents relating to this case could be found. These ill-gotten gains may have been invested in another jurisdiction, outside the reach of the court; evidence suggests that the VanWormers had extensive family and business connections in New York State. Whichever of these possibilities is correct, this case illustrates the problems that married couples could create for their creditors.[20]

If they absconded, Lida and Clemson eventually returned to Toronto; in February 1889 Lida once again found herself in court, in this case as the plaintiff in an action for assault and damages. In her statement of claim she asserted that she was the proprietress of the Grand Pacific Hotel and that the defendant was a butcher who had 'falsely, maliciously and without reasonable and probable cause assaulted and [beaten] the plaintiff.' She had been forcibly removed from her hotel on charges of fraud and imprisoned in the city jail until her husband had produced bail. The defendant claimed that Lida had removed goods from the hotel in order to prevent her creditors from making good on debts held against her. Lida argued that she was innocent of all fraudulent intent and that she had suffered 'pain, disgrace, annoyance and loss of time, credit and expenses.' She claimed $2,000 in damages.

In his statement of defence Jacob Levin claimed that he had supplied Lida's hotel with meat and provisions and that she had refused to pay him for these goods. He had been informed 'by reliable sources that she was secretly removing and disposing of her goods and chattels with intent to defraud her creditors and was about to leave the city of Toronto for the USA at once unless apprehended.' His intentions, he claimed, were in no way malicious and against her claim for damages he asserted that she had as yet outstanding debts to him of $181.61. Lida had established a reputation as a married woman with whom creditors could deal only at their peril. In the context of Lida's previous behaviour, Levin's assertion that she was about to abscond was not farfetched. This case did not come to trial. It is possible that Lida dropped the charges because she believed she had cowed Levin into refraining from any legal action to make good his debt. It is also conceivable that she sought refuge outside the province and beyond the reach of the court and her creditors. It is clear, however, that Lida, an astute if unscrupulous businesswoman, had achieved some economic independence on the basis of her ownership of property. She also demonstrated considerable knowledge of the law and of legal proceedings.[21]

Even though the act of 1884 ostensibly made women like Lida fully liable on contract, considerable scope for fraud existed and was exploited by unscrupulous couples such as the VanWormers. It is clear that Lida did not simply passively allow her husband to use her property for fraudulent purposes, but actively engaged herself in the economy and deliberately defrauded her creditors and manipulated her statutory property rights for her own benefit and that of her husband. The Van-Wormers manipulated the concept of agency, misrepresented ownership of family property, and made use of loopholes in the law to avoid their legitimate debts. Without any legal recognition of the economic partnership that was central to marriage and to such manipulation of the statutes, without joint ownership of family property and joint liability for family debts, creditors were often left empty-handed even when the court rendered judgment in their favour. This inability of the court to meet the needs of creditors was not due to judicial indifference, however. Decisions that favoured the wife over her husband's creditors, which had predominated in the 1870s, declined dramatically in the 1880s, in particular after the passage of the act of 1884. This change in emphasis occurred because judges were disgusted by the audacity with which couples attempted to defraud their creditors and because, in the light of the behaviour of women such as Lida VanWormer, they gradually recognized that assumptions about women's lack of business acumen were erroneous.

As the emphasis and sympathy of the court shifted, an increasing number of couples chose to settle their cases out of court.[22] Two cases involving the same defendants, Thomas and Emily Crittenden, illustrate the conditions under which some married couples entered into such agreements. In the first of the cases against the Crittendens, Charles Miller obtained judgment against Thomas Crittenden in 1890 for $353.53. The plaintiff argued that Crittenden, while largely indebted, had purchased properties, registered in the name of his wife, on which he had made large improvements: 'He has continuously since his marriage with his co-defendant placed in her name all properties he has acquired and as soon as acquired for the purpose and intent of placing them beyond the reach of his creditors and he has thus denuded himself of all his property and made his co-defendant ostensible owner of a large amount of property.' Included with the plaintiff's statement of claim was an affidavit of a clerk of the court asserting that Emily Crittenden had deliberately avoided the service of both her writ of summons and a subpoena.

In their defence both Thomas and Emily denied any fraudulent intent. At neither the time of the purchase nor the time of the conveyance, they claimed, had Thomas Crittenden been in insolvent circumstances. Emily attempted to establish that the money used to purchase the property was her separate estate, inherited from relatives in England. She claimed that on several occasions she had traveled to England to collect money from her family. She had never placed any of the money in the bank, but had kept it 'in a bag in her bedroom' and had 'always let Mr. Crittenden handle the money.' He did so, she claimed, only as her agent. In an attempt to exploit stereotypes about women's lack of business sense and knowledge, she also claimed that at the time of her marriage, and up until the time of the suit in question, she knew nothing of her husband's business affairs:

Q: You know he is insolvent and unable to pay his debts?

A: No, I know nothing at all about my husband's affairs.

Q: Do you mean to tell me that you do not know that your husband is insolvent?

A: No, I do not.

Her husband, a contractor, had superintended the construction of several brick buildings on her property, but the building materials, she asserted, had been paid for out of her separate estate. She also claimed that she had specifically insisted on holding the property in her own name because 'he was drinking at that time and wasting my money.' While she insisted that she was ignorant of her husband's business dealings, therefore, she simultaneously asserted that she had dealt with her own money in a knowledgable and responsible manner. Neither party in this case could have been sure of victory. Emily Crittenden's proof of ownership of separate estate was weak and her attempts to avoid the service of writs were suspicious, but her claim that her husband drank and squandered their money would have aroused the chivalric sympathy of the judiciary. In June 1891 judgment was rendered against the male defendant, although no decision was made with regard to the separate estate of Emily Crittenden. The decision against Thomas was of course fruitless, as he was insolvent. In July 1892 the action against Emily was dismissed at the consent of both parties. Unfortunately, the terms of the settlement are not extant.[23]

In a similar case in 1893, William and John Maguire, who had obtained judgment against Thomas Crittenden for $149.73 for the purchase of materials used in the construction of buildings on Emily's land, attempted to have the conveyance of the land from Thomas to Emily declared fraudulent and void. In their statement of defence the Crittendens reiterated many of the claims advanced in their earlier suit. Emily Crittenden also asserted that 'the defendant Thomas Crittenden has never claimed or exercised any ownership' over the property and that if the plaintiffs had advanced him materials on this basis they were neglectful. Moreover, she had not entered into any contract with the plaintiffs and had not given her husband agency to obtain credit on her property. The materials he had purchased from the defendants were to have been used in his other building projects, and if any had been used on her property, 'the said materials were furnished by the said plaintiffs solely upon the credit of the said T. Crittenden and upon his responsibility and the plaintiffs looked to him entirely for the payment therefor.' In other words, she indirectly accused her husband of fraud, comfortable in the knowledge that as an insolvent any judgment against him was fruitless anyway. She claimed that she had 'never contracted or agreed to purchase the said materials' and that she had no knowledge whatever of the transactions. In this argument she attempted to establish that her husband, if he had contracted debts with reference to her property, had done so irresponsibly and without her knowledge or consent. She sought to use the married women's statutes to assert her right to own and control the property, but used the common law concept of agency to deny responsibility for her debts. It is interesting to note that this was precisely the opposite claim to that used in her statement of defense against Charles Miller. In that suit Emily had argued that her ownership of the separate estate was confirmed by the fact that all the materials used in the construction of buildings on the property had been paid for by her. In this case, in order to avoid paying for such building materials, she claimed that her husband had purchased the materials without her consent. Although she attempted to use stereotypes regarding women's lack of interest in and knowledge of business to her advantage, clearly she was aware of the particulars of these business transactions and of the technicalities and loopholes of the law. In 1894 this case was also settled out of court.[24]

The needs of married women and the original legislative mandate of protection were difficult to reconcile with such evidence of fraud and manipulation of the statutes. Women like Emily Crittenden and Lida VanWormer defied the stereotypes of female economic passivity and lack of business interest and knowledge; they were victimizers, not victims, and such behaviour undermined the judicial incentive to protect women. Despite mounting evidence of female agency, however, the court remained willing to ignore the demands of creditors when circumstances warranted such action, as when women who fit traditional stereotypes required protection. This willingness is illustrated by a case decided in 1894, *Sheratt v The Merchants' Bank of Canada*.

Mrs Sheratt sued the bank for $5,000 and interest. The money had orig-
inally belonged to her husband, and shortly after the deposit was made in
her name he had been allowed by the defendants, without her knowledge
or consent, to draw money from the account. Her husband died in 1889,
and although she had made no claim to the money during his lifetime she
demanded payment in 1890. The case had originally been heard in Perth
and had been decided in favour of the plaintiff. On appeal the decision
was upheld. This judgment ultimately hinged on Osler JA's perception
that Mrs Sheratt was honest, that her husband and the bank had acted in
collusion to defraud her of property that had ostensibly been granted to
her as separate estate, and that she was therefore deserving of the protection of the court:

The delay which occurred in bringing the action is no doubt a fact to be considered in weighing the bona fides of the plaintiff's claim, as it suggests that she may
have known of her husband's dealings with the receipt, and that she was an
assenting party. But it is by no means conclusive, and in the case of an ignorant,
illiterate woman, ignorant of her rights, or how to enforce them, who had been
told by the defendants' manager when she went to enquire about the receipt after
her husband's death that there was no receipt or money of hers in the bank, it
would be unsafe to press the fact of delay too far, particularly when the conduct
of the bank in dealing with the receipt, prima facie the plaintiff's property, is
shewn to have been careless if not altogether irregular.[25]

Despite the fact that Mr Sherratt had probably granted his wife this
money only to protect it from his potential creditors, to deny her the right
to reclaim it would be to undermine the original intent of the legislation –
the protection of married women from coercion and abuse at the hands of
their husbands. It is interesting to note that this case was reported. In the
1870s the majority of cases had been decided in favour of the wife, and
those chosen for reporting had been cases that illustrated the problems
that early legislation had created for creditors. Only two decades later,
the majority of unreported cases were decided in favour of creditors, and
this case was reported to remind judges and other members of the legal
profession that in some circumstances wives were innocent, ignorant of
the law and the business world, and in need of protection. Within twenty
years the emphasis of the court, and of court reporters, had changed dramatically. This fact illustrates also the dangers inherent in an exclusive
reliance on reported cases when studying nineteenth-century law and its
interpretation and impact.

Growing judicial recognition of female potential for astute and at times fraudulent business dealings was not matched by any recognition of the economic partnership that was central to marriage. Individual women might be astute, but women – wives in particular – were not considered the equals of their husbands. An 1886 case that illustrates this central limitation of the legislation. Robert Smith had obtained judgment against George Lewis in the Court of Queens' Bench for $933.28, but the debt remained unsatisfied. George's wife and co-defendant, however, owned considerable separate property. Smith claimed that the separate estate of the wife had been transferred to her by her husband when both parties were aware that George Lewis was 'largely indebted.'

In their defence George and Eliza Lewis argued that the property had been purchased with the proceeds of a business in which husband and wife had laboured together. They had owned a store in which the wife had worked as a clerk, and she argued that 'it was my work the same as his, and more so, because I spent more time in the store than himself, and took a deeper interest in it.' She had hired another woman to perform her household chores so that she could devote herself more completely to the business. The business had originally been set up with the husband's money, and the property in question had been purchased with the proceeds from the sale of the store. Both defendants argued that the husband had been solvent at the time of the conveyance of the property to the wife and that the conveyance had been made in consideration of her labour in the business.

The plaintiff's solicitor challenged the defendants' assertion that a wife had a legitimate stake in a family business:

Q: You think that it is a fair division that the wife and husband should work together, but that the wife should have everything?

A: It is fair that way: that is the way it is now.

Q: You don't think a wife should do any work for her husband?

A: I did work for him.

Q: But you think she should be paid. You do not think she is under any obligation to work for her husband?

A: I do not think that is a proper question to put to me.

The plaintiff's solicitor sought to manipulate the traditional assumption that a wife was obliged to assist her husband in his work in order to discredit Eliza's claim to the property.

Eliza and George, however, were able to produce books from the business to prove that George had not been indebted at the time of the conveyance. George asserted that the property had been conveyed to his wife as the result of a longstanding promise that he would put their home in her name for added security; without this promise, he argued, she would not have married him. Of equal importance, at the time of the conveyance George Lewis was leaving on a trip to England and he wanted his wife to have clear title to their property. He had no intention of going into any speculative business and could not have foreseen that he would subsequently become indebted:

My intention was simply – I was in no ways liable to anybody, and I had a perfect right to do as I liked with my property ... I was a free man ... I was going away ... the ship might have sunk and taken me down and my wife would have been left and would have had to run a certain amount of law business, which I wanted to avoid ... I thought to myself 'Now, George, you are going away. You have promised this thing to your wife for years. You are going to do this for her: she has worked solidly for you ...' That is my sole and true intention in doing it. I did not know that I owed money that I could not pay, and my intentions were to pay every man every dollar that I owed. I never wanted to defraud a man out of a cent.

The case was discharged at the consent of both parties in 1886 after an out-of-court settlement had been reached. Unfortunately, the terms of this settlement are not extant. However, George Lewis's closing comment during the hearing conducted by the court is revealing. Asked what evidence he had regarding his longstanding promise to convey property to his wife, whether or not such an intention was set out in any marriage settlement, George answered, 'I just wish there had been.'[26] Without the protection of a written marriage settlement, questions regarding the ownership of and liability for family property undermined both the protective potential of legislation and the security of creditors. Although George and Eliza seem to have had a relatively modern view of marriage as an economic partnership, this was not shared or even recognized by the court. Eliza's claim on the property, in the eyes of the law, arose not from the work that had helped the couple to accumulate wealth, but from her husband's right to provide for his wife through a protective settlement, a fact that illustrates the subordinate role women were still expected to play within marriage.

Such cases were far from uncommon. Despite the fact that reform represented a dramatic improvement over the common law and earlier remedial legislation, problems remained endemic in credit relations with married couples. The limitations of the act of 1884 were inherent within the concept of separate property itself. These problems had not been evident under the common law because all family property, while under the management of the husband, was liable for debts contracted by both husband and wife. Under remedial legislation, however, the concept of joint liability was abolished. A husband was not liable for debts contracted by his wife with regard to her separate property, nor was she liable for any debts he might contract. Unscrupulous couples could place assets and profits out of the reach of creditors by transferring nominal ownership of property, and profits from businesses, to a non-liable spouse and by using and abusing the concept of agency. Evidence from fraud cases suggests that the act of 1884 provided women who owned separate property with unprecedented scope for active involvement in the marketplace and the economy.[27] Undoubtedly, only a small minority of such wives were dishonest. Eliza Lewis's assertion that 'it was my work the same as his' is also suggestive of the slow change of attitudes facilitated by property law reform. Judicial and social recognition of women's commercial potential was incomplete, however, without the establishment of some form of joint ownership and joint liability. The failure of the law to acknowledge that marriage was an equal economic partnership ensured that creditors would be denied justice when husbands and wives were partners in fraud. It had even more disastrous consequences, however, for women themselves.

10

'Being Terrified and in Fear of Violence': The Limitations of Separate Property as a Protective Device

In 1887 Eliza Young sought the protection of the court because her husband had mortgaged property, purchased in part with money from her separate estate, against her will. Although she had paid $4,334 of the original purchase price of $8,103, the mortgaged property had been taken in her husband's name. Eliza explicitly argued that she had been coerced into turning over her property to an insistent and abusive husband:

I requested that the deed should be made in our joint names but my husband, who is an exceedingly violent man, objected to that being done and demanded that the deed be in his name and that he would then make a deed to me of the portion of the land to which I was entitled. Being terrified and in fear of violence should I refuse to do as he requested I consented that the deed be made as he asked.

She was afraid that the money he was about to obtain from the mortgage would be squandered. The court issued an injunction forbidding the sale of the land on evidence that her husband was 'a very violent man and addicted to the excessive use of intoxicating liquors and spends large sums of money in drinking and treating.' Although no explanation was given for her action, on 30 April of the same year the plaintiff 'consented to see the action dismissed.' The obvious trepidation with which she viewed her husband may explain this decision. If so, it underlines the limits of the married women's property acts as protective legislation. Despite the fact that Eliza had contributed to the purchase of the home, her husband did not have to petition the court for the right to use – or, more correctly in this case, to misuse – family property. Once the property was in her husband's name, Eliza was obliged to prove that she had been defrauded of her separate property; had she not paid a portion of the purchase price, she would have had no claim on the property whatsoever. Without joint ownership of the property accumulated by virtue of the joint labour of spouses, what protection did the act afford to wives who had limited opportunities for employment outside the home and who had not, unlike Eliza, ever owned or inherited property?[1]

The Married Women's Property Act of 1884 eliminated the role of the husband as trustee for his wife's separate estate, and therefore the most obvious and glaring problems that married women had faced under the common law and earlier legislation. Problems remained, however. Property brought to the marriage or inherited during it by the wife – property that was explicitly included in the wife's statutory estate – was often mingled with other family property in the daily struggle for survival. To avoid confusion for creditors, the court considered mingled assets to have been voluntarily given over by the wife to her husband. Such a wife could reclaim her rights of management and disposition over her property only by taking her husband to court as Eliza Young had attempted to do. The usefulness of such recourse to judicial proceedings depended, of course, on whether or not the husband had squandered or encumbered the property while it remained under his control. Most importantly, many wives owned no separate property as it was defined by this statute;[2] without a claim on property accumulated during marriage, they remained economically dependent on their husbands and trapped in abusive or unhappy relationships. Although judges continued to use their powers of discretion to protect wives, the concept of separate property was inherently limited. The legislation failed to provide women with the rights necessary to protect themselves because it was still based upon the belief that women, being 'weak and liable to be imposed upon,'[3] were incapable of self-protection.

The possibility was ever present that the husband might appropriate his wife's property through intimidation or more gentle means of persuasion. Once under his control, the wife faced considerable obstacles in reclaiming her separate property, since family property belonged exclusively to the husband. This problem is well illustrated in *Hopkins v Hopkins*. During the period of her marriage, Hannah Hopkins claimed to have transferred over $1,000 to her husband to help establish him in various businesses, all of which money he had refused to repay to her. Her husband, from whom she was now estranged, denied that any money had been lent to him and that his wife was or ever had been the owner of any separate estate. Ferguson J concluded that

> to enable a wife to recover from her husband for her money which she let him have during coverture, she must prove a contract for the repayment of it, and in the view that I have taken of this case it is not necessary for me to say whether or not she could in that case recover against him. This action is brought by the wife to recover money lent, as she in her pleadings says, to her husband, and she says that no time was specified or agreed upon for the repayment of the money, but that it was payable on demand.[4]

Because of evidence of fraud, by the 1880s the court required strict evidence of a contract between husband and wife in order to enforce repayment of loans; the very nature of marriage and the usual dealings of husband and wife would, in many cases, preclude the formal drawing up of such agreements. Unsubstantiated parol agreements could always later be denied by a husband. In his summation, Ferguson J recognized that this ruling brought hardship upon Mrs Hopkins: 'Under such circumstances I am of the opinion that the plaintiff cannot recover ... great as the hardship upon her may, in light of the facts incidentally disclosed, appear to be.'[5] In dismissing this action, Ferguson was admittedly concerned with protecting the rights of creditors; other lenders claimed the property that Silas's wife sought to recover, and it was always possible that the separation was itself a ruse entered into only in order to reclaim the property. As this case illustrates, however, the growing emphasis on the need to protect the rights of creditors was detrimental to the interests of some individual women. Without joint ownership, husbands and wives could act in collusion and commit fraud with impunity; husbands too could commit fraud against unsuspecting wives.

Hopkins v Hopkins was reported because it was an unusual case in which the interests of the wife were subordinated to those of creditors. More commonly, however, judicial discretion was used for the benefit of married women. These cases were not reported because they were perceived as uncontroversial. Judges were willing, when evidence proved conclusively that husbands were abusive or absent, to provide needy wives with the means for survival and for the support of their children. It is important to understand, however, that the exercise of such discretion was dependent upon proof of male irresponsibility; wives still had to petition the court for relief against the presumed rights of husbands.

For example, Sarah Beales had come from Northamptonshire, England in 1883. In England she had carried on a business running a public house that she had inherited from her first husband. At the time of their marriage, the defendant had been a widower with three children. He was also in straitened circumstances, and she had supported both her husband and his children after their marriage. He had not, she claimed, aided her in her business, which she had sold before coming to Canada. Upon their arrival in Canada her husband had persuaded her to let him deposit her money in a chartered bank, 'representing to her that it would be unsafe to carry such a large sum about her person.' They purchased property, and she paid the mortgage from her separate estate and earnings in the belief that ownership of the property had been taken in her name. Her husband, however, had handled the transaction and had surreptitiously taken ownership for himself. Since coming to Canada, her husband had refused to look for employment, 'preferring to live on his pension and the plaintiff,' and she had recently been forced to leave the home which her money had purchased 'owing to the ill-treatment of the defendant.' She presented convincing evidence, including the eyewitness accounts of neighbours and friends, to prove that her husband had beaten her severely and frequently, and that he was in the habit of insulting and humiliating her in public. While Sarah had found employment and was supporting herself, she was living in much reduced circumstances because of his refusal to convey the property to her, to account for the money that he had placed in the bank, and to return to her chattel property still in the home.

In his defence Robert Beales denied that he had been in straitened circumstances at the time of his marriage and argued that, once married, 'the business of the Inn was transferred to and carried on by' him. The plaintiff, he admitted, kept their common purse, but the money she held was, by law, his. In his opinion, she had left his home without just cause. Under cross-examination, however, Robert Beales admitted, 'I never interfered with the business after it came in my name.' Although he did not perform any of the duties of operating the inn, he argued that all profits therefrom were rightfully his:

Q: Did you consider it was your property absolutely or did you think that it was your property and your wife's jointly?

A: I say it was my property.

Q: Supposing that the plaintiff had not been your wife, supposing she is not your wife but simply your landlady and the property was sold just as it was done in this case and she comes to this country just as was done in this case and that money was put in this house and land, wouldn't you have thought ...

A: Circumstances alter cases.

Q: Do you not think that she would be entitled to that property supposing she was not your wife?

A: I see your point, that she is my wife.

Robert's answers emphasized the unique relationship between husband and wife and the wife's duty to perform household services, such as those required in a public-house business, for her husband. His answers were good legal answers, but in the course of the cross-examination other information came to light which probably determined the outcome of the case. Robert Beales admitted that his wife had laid assault charges against him and that he had been unemployed since his arrival in Canada. He had therefore failed in two ways to act as a responsible husband: he had been violent and unmanly, and his wife was the family breadwinner. In its judgment issued on 12 February, 1890, the court ordered the property to be sold, the remaining mortgages on it to be paid, and the money left after the payment of creditors to be split between husband and wife. The defendant was to pay his costs and those of the plaintiff, and the plaintiff was barred from bringing a suit against her husband for alimony and from pledging his credit.[6]

Judicial discretion is also evident in *Beckett v Beckett*, in which husband and wife contested the ownership of a lot and the home that had been built upon it. In her statement of claim Mary Jane Beckett argued that the property had been purchased for $450 and that $400 of that money had been paid out of her separate earnings, wages earned from intermittent domestic labour and laundry services. The conveyance of the property, however, had been taken in the name of her husband. With her separate earnings, she claimed, she had constructed a home on the property. Her husband had been unemployed for some time, and she argued that he 'was not at the time of the purchase of the said property nor has he been at any time since, in receipt of a stated income and has never contributed regularly to the maintenance of the said Plaintiff and the children of their marriage.' Although she had lived with the defendant for many years despite his failure to support her, she had finally been driven from the home that she had purchased because of life-threatening abuse; she had been beaten with a fire-iron, horse-whipped, scalded with a kettle of boiling water, and half-strangled with her husband's suspenders.

In his statement of defence Henry Beckett denied that any of the purchase money had been paid by his wife and argued that she had 'no interest in said lands whatsoever except her right to dower.' He could not, however, provide proof of his own employment. His central line of argument against the action of his wife was that she had issued a writ of summons against him in April 1890 in an action for alimony; since this suit was still pending, he claimed, 'the Defendant alleges that the Plaintiff is estopped from claiming the said lands as her own.' The actions were contradictory, because in the suit for alimony Mary Jane claimed support out of this land, while in this case she claimed ownership of it for herself. In her suit for alimony Mary Jane had asserted not only that her husband was abusive, but that he was a drunkard and was living in open adultery with a woman he referred to as his wife. She also claimed to be surviving only on the charity of her six children, 'without whose help she would not have been able to support herself.' In his statement of defence in the alimony case Henry Beckett argued that his wife owned a lot, her separate estate, which was sufficient for her maintenance; this was the same land which in the later suit he claimed as his own. Clearly he wanted to use any possible technicality to relieve himself of his duty of support. An affidavit from the plaintiff's solicitor was filed in the alimony case, asserting that the defendant had deliberately attempted to avoid the service of a summons. Probably in order to pursue her claim under the Married Women's Property Act, Mary Jane discontinued her alimony suit in 1892.[7] In the married women's property case, Henry Beckett made no attempt to deny his wife's charges of ill-treatment, asserting that he couldn't live with her because of her 'habit of self-pollution' and arguing that she could not prosecute him in two contradictory actions. He also asserted that he owned no other property with which to support himself should Mary Jane's claim be granted.

Mary Jane responded by asserting that she had not continued in the proceedings for alimony, and that at the time of the alimony suit 'she was unaware that further remedy was available to her.' This case involved two central questions. It was clear that title was held by the husband, but who had paid for the property? If Mary Jane had provided the purchase price, under what terms had title been taken by the husband? If Henry Beckett had paid the original purchase price, his wife's only legal claim on the property would be for dower. If Mary Jane had paid for the property and transferred it to her husband as trustee, it was within her rights to reclaim absolutely the eight-ninths of the purchase price that she claimed to have paid; but if she had given the property to him as a gift she could not reclaim anything. The evidence with regard to the payment for the property and the nature of the transfer was inconclusive. Despite problems of evidence, the judges responded to Mary Jane's petition with sympathy; whoever had paid for the property, the court did not wish to see her left destitute. Moreover, Henry Beckett was admittedly abusive, and it was clear that Mary Jane could not, in safety, return to live with him. The judges used their discretionary powers to fashion a decision that would protect Mary Jane's interests without leaving her husband destitute. She was granted half of 'the land in question free from the claims of the defendant for curtesy.' Henry was granted the other half of the property, which was freed from any claim for dower, and he was ordered to pay half his wife's court costs.[8] This decision did not follow any established precedent, and illustrates the extent and importance of judicial discretion in married women's cases.

Although under section 15 of the Married Women's Property Act of 1884 judges had the right to determine questions 'between husband and wife as to the title to or possession of property,' in neither of these cases had application been made to the court under this section of the act. Judges, however, used their wide powers of discretion to 'make such an order with respect to the property in dispute ... as [they thought] fit,'[9] and considered not only legal issues but the conduct of the parties, particularly the husband, in making their decisions. The court was willing, as these cases make clear, to provide protection for battered and deserted wives and to ignore precedent when to do so ensured the protection of women the judges deemed to be both vulnerable and innocent. The decision in *Beckett v Beckett*, in particular, was anomalous; Mary Jane was granted half of the family property, a portion more than her widow's share, or dower, and this during the life of her husband.

Beckett v Beckett was not the only case in which judges demonstrated such sympathy for wives. In *Donnelly v Donnelly* a married woman sought an injunction to restrain her husband from interfering in her business as a hotel-keeper. The husband did not enter a statement of defence, and the evidence presented provided clear proof that the property was her separate estate. She had owned the property from before the time of her marriage; her husband had never worked with her, although both husband and wife resided at the hotel. The husband had been 'taking the receipts from the bar, interfering with the servants, and maltreating the plaintiff personally; and just previous to this application being made struck her with his closed fist in the face and about the head, catching her by the hair, and inflicting painful injuries upon her person.'[10] Rose J not only granted the plaintiff the injunction which she sought, but further stated that although she had not requested an order excluding her husband entirely from the hotel, such an injunction, if necessary, could be issued:

In this case the order asked for is not to exclude the defendant from the house. Had such relief been asked, I think, on the facts, I would have granted it. I cannot see what right a man has to enter a house owned by his wife for the purpose, not of seeking the comforts of a home, but to abuse, annoy, injure, and maltreat her, destroying her comfort and peace of mind, and putting her in peril of her life and health. By marital rights it cannot be meant the right of a man to act as a brute towards a woman, in most cases practically defenceless.[11]

Mr Donnelly was prevented from interfering with his wife's business and from removing her chattels from the hotel.

On the surface, this decision conflicts with the judgment in *McGuire v McGuire*, in which Gwynne J denied the wife relief and the right 'to prosecute her husband as a trespasser if he continues in her house after having received orders from her to leave it' on the basis of the fact that she had, in his estimation, left her husband's home without 'just cause.'[12] When it is acknowledged, however, that the outcome in cases between husband and wife hinged primarily on the behaviour of the husband, it becomes clear that these cases are complementary, not contradictory. Mr Donnelly, not his wife, had 'violate[d] the marriage contract.'[13] Mr Donnelly did not seek the company of his wife or the right to perform his marital duties, but only to seize and squander the property which Mrs Donnelly required to maintain herself. Moreover, she was forced to support herself because of his failure to perform his duty as the family breadwinner. By his assertion that the wife might exclude her husband entirely from the hotel, Rose J implied that she had the right to deny her husband his marital rights not only over her property, but over her person; this extension of the rights of the wife probably explains why this case was selected for reporting.

The rights granted or implied in such cases, however, were discretionary only. The wife was deemed 'practically defenceless' and the court upheld her right to protection from mistreatment, not any right to independence. Moreover, nothing guaranteed that all judges in all cases would respond to women with sympathy. In essence, these cases were contests of character. The wife sought to prove that her husband was abusive and that she was innocent; in response, husbands tried to impugn the reputations of their wives and to assert that they had behaved in accordance not only with the common law duty of 'maintenance and protection' but with wider social definitions of manliness. Without general rights and an inalienable claim on family property, the possibility always remained that a particular judge might deny a needy woman relief. In fifteen of the seventeen post-1884 cases litigated between husbands and wives that were found in the unreported court documents, judges used their discretionary power to the benefit of wives. Their decisions favoured wives when evidence was clear and convincing that husbands had behaved in an irresponsible manner, but the two cases in which wives' needs were not met are important in exploring the limits of judicial sympathy.

In the first of these two cases, Ann Healy was denied the security that her separate property should theoretically have provided for her. She claimed that she was the owner of land in Perth, 'in my own right and independent of any claim of my husband.' She had purchased it in 1886 with money she had inherited from her father's estate. On this lot were considerable timber stands and sand pits, and for some time her husband had 'been drawing sand out of the sand pit on the said lot and ... cutting timber therefrom and has applied the proceeds to his own use and has neither directly nor indirectly accounted to me for said material or given me any benefit whatever from the proceeds thereof.' She had repeatedly told him to desist, and had obtained an injunction against him. He had responded by increasing the number of workers employed in denuding her estate:

Before the service of the said notice on my telling him that he had to stop drawing away material from said property he repeatedly said that he would not stop and that nobody could stop him and after having been served with this notice on February 3 he admitted that he had been served with the notice but further said then that he would not stop and that he could not be stopped.

Ann sought a continuance of the injunction and was afraid that the value of her property had been greatly reduced by her husband's actions.

Dennis Healy argued that the property in question was rightfully his. He claimed that it had been purchased by his father-in-law, who had given over management of the lands to him. He had assumed that the deed for the lands was in his own name and, on this understanding, he had erected buildings on the land and had cleared, fenced, and cultivated it. When his father-in-law died, according to Dennis Healy's version of events, his wife had purchased the land from his estate and he had held and managed the estate for her in trust in a responsible manner. He denied having removed timber from the lands, and argued that 'sand and gravel are being drawn by me [in winter] to get money to support my family.'

Ann Healy's petition was dismissed. Her husband retained his right to manage her property, or to mismanage it, as the case might be, despite the passage of the act of 1884, because she was deemed to have voluntarily placed the property under his control. Moreover, Dennis Healy's argument that any sale of goods from the land was only to provide an income to support their family of ten children was taken as evidence that he was acting in a responsible manner. Perhaps most important, although the marriage was clearly troubled, Ann did not at any time claim that Dennis was abusive. Since it was unclear to whom the property rightfully belonged, judicial discretion was used to uphold the rights of the husband, as he was not perceived as having failed in the performance of his marital duties. Ann was unable to leave what she admitted was a 'very unhappy marriage,' but she was at least not in physical danger, and was being supported, albeit minimally, by her spouse.[14] Agnes Sandford was not so lucky.

Agnes and Michael Sandford had been married in 1863. In 1886 Agnes left her husband because of his cruelty and began alimony proceedings against him. In order to avoid the publicity of a court case, Michael conveyed a lot to his wife 'for [her] own sole property and for [her] support in lieu of any provision that [she] might have obtained by proceedings at law.' The property so conveyed included the family home. Under the agreement, Michael was to have vacated the premises; however, he refused to do so. Agnes claimed that he was 'taunting her with having conveyed the place for [her] own support and security and at the same time interfered with [her] support while refusing to supply [her] with the necessaries of life.' Eventually, despite the agreement, she left the farm and took refuge with a grown son. She claimed that her husband threatened to 'remain on the place until he is put off' and that, while enjoying the property, he had not paid the mortgage, which had been placed in her name, and had declared that he would 'let the said mortgage eat up the said land.' Agnes's son, with whom she was living, gave evidence that his father had mistreated his mother for years.

Michael Sandford contested his wife's charges of ill-treatment and asserted that they had been reconciled shortly after the 1886 agreement and that the agreement had thereby been nullified. He claimed not to have been violent with his wife since the reconciliation and that Agnes, having forgiven his earlier misbehaviour, had now left him without just cause. A second son gave evidence that this reconciliation had indeed occurred; in the course of his cross-examination he was prevented from discussing the reasons why his mother had initiated a suit for alimony:

HIS LORDSHIP: It is not an action for alimony.

Q (posed by defendant's lawyer): After that deed was made your father and mother went home together and they lived upon the place and he was the head of the family afterwards the same as before? Did he say that if he gave her the deed he thought it would keep her quiet?

A: Yes, and not break up the house.

Q: That was what it was given for?

A: For peace and quietness.

Q: It was the intention to keep her on the farm?

A: Yes.

Agnes Sandford countered these arguments with the assertion that it had never been their intention to reconcile and that her husband had simply refused to vacate the property. She had worked the farm herself, with the help of her two sons, until her husband's beatings again became so severe that she had fled to the home of another son, with whom the younger children had also taken refuge. She had not begun new alimony proceedings:

Q (posed by defendant's lawyer): In consequence of these actions [his alleged beatings] did you do anything?

A: No, I did not do anything. I was ashamed and it was kept quiet.

The defendant's lawyer suggested that this failure to bring the husband's abuse to the attention of the community proved that 'his beatings were not of a severity sufficient to justify her in leaving her husband's home.'

The discretionary power of Armour J, who had interpreted the married women's statutes liberally in a number of important fraud cases, did not serve the interests of the wife. He held that the husband was de facto owner of the land, that the cohabitation had nullified any agreement between the parties, and that evidence regarding the circumstances of the cohabitation and second separation was not admissible:

HIS LORDSHIP: He put in the crops and he took them out. I don't know that I should make any order about the crops.

MR. MAYBEE (for the defense): The plaintiff if not entitled to possession under the statute.

HIS LORDSHIP: Show me the statute. I suppose this leaves the law as it was before, and the wife cannot bring an action for ejectment against the husband.

MR. MORPHY (for the plaintiff): I ask for judgment upon the evidence as if for alimony.

HIS LORDSHIP: You do not pray for alimony and I don't like to change an action into an action of another kind altogether.

MR. MORPHY: Then there is the question of the mesne profits.

HIS LORDSHIP: I think you wouldn't be entitled to mesne profits. If the statute covers it you would not be entitled to turn him out, and he would be entitled to mesne profits. I will have to direct judgment accordingly ... I refuse costs (to the husband) only on the ground that she is a married woman without separate estate.

Agnes Sandford was left dependent upon the largesse of her son. Her husband was not forced to maintain her or to grant her any share in the farm property that her labour had helped to accumulate. Michael had made himself the de facto owner of the property by refusing to comply with a supposedly legally binding agreement and by the use of physical power and intimidation. Obviously, judicial discretion could not serve as an absolute or complete solution to the problems wives faced.[15]

Ironically, Agnes Sandford was, in theory, in a better position than most wives. She at least had legal grounds for a claim because she had, at the time of the agreement of 1886, owned separate property. Most wives did not possess significant amounts of separate property and could not make any claim upon family property, except for alimony. Without rights to family property equal to the rights of husbands, wives could not protect themselves. Family farms, businesses, and even the marital home, which might have been purchased partially with a wife's separate estate and which was certainly usually maintained by the wife, were all the exclusive property of the husband. The Married Women's Property Act, 1884, granted wives rights to their separate property that approached those of men, but did nothing to correct the underlying imbalance of economic power within nineteenth-century marriage. In practice, therefore, despite the symbolic importance of these acts as the first legal recognition of married women's rights to property, they did little to improve the plight of most wives, who did not have either separate incomes sufficient for their own support or significant inheritances. Without ready cash, wives remained trapped with abusive and domineering spouses. Formal legal equality, in other words, was of limited, and class-specific, value in a context of continuing economic and social inequality.

Conclusions and Epilogue

In his statement of defence in an 1873 alimony suit, Isaac Watts asserted that his wife had no claim, other than minimal maintenance, on the home and other property that her labour had helped him to accumulate: 'The plaintiff has only worked with and assisted me in the way any working man's wife is accustomed to work with him and assist him by managing and attending to his household duties.'[1] Such work, the court concurred, was simply part of the labour that a wife owed to her husband. Fully one hundred years later, in 1973, the Supreme Court of Canada upheld this antiquated view of marital relations, ruling that Irene Murdoch was not entitled to a share in the ranch property held in her husband's name because her work was 'just about what the ordinary rancher's wife does.'[2] The Married Women's Property Act of 1884, which granted wives rights over their separate property that approached those of men and single women – formal legal equality – had done nothing to address the fundamental imbalance of economic power within most marriages or to deconstruct the social belief in marital unity, male authority, and wifely obedience, to achieve more substantive equality between spouses. Separate property – narrowly defined as wages and inherited land, money, and chattels – was inherently limited. In a society in which most women were housewives, men continued to own the vast majority of family property. Without a legal recognition of the economic value of domestic labour, most wives were denied the benefits of property ownership.

Upper Canada inherited a common law of feudal origins that empha-

sized and enforced the authority of the husband and the subordination of
the wife. Judaeo-Christian teaching reinforced such ideas, and stressed
the indissoluble unity of marriage. Although these beliefs remained
important throughout the nineteenth century, changing economic and
social conditions created an atmosphere conducive to reform that would
reduce the scope for male abuse of marital privilege. The belief that husbands and wives could and should be companions and friends to each
other made cruel and neglectful behaviour on the part of husbands
increasingly offensive. A culture of sentimentality and protectiveness
encouraged legislative and judicial interference in the privacy of the
home. Economic conditions in a frontier community were unstable, and
high rates of transiency ensured that husbands could easily disappear.
The practical problems faced by deserted wives, who were denied both
the support assumed by the common law and the legal means to earn a
living for themselves, encouraged reform. By reform – in Chancery and
later under statutes – fathers, women, judges, and legislators acted to
reduce the hardships faced by women who were married to irresponsible
and abusive men, not to eliminate male marital privilege itself. Throughout the century, reform was predicated on a persistent belief in the innate
dependency and inferiority of women.

In this context it should not be surprising that changes were enacted
incrementally and reflected a practical concern to remedy particular
injustices without changing anything fundamental about marriage. Legislation would not have been passed had the statutes been perceived as
being incompatible with traditional family relations, masculine authority,
and property regulations. This protective theme emerges clearly in legislation itself and in the ways in which judges interpreted the married
women's acts. Legislators were careful to distinguish between women's
rights, which they opposed, and wrongs committed against women,
which they sought to correct. Judges interpreted the married women's
property statutes liberally when wives could prove that their husbands
were abusive or economically irresponsible, but limited the scope of legislation when women used their property to challenge masculine authority in the family. Decisions hinged primarily on judicial perceptions of the
character of the husband and wife.

A second theme that emerges from an examination of the various acts
is a tendency of legislators to generalize practices begun as individual
remedies to particular problems. By the introduction of the Court of
Chancery in 1837, Upper Canadian wives gained access to alimony in
cases of abuse, desertion, and adultery on the part of the husband. Mar-

riage settlements became available, and a few families gave their daughters protection against the loss of their property through fault or misfortune on the part of their husbands. The act of 1859 democratized this practice, granting all wives the right to hold the property they owned before marriage or inherited during coverture. This act also sought to provide a source of support for working-class wives who were unlikely to inherit property adequate for their support or to be able to afford to take their husbands to court for alimony; in cases of abuse and abandonment wives could apply to the local magistrate for control of their own earnings from labour performed outside the home. The act of 1872 generalized this practice, giving all wives control over their earnings without the necessity of a protection order. It also allowed wives to alienate their chattels and money, to use their separate property, other than real estate, for their day-to-day support and maintenance. The act of 1873 allowed wives to apply for the right to dispose of their separate real estate when necessary. The act of 1884 generalized this practice, granting all wives dispositive powers over their separate real property; it also provided a mechanism, analogous to earlier protection orders, by which wives could claim the wages of dependent children, since such wages were often necessary for family survival when husbands were absent.

Specific individual remedies were ultimately granted to all wives for two reasons: first, husbands and wives manipulated the statutes to avoid the payment of legitimate debts, and fraud could be reduced, if not eliminated, by giving wives greater rights and liabilities with regard to their property; second, it was recognized that without dispositive powers over their separate property wives could not use their money, chattels, and land for their own support and protection. Even under the most liberal of these acts, however, male rights of control over the property accumulated during marriage went unchallenged. In exceptional circumstances wives could petition the court to reclaim separate property that had been mingled with other family assets; in such cases the rebuttable presumption remained that all family property belonged to the husband, and women were granted rights only at the discretion of the bench, although they also retained the right established in Chancery to claim maintenance in the form of alimony. Both of these remedies, however, continued to be based upon the assumption that the role of the husband was to provide for his wife and family and that it was the duty of the wife to obey and cohabit in all but the most extreme of circumstances. Such a legal framework and ideology could not, and did not, liberate wives. Evidence of male misbehaviour was central to rulings favouring women, and in effect the court assumed the role of intermediary, or overruling patriarch. It is highly ironic that the legislation had limited success in achieving its basic stated purpose – 'the better protection of married women'[3] – and yet simultaneously allowed some women, those who did not need protection from husbands but acted in collusion with them, to participate actively in the economy, defying the very stereotypes that had been central to the reform impulse.

There is no denying that truncated rights for women were preferable to none at all. Moreover, such changes promoted tangible benefits for some individual women as well as symbolic improvements in the status of all wives. In practical terms, however, separate property was inherently limited as a protective device because most housewives simply owned little property of their own, and the separate property regime denied them any claim on the property accumulated during marriage. These limitations, however, were not readily evident in a community in which divorce and separation remained extremely rare, particularly since judges were willing to use their discretion to expand women's claims to property in cases of particular hardship. By providing such discretionary justice they not only assuaged their own consciences, but obscured the enduring patriarchal nature of the law, perhaps contributing to a delay in further legal reform. Even George Holmested, the most vociferous advocate of continued reform after 1884, did not recognize the fundamental limitations of the concept of separate property. In his 1905 treatise on the law of married women and their property, he provided a list of recommendations aimed at eliminating the problems faced under the law by both married women and their creditors:

1. A married woman may enter into and shall be bound by any contract or engagement as fully as if she were a feme sole, and shall be liable in respect of her ante-nuptial contracts as if she had remained a feme sole.

2. A married woman shall be liable for her torts whether committed before or after marriage as if she continued a feme sole.

3. A husband shall not, by reason of marriage only, be liable for his wife's contracts or torts, whether entered into or committed before or after marriage.

4. A husband shall not, by reason of marriage only, be entitled to any estate or interest in his wife's property, real or personal, except, in the event of surviving her, his distributive share of her undisposed property.

5. A wife shall not, by reason of marriage only, be entitled to any estate or interest

in her husband's property, real or personal, except in the event of surviving him, her distributive share in his undisposed property.

6. Upon the decease of the wife, if her husband survive her, he shall be entitled to the same and no greater interest in his wife's property, real or personal, as a widow is now entitled to in the property real or personal of her deceased husband.

7. All restraints against anticipation by married women of property settled to their separate use shall be invalid against the creditors of married women to whom any such restraint may relate.[4]

These improvements to the law would have granted wives responsibilities and liabilities with regard to their separate property equal to those of men and unmarried women.

The proposed amendments, however, did not consider the social inequalities that limited the practical impact of reform. Many wives simply did not own separate property – inherited property or wages – and therefore were denied the protection that legislation purportedly afforded. The economic reality of marriage remained that most wives worked in the home and that such labour was unpaid. Marriage was not considered an economic partnership, and the contribution of the wife as mother and homemaker was not granted legal recognition, despite the cult of domesticity and the nineteenth-century veneration of motherhood. Without 'any estate or interest in her husband's property,' in the property accumulated during marriage but which by law belonged exclusively to the husband, wives remained economically dependent upon their husbands and vulnerable when men were abusive and domineering. Although men could protect their wives by placing property in their names, this decision remained at the discretion of individual husbands. The Law Reform Commission of Canada, established in the wake of the feminist pressure inspired by the decision in *Murdoch v Murdoch*, acknowledged in 1975 that under the separate property regime

no doctrine exists that the value of a contribution towards the family home, farm or business by way of management, physical labor, cooking, housekeeping, or child care is sufficient to give a spouse making such a contribution – and these are almost invariably wives – any share in the business, farm, home or property.[5]

Such problems were based upon the nineteenth-century conception that the wife's labour, while central to family maintenance and happiness, was part of the marital duties that a wife owed to her husband, and was therefore undeserving of economic remuneration.

Although a number of the reforms advocated by George Holmested were enacted over the course of the twentieth century, and although women slowly acquired an increased claim upon the marital home in particular,[6] it was not until the passage of the Ontario Family Law Act of 1986 that an explicit attempt was made to overturn this longstanding undervaluation of female labour in the home:

to recognize that child care, household management and financial provision are the joint responsibilities of the spouses and that inherent in the marital relationship there is equal contribution, whether financial or otherwise, by the spouses to the assumption of these responsibilities.[7]

Even this act, however, does not guarantee wives material compensation for the career sacrifices often made for the benefit of the family as a whole, and does nothing to provide wives with access to cash in ongoing marriages, a problem that continues to limit women's options in abusive relationships. Substantive equality between spouses has yet to be achieved either in law or in the economy.[8] Despite these problems, and despite a continuing need for reform, the importance of the Family Law Act, 1986, for Ontario wives can be much more fully appreciated when the nineteenth-century assumptions that the act explicitly seeks to overturn are understood. That these changes were one hundred years in the making ought not to be forgotten. This fact should serve as a salient reminder of the necessity for feminist legal knowledge, vigilance, and political action. Good intentions and judicial sympathy, as the history of married women's property law reform illustrates, are insufficient to meet women's needs. But law reform, as these cases also illustrate, is not in itself a panacea. The various nineteenth-century married women's property laws were irrelevant to wives, and husbands, who owned nothing and who earned wages insufficient for basic family needs. Similarly, modern legal reform will be of limited impact unless accompanied by a transformation of societal values, an expansion of the economic opportunities available to women, and a recognition of the obligation of the state to provide support and shelter for women who must flee domestic abuse.

Notes

ABBREVIATIONS

AO   Archives of Ontario
CIHM   Canadian Index of Historical Microfilm
Gr.   Grant's Chancery Reports
OAR   Ontario Appeal Reports
OR   Ontario Reports
UCCP   Upper Canada Common Pleas
UCQB   Upper Canada Queen's Bench

INTRODUCTION

1 Similar reforms were enacted earlier in other common law jurisdictions, as will be discussed throughout this book. It should also be noted that First Nations' legal perspectives, ultimately superseded in Ontario by the Anglo-American tradition, were much more progressive on this point. For further information on First Nations' law regarding marriage, see Van Kirk, '*Many Tender Ties*'; Morse, 'Indian and Inuit Law'; Jamieson, *Indian Women and the Law*; and Backhouse, *Petticoats and Prejudice*.
2 Macqueen, *Rights and Liabilities*, 342.
3 Salmon, *Women and the Law of Property*, xii.
4 Constance Backhouse began the process of examining married women's property law in Canada with a groundbreaking article illustrating the central

themes of reform in the common law provinces of the nation. Because of its wide scope, her work did not examine any one jurisdiction in extensive detail, and this study is intended to fill this void: Backhouse, 'Married Women's Property Law.' It is to be hoped that further case studies in the future will allow comparisons between Canadian provinces.

5 Preamble to An Act to secure for married women certain separate rights of property, (1859) 22 Vict., c. 34.

6 *Mitchell v Lizard*, RG 22, Chancery, 515/19/3/11–462/1884, AO, and Holmested, *Married Women's Property Act*, 8.

7 The manuscript begins at 1837 because it was in this year that the Court of Chancery was established in the colony providing the first forum in which women could assert some rights over property, and, as will be discussed in chapter 2, claim alimony against abusive or deserting husbands. The year 1900 was selected as an end date for more arbitrary reasons. The state of the law remained unchanged, in substantive terms, for several decades after this time, but to examine all the cases of the twentieth century would have required several further years of research.

8 While this cannot pretend to be a complete record of all court cases, since records from some counties are missing entirely, every relevant extant case at the Archives of Ontario was examined, and it is assumed that the extant cases are representative.

9 Snell, *Shadow of the Law*, 75.

10 See in particular Backhouse, 'Married Women's Property Law,' and Backhouse, 'Pure Patriarchy.'

11 This argument is also made by Veinott, 'Changing Legal Status of Women,' Girard and Veinott, 'Married Women's Property Law,' in Guildford and Morton, *Separate Spheres*.

12 Of previous historians who have looked at married women and property law, only Marylynn Salmon and Rebecca Veinott have utilized unreported court documents: Salmon, *Women and the Law of Property*, and Vienott, 'Changing Legal Status of Women.' Both Norma Basch and Constance Backhouse rely only on reported cases, supplemented in places by newspaper accounts of cases that were particularly notorious: Basch, *In the Eyes of the Law*, and Backhouse, 'Married Women's Property Law'; and Backhouse, *Petticoats and Prejudice*. It is not surprising, given the arguments that follow, that the use of unreported sources has led me to conclusions at least partially at odds with those of Backhouse and Basch. With regard to other aspects of women and law, both Dubinsky, *Improper Advances*, and Strange, *Toronto's Girl Problem*, have utilized unreported court documents, although neither has engaged in a direct comparison of the outcome in reported and unreported cases.

13 Snell, 75.
14 For an excellent defence of the use of such sources despite their limitations, see Linda Gordon, 'Review of *Gender and the Politics of History*,' and 'Response to Joan Wallach Scott.' The limitations of such sources are detailed in Joan Wallach Scott, 'Review of *Heroes of their Own Lives*'; and Joan Wallach Scott, 'Response to Linda Gordon.' All of these reviews are to be found in *Signs* 15, no. 4 (Summer 1990).
15 This definition of a feminist historical perspective is drawn from Smith, 'Feminism,' 370.
16 Preamble to An Act to secure for married women certain separate rights of property (1859) 22 Vict., c. 34.
17 Graveson and Crane, *A Century of Family Law*, 140.
18 This suggests that in Ontario, as Norma Basch has illustrated in the context of New York State, the population was actively concerned with learning about the state of the law. She suggests that the use of do-it-yourself legal manuals, most of them simplistic versions of Blackstone, was common. See Basch, *Eyes of the Law*, 66–8. Although research uncovered no evidence of such Canadian manuals, American books probably circulated in Ontario.
19 Recent microeconomic studies reinforce this assertion by illustrating the increasing involvement of married women in the economy after the passage of reform. It is not surprising that at least a small proportion of these new agents in the marketplace were dishonest. See Baskerville, 'Already Hinted at Board.'
20 Conley, *Unwritten Law*, 204.
21 Millett, *Sexual Politics*, 37.

CHAPTER 1

1 *Blackstone's Commentaries*, vol. 2, 1803, 242. Although *Blackstone's Commentaries* presented a simplified version of the common law, Norma Basch has argued forcefully that this simplified form became the educational staple of a generation of American lawyers and informed basic interpretations of the law: Basch, *Eyes of the Law*, chapter 2. Blackstone was similarly important in the education of Upper Canadian lawyers: Baker, 'Legal Education in Upper Canada.'
2 *Blackstone's Commentaries*, vol. 2, 433.
3 Single women did not have political rights, and, like their married sisters, were denied the right to vote into the twentieth century.
4 Basch, *Eyes of the Law*, 111.
5 'For My Daughter Julia,' *Farmers' Journal*, 10 September 1828. This article had originally appeared in 'Letter From a Lady to Her Daughter' in the *York Weekly Register*, 24 March 1825.

6 In addition to Blackstone, this account of the common law is based upon Dicey, *Law and Public Opinion*; Holdsworth, *History of English Law*; Jenks, *Short History of English Law*; Graveson and Crane, eds, *A Century of Family Law*; Redman, *Law of Husband and Wife*, Underhill, *Law Reform*; and Wharton, *Exposition of Laws*.

7 For a detailed description of the impact of the church on married women's status, see Daly, *The Church and the Second Sex*, 74–106.

8 *Blackstone's Commentaries*, vol. 2, 242.

9 Genesis 2:24.

10 *Blackstone's Commentaries*, vol. 2, 433.

11 Ephesians 5:22.

12 Ephesians 5:25.

13 Ephesians 5:28–9.

14 Bingham, *Infancy and Coverture*, 162.

15 This argument is also made by Girard and Veinott, 'Married Women's Property Law.'

16 For a detailed and interesting discussion of women's economic roles on Upper Canadian farms and the limitations on women's actions imposed by property laws, see Cohen, *Women's Work*.

17 An Act to establish a Court of Chancery in this Province (1837) 7 W IV, c. 2, section 3.

18 Matrimonial Causes Act, 20 & 21 Vict., c. 85.

19 Gemmill, *Practice of Parliament*, 52.

20 Ibid.

21 Provinces that entered Confederation after 1867 adopted the Matrimonial Causes Act of 1857. This left only Ontario and Quebec without judicial divorce, since both of the original Maritime provinces had pre-existing mechanisms for divorce which were allowed to continue to operate under the British North America Act. For further information regarding divorce in the Maritimes, see Owen and Bumsted, 'Divorce in a Small Province,' and Veinott, 'Child Custody.'

22 Owen and Bumsted, 'Divorce in a Small Province,' 86.

23 Gemmill, *Practice of Parliament*, 150–1; 194–245.

24 For a detailed discussion of divorce in the early twentieth century, see Snell, *In the Shadow of the Law*. For a further discussion of the implications of the failure to provide a forum for divorce for nineteenth-century wives, see Backhouse, 'Pure Patriarchy,' and Backhouse, *Petticoats and Prejudice*.

25 'Woman's Rights in Ontario,' Toronto *Daily Mail*, 24 September 1872, 2.

26 This requirement for a separate examination of the wife was not abolished until 1873: Married Women's Real Estate Act (1873) 36 Vict., c. 18.

27 Walkem, *Married Women's Property Acts*, 64.

28 For a deed of sale to be valid, a wife had to give her consent to any transaction entered into by her husband by formally barring her dower. During this procedure she was examined by a magistrate to guard against coercion. If a wife had failed to bar her dower or had done so only on the basis of coercion on the part of her husband, she could petition to reclaim such property upon her husband's death. Dower, therefore, provided a serious impediment to the free trade of land and a damper on the development of a commercial economy. In several American states dower was abolished in order to facilitate the sale of real estate: Salmon, *Women and the Law of Property*, chapter 7. It is significant that Upper Canadian legislators steadfastly refused to interfere with the wife's right to dower. It was argued in the Legislative Council in 1860 that to abolish this protection would be to undermine the position of most widows: 'The loss by a poor widow of her dower would perhaps leave her penniless. And in many instances the wife contributes just as much to enhancing the value of the property as the husband ... It would not be right to leave the widow completely at the mercy of her offspring ... Often it happened that this very matter of dower was the only thing that prevented a man in these circumstances [a drunken or abusive husband] from selling his property ... The restriction in this case was a very valuable one': *Parliamentary Debates*, Newspaper Hansard, reel 2, Legislative Council, 13 April 1869, 34.

29 Not only did dower extend his responsibility for his wife beyond the grave, but under a will a man might extend control over his wife beyond the grave, by providing, for example, that her rights over personal property and for support out of the family estate would cease upon remarriage. For further examples and explanation, see Davies, 'Patriarchy from the Grave.'

30 For more information regarding the law of dower in Upper Canada/Ontario, see Cameron, *Law of Dower*.

31 'The Law of Dower,' *Upper Canada Law Journal* (November 1857), 209.

32 Ibid. It should be noted here that the editors decried not the role of the husband as the protector and head of the family, but the failure of the law to give widows the right type of property to ensure support.

33 For some particularly poignant examples of this problem, see Backhouse, 'Married Women's Property Law.'

34 *Blackstone's Commentaries*, vol. 2, 442.

35 Ibid.

36 Notice of Philip Mark, *Correspondent and Advocate*, 14 December 1833. Any random sampling of nineteenth-century newspapers will reveal that this practice was not uncommon.

37 The irrevocable right of the husband to his wife's sexual services was clarified

by the codification of the Criminal Code in 1892, under which marital rape was exempted from prosecution. For further information on marital rape, and rape in general, see Backhouse, 'Nineteenth-Century Canadian Rape Law.'

38 *Blackstone's Commentaries*, vol. 2, 392.

39 The husband was not automatically liable for criminal acts committed by his wife, but the wife could use her husband's authority and influence as a defence against her own liability if she committed a criminal act in the presence of her husband or under duress imposed by him.

40 Moderation, of course, was subjective and difficult to define. *Blackstone's Commentaries*, vol. 2, 444–5.

41 Ibid., 445. It is interesting to note that George Tucker, the editor of this 1803 American edition of *Blackstone*, protested against this assertion, taking issue with many of the provisions for married women: 'I fear there is little reason to pay a compliment to our laws for their respect and favour to the female sex.'

42 Gagan and Mays, 'Historical Demography,' and Gagan, *Hopeful Travellers*.

43 The myriad ways in which men could squander such cash, leaving their families destitute, are illustrated in Bradbury, *Working Families*.

44 For a description of the extent of transciency at mid-century, see Michael Katz, 'Social Class.'

45 Shorter, *The Modern Family*; Stone, *The Family*; and Trumbach, *Egalitarian Family*. On the growth of companionate marriage and changes in courtship rituals, see Rothman, *Hands and Hearts*.

46 Shorter, *The Modern Family*, 227.

47 Ephesians 5:24.

48 Alcott, *The Young Wife*; Ellis, *Women of England*.

49 This difference can be observed in many of the great social movements of the nineteenth century; it explains, for example, why many abolitionists could simultaneously find slavery abhorrent but continue to believe that blacks were innately inferior to whites: Stouffer, *Light of Nature*.

50 'Maxims for Married Women,' Barrie *Northern Advance*, 13 November 1856, 1.

51 'Husbands and Wives,' Toronto *Daily Mail*, 11 April 1876, 2.

52 'Husbands and Wives,' Toronto *Daily Telegraph*, 26 May 1868, 1.

53 For a more detailed discussion of the discourse surrounding wives and mothers, see Errington, *Wives and Mothers*. For an interesting discussion of the language and imagery of gender in Upper Canada during this pivotal period, see Morgan, 'Languages of Gender.'

54 Lasch, *Haven*.

55 Welter, 'Cult of True Womanhood,' and Douglas, *Feminization of American Culture*.

56 Cook and Mitchinson, eds, *Proper Sphere*, 9.

57 'The Christian Mother,' *The Witness Weekly Review and Family Newspaper*, Montreal, 1846.

58 Women were consistently paid lower wages than men on the assumption that they worked only to provide themselves with luxuries, since women were expected to be supported by men, either their fathers or their husbands.

59 Work was available in rural communitites, but it was limited in scope and nature and did not provide wages adequate for independent living. See Errington, *Wives and Mothers*.

60 For a description of such strategies, see Bradbury, *Working Families*.

61 With the gradual expansion of women's higher education, by the end of the nineteenth century a small minority of middle class women were opting out of marriage and motherhood, instead supporting themselves in the emerging women's professions, particularly teaching. This profession, however, remained underpaid. For a detailed discussion of the specific middle class beliefs that shaped the domestic ideal, see Davidoff and Hall, *Family Fortunes*.

62 Cott, *Bonds of Womanhood*, 200.

63 Grossberg, *Governing the Hearth*, 300. See also Backhouse, *Petticoats and Prejudice*; Backhouse, 'Married Women's Property Law'; Veinott, 'Changing Legal Status'; Basch, *Eyes of the Law*; and Salmon, *Women and the Law of Property*.

64 'Woman's Rights,' *Toronto Globe*, 19 January 1857.

65 This said, however, the laws as promulgated did not distinguish between women of different classes. Further reform was probably not forthcoming, at least in part, after 1884, because this act provided women with property – those who also had the influence to assert the need for change – with rights parallel to those of men. The fact of unequal access to the protection of separate property would have been unapparent to many reformers, and, in the context of nineteenth-century beliefs about the nature of law, would have been perceived as outside the purview of legal reform.

CHAPTER 2

1 RG 22, series 372 (box 20, file 17), Niagara, Court of the Quarter Sessions, 1835, Archives of Ontario. Unfortunately, it is not clear what ultimately happened to Ellen – whether the magistrates refused to issue the peace bond or whether it was issued but proved to be futile in a community lacking a modern police force. Either way, Ellen's future appeared to be bleak. I am indebted to Ed Montigny for bringing this case to my attention.

2 The peace bond remedy was limited before mid-century because of the geographical isolation of many communities and the lack of police services, even in larger centres. Moreover, the interpretation of the law depended greatly

upon the beliefs of individual magistrates. Before the magistrate, as before the chancellors, women's options were limited by their economic dependence on the husbands they wished to prosecute. In a rural setting, women such as Ellen Fitzgerald had no claim on family farms and other property, and in an urban setting, many women could not afford to send their husbands to jail because of the importance of the male wage in the family economy: Harvey, 'Amazons and Victims;' and Harvey, 'To Love, Honour and Obey.'

3 The extreme vulnerability of abused wives under the common law is also well described in the chapter entitled 'Divorce and Separation: Esther Hawley Ham' in Backhouse, *Petticoats and Prejudice*. This case was heard in 1826, and in it Esther Hawley Ham's father claimed costs against the husband, since he had been obliged to support his daughter since she had fled the marital home due to physical and emotional abuse. It was not until the establishment of the Court of Chancery in Ontario, in 1837, that women themselves would have the right to claim alimony.

4 Economic opportunities for all women were more limited than those available to men, particularly outside the family unit. In rural areas women earned cash by producing goods for the market such as cheese, butter, and other essentials; but, since the farm was owned by her husband, a wife could not continue such production and income after separation. See Cohen, *Women's Work*. More opportunities existed in the growing urban centres of Upper Canada, but few provided incomes sufficient for women to support their children, and ideological opposition to the employment of married women remained strong.

5 Self-divorce, of course, did not provide couples with the legal right to remarry. However, the economic importance of both male and female contributions to the family economy, particularly on the farm, would have encouraged the formation of new, illicit, but possibly publicly accepted or at least tacitly ignored unions. James Snell, with regard to a later period, asserts that bigamy was common and was, at least to some degree, tolerated in the community: 'There was a certain amount of *de facto* tolerance of bigamy, both within local communities and among authorities. One reason for this tolerance was that a challenge to the validity of a second marriage was often an attack on an active, functioning, "successful" marriage, one in which children were often present.' Snell, *Shadow of the Law*, 234.

6 An Act to establish a Court of Chancery in this Province (1837) 7 W IV c. 2, section 3.

7 *Soules v Soules* (1851), 2 Grant 299, at 300. This is the first reported alimony case in Upper Canada. Of course, since this case firmly established the jurisdiction of the court to grant decrees of alimony, it was precedent-setting and worthy of being reported. It is suggested in the report, however, that the court

had been granting such relief from its inception. Further evidence to support this assertion is provided by unreported court documents. The benchbooks of William Hume Blake for the period 1849–59 contain ten cases of alimony litigation, and *Soules v Soules* is not the first of these: RG 22, series 390, box 55, AO.

8 *Soules v Soules*, 299.

9 Ibid., 300.

10 Ibid.

11 *Severn v Severn* (1852), 3 Gr. 431 at 432.

12 An Act respecting the Court of Chancery, (1859) 22 Vict., c. 12, section 29. It is perhaps not coincidental that this was also the year in which the first married women's property statute was passed.

13 In the earliest years of the operation of the court it appears that Chancery held its hearings only in Toronto, but few of the cases still extant were heard during this period. Once the rotating basis was established, however, Chancery hearings coincided with the quarterly assizes, which dealt with criminal and civil cases. At this level the cases would be heard by a single chancellor; when an appeal occurred, it was heard by the full court in Toronto, consisting of the chancellor and two vice-chancellors.

14 In the twelve cases in this sample in which the costs were explicitly enumerated, they varied between $20.00 and $292.79, and averaged $141.95.

15 *Soules v Soules*, 118–19.

16 The value of the property so enumerated varied dramatically. In two cases women claimed that the real estate owned by their spouses was worth in excess of $30,000: *Burgess v Burgess*, RG 22, Chancery 510/11/3/4–482/1878; and *Beatty v Beatty*, RG 22, Chancery 510/9/2/6–390/1875, AO. At the opposite end of the scale, one woman sought to prevent her husband from selling a lot, the only property owned by the couple, worth only $600: *McCulloch v McCulloch*, RG 22, Chancery 510/6/4/14–42/1872, AO. The class status of many of these couples is therefore ambiguous. Subsistence farming is not a middle-class activity, and several of the farming husbands in this sample had to supplement the earnings from the land by seeking employment in what can only be considered working-class areas of employment. Moreover, working-class families are represented here, although the most poverty-stricken elements of the community would have had little access to the court process and such wives would have had no hope of obtaining support since the husband's earning could barely support a family under one roof, let alone two.

17 The Court of Chancery had the right to issue a *lis pendens* – a notice that property was subject to litigation and therefore could not legally be sold – at the filing of the bill of complaint. However, this is known to have been done in only twelve cases. When implemented, the *lis pendens* was an effective weapon.

Property that could not be sold before the hearing would be available to satisfy a judgment against the husband. This was true even when husbands left the country. A notice that a *lis pendens* was being requested, however, preceded its issue in all cases, and it is likely that only twelve decrees of *lis pendens* were issued not because the court was hesitant to support these wives, but because husbands had *already* sold and absconded, leaving no property behind.

18   The chancellors were drawn from the élite ranks of the community. Between 1837 and 1881, the period during which alimony cases were heard exclusively in the Court of Chancery, the following men served as Chancellors: R. Jameson, J. Godfrey Spragge, Oliver Mowat, J.C.P. Esten, P.M.S. Vankoughnet, Samuel Henry Strong, W.H. Blake, William Proudfoot, and John Alexander Boyd. Robert Jameson, the first vice-chancellor (in the early years the chancellor was a nominal head of the court only), was the last attorney-general of Canada appointed by the British government. He is now less well known than his wife, Anna Murphy Jameson, the author of *Winter Studies and Summer Rambles in Canada*. This book was the product of a short period spent in Upper Canada in an attempt to reconcile with her husband, from whom she had separated before he left England. This attempt was unsuccessful and Anna Jameson returned to Britain alone, having secured an annuity and a separation agreement from her husband. Although he could by law have claimed all his wife's earnings from her successful career as an author, Robert Jameson did not do so, and it is possible that his own unhappy marital experience made him particularly sympathetic towards the women who came before the Court of Chancery seeking relief. John Godfrey Spragge, a former student of John Strachan, later served as chief Justice of Ontario. Philip Michael Matthew Scott Vankoughnet was a partner in the firm of Oliver Mowat and Robert Easton Burns, and specialized in equity practice before being called into Chancery. William Hume Blake was not only the first chancellor of the reformed court, he also served as solicitor-general in the Baldwin–Fontaine government, was a pioneer in Canadian legal education, and was instrumental in much of the legislation that transformed the legal system at mid-century. While he never became a chancellor, Edward Blake, William Hume's son, was later premier of Ontario and presided over the passage of the Married Women's Property Act of 1872. Oliver Mowat, also a Liberal premier of Ontario, presided over the fusion of equity and the common law and the passage of the Married Women's Property Act of 1884. His experience in Chancery may have made him more aware of the problems women faced.

19   More cases than women exist because several women submitted multiple petitions to the court.

20 It is unclear from the cases in which litigants were able to affix their names to legal documents to what further extent they would have been considered literate. Not surprisingly, the numbers of illiterate men and women coming before the court declined dramatically in the last quarter of the century.

21 The majority of the husbands in this group were farmers, but a significant minority laboured in what were clearly working-class jobs such as tinsmithing, hotel-keeping, blacksmithing, taxi-driving, and itinerent labouring. The vast majority of wives, in this context, were able to afford lawyers, not surprisingly, only when they had the economic and emotional support of family and friends.

22 Hay, 'Property, Authority.'

23 The chancellors may have seen controlling abusive husbands as simply one facet of controlling the dangerous masses. They asserted, despite the variety of backgrounds from which the wives who came before them were drawn, that wife abuse was a class-specific problem associated with intemperance; thus they avoided questioning the larger economic and social issues that made wife abuse prevalent.

24 *Rodman v Rodman*, 20 Gr. 429, at 447.

25 Although these findings challenge previous Canadian writing on this topic, such studies were entirely based upon reported cases, and the contrast between reported and unreported cases is central to this difference in interpretation. See in particular Backhouse, 'Pure Patriarchy.' Judith Fingard, although she does not examine court records themselves, argues that the Nova Scotia Society for the Prevention of Cruelty provided a middle ground for women who did not want to publicly proclaim their husbands' sins in court. The SPC was popular with such women and focused on marital compromise, reconciliation, and negotiated settlements. Although she rightly asserts that the court did not impose severe enough sentences on wife abusers, these same women might have gotten a favourable hearing if they had chosen to seek alimony from their husbands, a possibility she does not explore. See Fingard, 'Prevention of Cruelty.' James Snell's work on divorce in Nova Scotia, the only Canadian province that allowed cruelty as a basis for divorce, suggests that this term was interpreted in a varied manner. He does not consider, however, the fundamental difference between divorce and separation, in that while judges might well hesitate to grant a divorce without overwhelming evidence, they might have been favourable to a middle-ground option, such as alimony, which allowed women to live apart from their husbands without the right of remarriage. As he asserts in his monography on divorce, separation was viewed quite differently from divorce specifically because divorce was permanent and allowed remarriage, which was widely perceived as state-

sanctioned adultery. See Snell, 'Marital Cruelty,' and *In the Shadow of the Law*. Moreover, in other jurisdictions, where some study of unreported cases has also begun, similar findings are emerging. For example, in his study of divorce, James Hammerton found that the courts were increasingly intolerant of men's physical abuse of their wives. However, less obvious forms of psychological and emotional cruelty were not recognized by the court. See Hammerton, 'Victorian Marriage.' In her pathbreaking study of family violence, *Heroes of their Own Lives*; Linda Gordon also argues that the response to battered wives, while well-meaning, was ineffective and condescending.

26 By English precedent, adultery was sufficient cause for divorce only for men. Women had to prove aggravated adultery – bestiality, the presence of a concubine in the home, or abuse, as well as the act of adultery itself – in order to qualify for relief. It is unclear to what degree this standard was challenged in Upper Canadian cases, since in all extant cases wife abuse accompagnied adultery; the chancellors, however, expressed consistent disgust with adulterous husbands.

27 The 'unnnatural acts' to which Ellen Conroy objected seem to have been fellatio and anal sex, although the language she used in describing these acts to the court was, not surprisingly, obtuse. Sodomy, whatever the gender of the participants,was illegal at this time. This parallels the findings of Robert Griswold, who has asserted that the courts in California were increasingly willing during this period to recognize sexual cruelty as a reason for divorce: Griswold, *Family and Divorce*.

28 *Conroy v Conroy*, RG 22, Chancery 510/4/3/14–257/1869, AO.

29 *Howey v Howey* (1879), 27 Gr. 57, at 59.

30 The widespread concern with desertion is also revealed by the passage of the An Act respecting the Maintenance of Wives deserted by their Husbands (1888) 51 Vict., c. 23. This act created a mechanism by which deserted wives could petition for support in the local magistrate or police court without having to incur the expense and annoyance of a proceeding for alimony. This act was explicitly intended to allow working-class wives access to spousal support, since the proceedings in the higher court were acknowledged to be beyond the means of such women. Given that only the federal government had the power to create new mechanisms for divorce or separation under the BNA Act, the consititutionality of such proceedings was highly questionable. None the less, this legislation was extended in 1922 when the provincial government made deserting fathers also liable for the support of the children they left behind: Deserted Wives' and Children's Maintenance Act, SO (1922), c. 57.

31 Evidence suggests that bigamy was widespread in Upper Canada. See Backhouse, *Petticoats and Prejudice*.

32 *Severn v Severn* (1852), 3 Gr. 431, at 448. Aureta Severn had been subjected to considerable violence. Her husband argued that his violence was justified by her drunken and disreputable conduct, but the chancellors rejected his plea. In 1859 Mrs Severn applied for and was granted an increase in her alimony because of her husband's improved financial situation: *Severn v Severn* (1859), 7 Gr. 109. The decree for alimony was itself overturned in 1867 when her husband proved to the satisfaction of the court that his wife had been guilty of adultery. By this point, however, Aureta Severn had established a stable common law marriage with her paramour and was being adequately supported by him: *Severn v Severn*, 14 Gr. 150.

33 *Rodman v Rodman* (1873), 20 Gr. 429 at 431.

34 *Bavin v Bavin*, 27 Gr. 571, at 580.

35 The fact that a man such as John Haffey could serve as justice of the peace and police magistrate illustrates the perils of leaving the relief and protection of women dependent upon judicial discretion.

36 Haffey was also ordered to pay his wife's costs, $238.86.

37 *Haffey v Haffey*, RG 22, Chancery 510/9/2/11–283/1876, AO.

38 *Rodman v Rodman* (1873), 20 Grant 435–6.

39 Ibid. 435.

40 Ibid. 437.

41 Ibid. 435.

42 Ibid. 437.

43 Ibid. 431.

44 Ibid. 439.

45 Ibid. 445.

46 *Re: Rodman infants*, RG 22, York Matters, 110/24/2/21–18-R, 1873, AO.

47 *Malloch v Malloch*, RG 22, Chancery 515/9/3/14–329/1881, AO.

48 It is interesting to note that Georgina Malloch was successful in her petition for custody while Ann Rodman was not. Georgina presented a joint petition for alimony and custody, and focused on the moral threat to her children's well-being created by the presence of a drunken parent; Ann Rodman never claimed that her husband was a bad father.

49 *Carr v Carr*, 2 Chambers Reports 71.

50 *Barker v Barker*, RG 22, Chancery, 510/9/2/4–261/1875, AO.

51 *Holmes v Holmes*, RG 22, Country Causes, 58/10/2/16–H-20, 1887, AO.

52 For further information on the Insolvent Act of 1869, see Edgar, *The Insolvent Act of 1869*. Other contemporary works outlining insolvency provisions and the frequent amendments to this field of law include Clarke, *The Insolvent Act of 1875*; Edgar, *The Insolvent Act of 1864*; MacMahon, *The Insolvent Act of 1875*; and Stevens, *Insolvent Act of 1875*.

53 *Fell v Fell*, RG 22, Chancery 510/14/1/3–224/1877, AO.

54 *Richardson v Richardson*, RG 22, Chancery 510/11/3/1–208/1878, AO.

55 In all likelihood this is because Negro men and women were unlikely to possess adequate property for either the right of alimony or the various amendments to married women's right to own property to have much practical meaning or impact in their lives. The black population of Ontario, composed of the former slaves released when slavery was abolished in 1833, those who had emigrated to the colony after 1793 when the importation of new slaves was forbidden, and those who escaped from the United States on the underground railway, faced discrimination in Upper Canada/Ontario, which made economic advancement very difficult. For a discussion of attitudes towards people of colour in nineteenth-century Ontario, see Stouffer, *Light of Nature*.

56 *Melville v Melville*, RG 22, Chancery 510/9/3/2–111/1880, AO. In 1884 she applied for and was granted the right to dispose of this real estate without the consent of her husband: RG 22, York County, Married Women's Real Estate Act Files, AO.

57 *Watts v Watts*, RG 22, Chancery 510/9/1/10–360/1873, AO.

58 *Bavin v Bavin*, RG 22, Country Causes 58/9/1/4–B-79, 1895, AO.

59 *Lalonde v Lalonde*, RG 22, Chancery 510/9/1/8–244/1873 and 510/10/4/16–117/1878, AO.

60 *Dainard v Dainard*, RG 22, Chancery 510/36/4/14–749/1879, AO.

61 *Mills v Mills*, RG 22, Chancery 515/19/3/5–647/1883, AO.

62 When his ill-treatment recommenced, Caroline once again left John and filed a new bill of complaint; this bill was also later dropped: *Scott v Scott*, RG 22, Chancery 510/9/1/7–165/1873, AO.

63 An Act respecting the Custody of Infants, (1855) 18 Vict., c. 126. For a full discussion of the changing law of child custody in this era, see Backhouse, 'Shifting Patterns.'

64 'The Law as to Custody of Children,' 199.

65 *Russell v Russell*, RG 22, Chancery 515/20/4/1–402/1887, AO.

66 *Beatty v Beatty*, RG 22, Chancery 510/9/1/14–212/1874; 510/9/1/15–267/1874; 510/9/2/6–390/1875, AO. It is interesting to note that although the couple resumed cohabitation, in 1879 Mrs Beatty petitioned the county court in York for $400 out of the estate of her husband, who was now in proceedings for bankruptcy. She stated that the payment of such a sum had been a condition of cohabitation, but that her husband had not ever lived up to this promise, and that he now refused to sign documents acknowledging the promise unless she guaranteed to him that she would give him the money. It is unclear, unfortunately, whether she made this claim of attempted coercion on the part of her husband in order to obtain funds to enable her to leave the marital

home, or in consultation with him in a joint attempt to preserve some of the marital property: Married Women's Real Estate Act Files, York County, Archives of the Law Society of Upper Canada.

67 *Strong v Strong*, RG 22, Chancery 510/9/3/2–105/1880, AO.

68 *Turner v Turner*, RG 22, Chancery 510/10/4/10–350/1877, AO.

69 *Vardon v Vardon*, RG 22, Chancery 515/18/2/13–700/1882, AO.

70 *Coulson v Coulson*, RG 22, Chancery 516/29/3/2–42/1893, AO.

71 *Gracey v Gracey*, RG 22, Chancery 510/5/1/1–431/1869 and 17 Gr. 113. Minnie Gracey had previously been awarded relief, but this decision was annulled when her husband proved to the satisfaction of the court that Minnie had been guilty of adultery subsequent to the decree. Also *Edwards v Edwards*, RG 22, Chancery 510/9/1/1–198/1872 and 20 Gr. 392; *Campbell v Campbell*, RG 22, Chancery 510/9/1/2–269/1872 and 22 Gr. 322; *Smye v Smye*, RG 22, Chancery 510/9/2/5–323/1875; and *Graham v Graham*, RG 22, Chancery 510/6/4/12–328/1871, AO. When a wife committed adultery, whatever the behaviour of her husband, she forfeited her claim upon him for marital support. Mary Jane Edwards was denied relief because evidence presented in the hearing suggested that she had voluntarily left her husband's home; Chancellor Spragge deduced that 'she deliberately preferred living apart from her husband.' Such behaviour could not be given the sanction of the law, as she alleged no mistreatment that would justify her leaving her husband's home. Such limitations on who could be awarded alimony were entirely consistent with the companionate model of marriage and the doctrine of separate spheres. In the context of these beliefs, it is perhaps not unreasonable that the chancellors refused to award maintenance to women who were receiving such support from new 'husbands.' Interestingly, in one of these cases, *Campbell v Campbell*, the wife was later granted a separation by act of Parliament: Gemmill, *Practice of the Parliament*, 74.

72 *Rodman v Rodman*, 20 Gr. 428; *Henderson v Henderson*, 19 Gr. 465; *Howey v Howey*, 27 Gr. 57.

73 The lopsided and unrepresentative nature of the reported cases, however, also raises the possibility that with time, as the chancellors who had been sympathetic to women's needs were replaced by a new generation of judges, the interpretation of what constituted cruelty and what conditions legitimated a wife's claim for alimony may have narrowed. After all, during the nineteenth century the nascent women's movement, and particularly advocates of temperance, were mounting a very visible campaign against both drunkenness and accompanying wife-abuse. As public interest in this issue waned, and if twentieth-century judges assumed that reported cases were representative, the prospects for abused wives may again have declined.

CHAPTER 3

1 This sale was illegal. Hannah should have undergone a separate examination by the magistrate or justice of the peace. Since Hannah's only interest in the land, at law, was her dower, the court would not intervene, despite the illegality of the sale, until dower itself became operative – that is, until her husband died.
2 *Nolan v Fox* (1865), 15 UCCP 576.
3 This case illustrates the central limitations of dower in that it could only protect the interests of the wife after the husband was dead; during his lifetime, the wife had no recourse or claim on family property.
4 Graveson and Crane, eds, *Century of Family Law*, 140.
5 Trusts were particularly useful as a means of protecting personal property; personal property required such protection because the husband had rights not only of management but of alienation over money and chattels acquired by way of his wife. It should not be surprising, therefore, that trusts emerged as a kind of alternative to dower, as a means of protecting the non-land property of the rising industrial class.
6 W. Harrison to Sir George Shee, (April 1806), PAC series Q, 305 at 119. As quoted in Brown, 'Equitable Jurisdiction,' 277. Theoretically, a Court of Chancery could easily have been established in 1791 along with the courts of the common law. As well, when the great seal of the province was delivered to the lieutenant-governor he assumed all the powers of chancellor and could legitimately have taken it upon himself to dispense equity in the province. It was on this basis that Courts of Chancery had been established in Nova Scotia, Quebec, and many American states: ibid, 276.
7 Spragge, *A Letter*, 12. Such concerns were widespread in England during this period, and the Court of Chancery was the subject of considerable public debate and criticism. Dickens's *Bleak House* provides an example of such an attack.
8 In New England early legislators explicitly rejected the example of the English Court of Chancery and established only common law precedents; in Pennsylvania certain equitable principles were adopted in a single system of common law; in the Canadian colonies equity was not rejected but developed only slowly. The reform-minded colonists in many of the early American colonies saw the Court of Chancery as a prime example of royal excesses and arbitrary rule, and therefore deemed the creation of such a court both unnecessary and undesirable: Salmon, *Women and the Law of Property*, chapters 1 and 2. With the emphasis on loyalty that characterized Upper Canada, however, it is unlikely that such reasoning explains the failure of legislators to establish such a court in this colony.

9 An Act to establish a Court of Chancery in this Province (1837) 7 W IV, c. 2, section 2.

10 Holdsworth, *History of English Law*, 5:309–15. The case cited by Holdsworth is *Avenant v Kitchin* (1581–2).

11 The account of equity law is based upon Dicey, *Lectures*; Holdsworth, *History of English Law*, vol. 1, Jenks, *Short History of English Law*; Graveson and Crane, eds, *A Century of Family Law*; Redman, *A Concise View of the Law*; Underhill, *The Law Reform*; and Wharton, *An Exposition of the Laws*.

12 Walkem, *Married Women's Property Acts*, 10.

13 Salmon, *Women and the Law of Property*, 118.

14 Walkem, *Married Women's Property Acts*, 4. It is interesting to note that Walkem's discussion of equity, although ostensibly applicable to Ontario, was based almost exclusively on examples drawn from English precedents. Walkem wished to see the Married Women's Property Act of 1872 interpreted in a liberal manner. Either he was unaware of the fact that the Upper Canadian Court of Chancery had not adopted these precedents or he deliberately ignored this fact in order to strengthen his own argument for a liberal interpretation of the acts of 1872 and 1873.

15 It is interesting to note that Salmon's own findings would support this argument, since in South Carolina, where divorce remained impossible throughout the nineteenth century and where the chancellors explicitly argued that they had a responsibilty to provide abused wives with relief through alimony, the idea of coercion remained embedded in law much later than in states that allowed divorce. See Salmon, *Women and the Law of Property*, chapters 4 and 5.

16 'Husbands and Wives,' Toronto *Daily Telegraph*, 26 May 1868, 1.

17 Basch, *In the Eyes of the Law*, 73.

18 Salmon estimates that in South Carolina between 1790 and 1810 only between 1 and 2 percent of married women had separate estates: Salmon, *Women and the Law of Property*, chapter 5. Holcombe estimates that only 10 percent of English women, during a slightly later period, had such estates: Holcombe, *Wives and Property*, chapter 3.

19 Undoubtedly further examples of marriage settlements could have been located by working through the personal papers of prominent Upper Canadians. I have not done this, however, for reasons related to economy of time, and have assumed that the settlements that came before the court are representative.

20 Mr Vankoughnet, *Parliamentary Debates*, reel 2, 13 April 1860, 34.

21 Of the twenty cases, the reasons for litigation were as follows: four were challenged due to problems that had arisen after the death of the beneficiary; one petitioner sought to validate a trust that had been drawn up in another juris-

diction; three trustees sought to have mistakes in the terms of the settlement clarified; six trustees found themselves in court in order to enforce the payment of mortgages due to the trust estate; and six petitioners sought to have the trustee named under the settlement changed and the management of the trust fund placed in more competent or honest hands.

22 Peter Ward discovered one settlement, not in the records of the court, in which the wife was given sole administrative powers over her separate estate: Marriage settlement, William Drummer Powell Jarvis and Diana Irving, 1 October 1850, Jarvis-Powell Papers, AO, as quoted in Ward, *Courtship*, 46. This appears to have been the exception, however, and the other three marriage settlements he found in the Powell-Jarvis papers gave wives only a yearly income from the trust fund. This exception illustrates that couples who wished more liberal terms were free to establish them.

23 Marriage settlement between Margaret Nelles and Dr William Ferris, Henry William Nelles, trustee, RG 22, Brant County, 25 January 1840, AO.

24 *Nolan v Fox*, 576.

25 *Hillock v Button*, (1881) 29 Gr. 490.

26 Ibid. 492.

27 Ibid. 491

28 This provision reveals the importance of family considerations in the drawing up of marriage settlements. Should the husband be allowed to retain such property after a second marriage, the collateral relatives of the wife could lose their inheritance to the offspring of the second wife, a most undesirable and unfair prospect: *Hillock v Button*, 491–2.

29 *Re: DeBruhl settlement*, RG 22, York Matters, 110/22/1/12–115/D, AO.

30 *Mullholland v Williamson* (1868), 14 Gr. 291, at 295.

31 *Jackson v Bowman* (1867), 14 Gr. 156, at 158–9.

32 This way of interpreting disputes between wives and their husbands' creditors continued under the Married Women's Property Acts of 1859 and 1872 until mounting evidence of fraud finally convinced the judges and the legislature that reform on the English and American model was necessary.

33 *Jackson v Bowman*, 160.

34 Spragge was referring here to the separate examination which was required under the common law in Ontario to ensure that a wife was parting with her dower rights freely and without coercion: *Royal Canadian Bank v Mitchell* (1868), 14 Gr. 413–14.

35 Ibid. 416.

36 Kent, *Commentaries on American Law*, vol. 2, 162.

37 Salmon, *Women and the Law of Property*, 117.

38 *Tripp v Martin* (1862), 9 Gr. 20, at 21.

39 Ibid. 22.
40 *Mitchell v Lizard*, RG 22, Chancery, 515/19/3/11–462/1884, AO.
41 *Torrance v Torrance*, RG 22, Chancery, 515/9/3/16–127/1881, AO.

CHAPTER 4

1 'Law of Dower,' Hamilton *Spectator*, 28 April 1858, 4. It was not uncommon
  during this period for men and women to submit letters to the editor either
  anonymously or under the guise of a pseudonym. This woman wrote to thank
  the *Spectator* for its opposition to a bill for the abolition of rights of dower. She
  argued that to remove the right of dower would be to deny women 'the only
  foothold that the Canadian wife has to cheer her through many years of toil,
  and often unkindness too.' If women did not have a claim to dower, what
  security would they have for their maintenance in old age? Moreover, the
  family farm, the property of most importance in the majority of cases, could
  only be successful due to the joint efforts of husband and wife: 'Though the
  property may have been made since their marriage, the wife assisting the husband both indoors and out, often with her child in her arms, has struggled and
  deprived herself of many comforts that the mother of a family particularly
  requires, to pay for those farms which the abolition of this law would give
  them no right in.' The *Spectator* was renowned as a Conservative paper, and
  the publication of this letter in this paper suggests the widespread nature of
  discontent with marital property laws.
2 Perhaps not surprisingly, property law reform was also the 'first point in the
  women's charter' in England: Holcombe, *Wives and Property*, 4.
3 Parliamentary debates were not officially recorded during this period, and
  newspapers, representing a wide range of divergent opinion, provided the
  basis for research in this chapter. The 1850s were marked by almost constant
  deadlock in the legislature of the United Canadas, and 1858 was the year of
  the abortive Brown-Dorion government. Despite instability and deadlock, the
  legislation achieved majority assent in 1859, a measure of its popularity and of
  the strength of public demand for reform.
4 Preamble to An Act to secure for married women certain separate rights of
  property (1859) 22 Vict., c. 34.
5 'The Legal Rights of Married Women,' Toronto *Globe*, 26 December 1856, 1.
6 Ibid.
7 'Woman's Rights,' Toronto *Globe*, 20 February 1857, 4.
8 'The Married Woman Question,' *Upper Canada Law Journal*, August 1857, 144.
9 'The Legal Rights of Married Women,' Toronto *Globe*, 26 December 1856, 1.
10 'Property Rights of Married Women,' Toronto *Globe*, 17 March 1857, 4.

11 'The Married Woman Question,' *Upper Canada Law Journal*, August 1857, 143.
12 Ibid. 157.
13 *Journals of the Legislative Assembly* (1852–3) 690.
14 See, for example, Basch, *In The Eyes of the Law*, and Holcombe, *Wives and Property*.
15 *Journals of the Legislative Assembly* (1854–5) 807.
16 *Journals of the Legislative Council* (1856) 230. For the New York Act of 1848, see Basch, *In the Eyes of the Law*.
17 This supposition is strengthened by the fact that some of the wording of the Upper Canadian petition seems to have been taken directly from the 1856 English petition: Holcombe, *Wives and Property*, 86, 237–8.
18 'Woman's Rights,' Toronto *Globe*, 19 January 1857, 1.
19 Unfortunately, it has proved impossible to trace the few women whose names are extant. The petitions by Anne Macdonald and Elizabeth Hawley do not even state the names of the towns in which these women resided, making the search for biographical material extremely difficult. The only woman about whom any other information is known is Elizabeth Dunlop. In the course of research regarding prostitution, Constance Backhouse discovered that this woman was actively involved in the creation and management of the Toronto Magdalen Asylum, an institution devoted to the goal of eliminating prostitution by rehabilitating prostitutes and training them as domestic servants. See Backhouse, *Petticoats and Prejudice*, 179, 234.
20 'Parliamentary Report,' Toronto *Daily Leader*, 17 March 1857, 2. While petitions to the Legislative Assembly are no longer extant, those to presented to the Legislative Council can be found in the NAC, RG 14, vols. 26, 42, 45, 54, 55, 57, 59, 60, 61, and 64. They are, however, almost illegible, and yield little specific information about the nature of the reform desired by the women and men who signed such petitions.
21 *Parliamentary Debates*, Newspaper Hansard of the United Province of Canada, reel 1, 6 May 1857, 84.
22 *Journals of the Legislative Assembly* (1857): Esquesing, 266: Galt, 503; Leeds, 377; Lochiel, 377; London, 377; Millbrook, 226; Nassagaweya, 226; St Catharines, 41, 273; Saugeen, 219; Waterford, 226; and York, 306. It is not unlikely that municipalities favoured such reform because deserted wives were a potentially heavy burden on local relief.
23 The importance of the law reform movement in Great Britain, particularly of the Law Amendment Society and the desire for a fusion of law and equity, has been recognized by other authors interested in the changes in the law of married women and their property: see, for example, Holcombe, *Wives and Property*, and Shanley, *Feminism*. The codification movement, and the desire to

strip the common law of its feudal trappings, are cited as impetus for reform in New York State: Rabkin, *Fathers to Daughters*, and Basch, *In the Eyes of the Law*.

24 'Codification of Law in America,' *Upper Canada Law Journal*, October 1860, 223.

25 Ibid.

26 Under the leadership of William Hume Blake, the Judicature Act, 1849, reorganized the court system and attempted to simplify and clarify procedure and to eliminate abuses in the Court of Chancery: Blackwell, 'William Hume Blake.' In 1851 Chancery standardized and published its rules and regulations, and by the mid-1850s, despite its early reputation as corrupt and inefficient, the court had earned considerable respect, and the principles it enforced were deemed essential to substantive justice: Cooper, *Rules and Practice*.

27 'Consolidation of the Laws of Upper Canada,' *Upper Canada Law Journal*, June 1858, 124, 125.

28 'Associations for the Amendment of Law,' *Upper Canada Law Journal*, October 1863, 281.

29 'Law, Equity and Justice,' *Upper Canada Law Journal*, July 1858, 171.

30 Basch, *In the Eyes of the Law*, chapter 4.

31 Girard, 'Married Women's Property,' 106–13.

32 Holcombe, *Wives and Property*, chapter 4.

33 'Associations for the Amendment of Law,' *Upper Canada Law Journal*, November 1863, 281, 283.

34 Mr DeBlaquiere, Legislative Council, *Parliamentary Debates*, Newspaper Hansard, reel 1, 30 March 1857, 47.

35 This argument has been particularly emphasized by authors attempting to explain the transformation of married women's property law in the United States: Friedman, *History of American Law*, 184–6; Chused, 'Married Women's Property Law'; and Basch, *In the Eyes of the Law*.

36 An Act to Extend the Provisions of the Act for the Abolishment of Imprisonment for Debt (1859) 22 Vict., c. 33.

37 'Shall We Have a Bankruptcy Law?' *Upper Canada Law Journal*, January 1858, 3.

38 Holmested, 'Married Women's Rights of Property,' *Canadian Law Times* 3 (February 1883) 64.

39 'Married Women's Property Bill,' Hamilton *Spectator*, 15 June 1850, 3.

40 Billa Flint was a self-made man with only six weeks of formal education. He served in the Legislative Assembly from 1847 until the election of 1851, was re-elected in 1854, and was elected to the Legislative Council in 1863. He was called to the Senate of Canada in 1867 and served in that capacity until his death in 1894. See *Dictionary of Canadian Biography*, vol. 12, 321–3.

41 *Debates of the Legislative Assembly of United Canada 1841–1867*, ed. Elizabeth Gibbs, vol. 9, part 2, 1850, 1197–9.

42 'A man, who of course has implicit confidence in the woman whom he intends to make a partner for life, [will be able] to transfer to her on the eve of marriage, all the real estate and personal property of which he may be possessed. This relieves him from all future contingencies, and any difficulties which may arise. The contract being private, of course, the public can know nothing of it; and the consequence would be that the man could contract what debts he chose, defraud his creditors as much as he pleased, and still enjoy the property which he had taken the precaution to place out of the reach of those to whom he was indebted': 'Married Women's Property Bill,' Hamilton *Spectator*, 15 June 1850, 3. This fear, which seems to largely have disappeared during the 1850s, would re-emerge with a vengeance in the late 1870s and 1880s, in great degree as a result of the very large number of frauds that were committed under colour of the statutes of 1859 and 1872–3.

43 Supra note 41, at 1197.

44 'Married Women's Property Bill,' Hamilton *Spectator*, 15 June 1850, 3. This article was written in response to the editorial comments of the *Journal*, which, unfortunately, are no longer extant.

45 *Journals of the Legislative Assembly* (1852–3) 870 and 1036.

46 William Morris died in 1858, before seeing married women's property law reform enacted. A staunch supporter of the rights and privileges of the Church of Scotland, Morris was also prominent in educational reform. His eldest son was married to a niece of Philip Vankoughnet, another supporter of married women's property law reform, who also sat in the Legislative Council and had experience as a chancellor. This family connection may have influenced Morris's views on this question. See *Dictionary of Canadian Biography*, vol. 8, 638–42, and vol. 11, 608–15.

47 William Hamilton Merritt was a central figure in the development of the Welland Canal. Perhaps more important in this context, he had married into the wealthy Prendergast family of St Catharines, and his own financial instability in the 1840s and 1850s may have influenced his views on the necessity of statutory separate property. See *Dictionary of Canadian Biography*, vol. 9, 544–8.

48 *Parliamentary Debates*, Newspaper Hansard, reel 1, 19 June 1856, 230.

49 It is not surprising that there was little, if any, difference between the assembly and the council on this question. Unlike the House of Lords in Great Britain, which would dramatically reduce the scope of married women's property legislation in the 1870s, the upper chamber in the United Canadas was, from 1856, an elected body.

50 *Parliamentary Debates,* Newspaper Hansard, reel 1, 15 May 1857; *Journals of the Legislative Assembly* (1857) 43, 549, 31, 444, 472, 698, 703, and 717.

51 Cameron served, at various times, under John A. Macdonald in the coalition governments of the 1850s, but was also quick to cross the floor and join the opposition when confronted with issues on which he disagreed with government policy. In the elections of 1858, although Cameron described himself as a reformer, he was challenged in his home riding of Lambton by another reform candidate, Hope Mackenzie, brother of the later Liberal prime minister, Alexander Mackenzie. Cameron served on the executive of the Sons of Temperance for many years and was a founder of the city of Sarnia. See *Dictionary of Canadian Biography,* vol. 10, 124–9.

52 For an extended example of Cameron's fiery temperance rhetoric, see 'Speech of the Hon. M. Cameron, delivered in Ottawa, February 1864,' published by the Bytown Division, Sons of Temperance, CIHM no. 50456.

53 'Property Rights of Married Women,' Toronto *Globe,* 17 March 1857, 4.

54 'House of Assembly Debates,' Hamilton *Spectator,* 4 April 1857, 1.

55 *Parliamentary Debates,* reel 1, 30 March 1857, 47.

56 Ibid. 47.

57 'House of Assembly Debates,' Hamilton *Spectator,* 4 April 1857, 1.

58 *Parliamentary Debates,* reel 1, 30 March 1857, 47.

59 Ibid.

60 Ibid., 22 May 1857, 109. It is interesting to note that a 'Bill to Abolish Primogeniture' was passed on this same day. Primogeniture, like the civil death of women upon marriage, denied the companionate belief in the spiritual equality, in their separate spheres and roles, of subordinate members of the household. In this same year, the *Globe* explicitly pointed to primogeniture as another archaic law, inherited from feudal times, which required revision: 'The desire to give the whole estate to one child to the exclusion of all the rest was the exception; the desire to divide it equally among all was the rule. While the law enforced the exception in all cases in which parents had been unable, had forgotten or had neglected to make a will, there was a crying injustice ... The same reasoning ... applies to the case in hand [reform of the married women's property law]': 'Property Rights of Married Women,' Toronto *Globe,* 17 March 1857, 4.

61 *Parliamentary Debates,* reel 2, 15 April 1858, 54. As Mr Vankoughnet argued when the bill was reintroduced for the consideration of the council in 1858, 'it was rather late when it came up last year from the Lower House, and he hoped from the early day in which it was introduced in this session, it would receive careful consideration and the bill would be made as perfect as circumstances would permit.'

62 This open-mindedness stands in stark contrast to the almost blind adherence to English models and precedents that came to characterize Ontario jurisprudence and legislation at the end of the nineteenth century and into the twentieth: Baker, 'Reconstitution,' 234. Ironically, the position of legal status of wives in Quebec seems to have declined in the wake of codification.

63 *Parliamentary Debates*, reel 2, 15 April 1858, 2.

64 'The Rights of Woman,' *Upper Canada Law Journal*, November 1856, 218.

65 'Woman's Rights,' Toronto *Globe*, 20 February 1857, 4.

66 'The Married Woman Question,' *Upper Canada Law Journal*, August 1857, 145.

67 'Legal Rights of Married Women,' Toronto *Globe*, 26 December 1856, 2.

68 For Upper Canadian comments on the New York act, see Hamilton *Spectator*, 15 September 1847 and 15 June 1850; London *Free Press*, 1 and 26 February 1857.

69 Basch, *In the Eyes of the Law*, appendix, Laws of New York, 1848, c. 200: 'S.1. The real and personal property of any female who may hereafter marry, and which she shall own at the time of marriage, and the rents, issues and profits thereof shall not be subject to the disposal of her husband, nor be liable for his debts, and shall continue her sole and separate property, as if she were a single female.' Wives had not had such rights of disposal in Upper Canada under marriage settlements, and legislators did not want to introduce new rights, but to democratize those which wealthy wives already possessed.

70 For comments on the agitation and the Matrimonial Causes Act, see Hamilton *Spectator*, 22 August 1857 and 10 October 1857; London *Free Press*, 22 September 1856 and 12 February 1857; Toronto *Globe*, 3 July and 3 August 1857.

71 Holcombe, *Wives and Property*, chapter 5. Holcombe argues that the passage of the Matrimonial Causes Act took the 'wind out of the sails' of the parliamentary campaign for wider reform of the married women's property law.

72 Matrimonial Causes Act [UK] (1857) 20 and 21 Vict., c. 85, section 21.

73 It is possible that the imperial government exerted some pressure on the provincial legislature to pass similar legislation. A short article published in the Kingston *Daily News* in 1859 referred to such direct imperial advice being given to the legislature: 'Imperial Advice on Divorce,' Kingston *Daily News*, 29 April 1859, 2. It is not clear, however, whether the imperial government was concerned with the protection of wives or the liberalization of divorce law, an impossibility in the United Canadas because of the solid block of opposition to divorce in Catholic Canada East.

74 Mr Vankoughnet, *Parliamentary Debates*, reel 2, 13 April 1860, 34.

75 'The Rights of Woman,' *Upper Canada Law Journal*, November 1856, 218.

76 'Bills of the Session,' *Upper Canada Law Journal*, May 1858, 107.

77 'Legal Rights of Married Women,' Toronto *Globe*, 26 December 1856, 2.
78 'Woman's Rights,' Toronto *Globe*, 20 February 1857, 4.
79 *Parliamentary Debates*, reel 2, 15 April 1858, 54.
80 *Journals of the Legislative Assembly* (1858) 355.
81 *Parliamentary Debates*, reel 2, 1, 11, 18 February 1859.
82 Ibid. 18 March 1859.
83 Ibid. 11 April 1859.
84 Oliver Mowat, later premier of Ontario (1872–96), was by 1859 a prominent
   member of the reform opposition. In 1858 he was provincial secretary in the
   two-day Brown-Dorion government. In 1864 Mowat was appointed vice-
   chancellor, and he remained on the bench until his return to politics as provincial premier. Although on the surface Mowat's opposition to certain reforms
   seems to contradict his sympathetic role in Chancery, his desire was to see
   legislation mirror Chancery precedents as closely as possible. Moreover,
   his experience in Chancery may have softened his opposition to reform by
   1872–3,
85 *Parliamentary Debates*, reel 2, 11 April 1859.
86 Interestingly, this was George Brown, editor of the *Globe* and critic of the
   common law. His mocking sarcasm during this debate reveals the limits of
   reformism.
87 *Parliamentary Debates*, reel 2, 25 April 1859.
88 An Act to secure for married women certain separate rights of property (1859)
   22 Vict., c. 34, section 1.
89 Ibid. section 4.
90 Ibid. section 5.
91 Ibid, section 6.
92 It is unclear, however, how many wives actually made use of such protection
   orders. These orders were issued at the local level, and few such records are
   extant.
93 An Act respecting the Court of Chancery (1859) 22 Vict., c. 12, section 29.
94 'Woman's Rights,' Sarnia *Observer*, 5 November 1857, 4.
95 Ibid.
96 'Married Woman's Rights,' Barrie *Northern Advance*, 20 April 1859, 2.

CHAPTER 5

1 'Women's Rights in Ontario,' Hamilton *Spectator*, 2 April 1872, 4. Victoria
  Woodhull and her sister, Tennessee Claflin, co-edited *Woodhull and Claflin's
  Weekly*, a free-love journal. Woodhull, who advocated free sexuality only in
  conjunction with love, still held perfectionist notions regarding the nuclear

family, although her views were considered scandalous in the 1870s. For more information on free-love advocates, see Sears, *Sex-Radicals*.

2 'The Rights of Married Women,' Toronto *Globe*, 18 May 1869, 4.

3 Ibid.

4 'Married Women's Property Bill,' Toronto *Globe*, 7 July 1870, 2.

5 'Protection to Wives,' *Local Courts' and Municipal Gazette* vol. 5 (February 1869), 22.

6 'Women's Rights in Ontario,' Toronto *Daily Mail*, 24 September 1872, 2.

7 Eighteen-fifty-five was the year of Lucy Stone's marriage to Henry Blackwell. At their wedding ceremony, they protested together against the manifold injustices inherent in nineteenth-century marriage, and Stone was censured by some other feminists, including Susan B. Anthony, for her refusal to take her husband's name. Their mutual statement of protest began: 'While we acknowledge our mutual affection by publicly assuming the relationship of husband and wife, yet, in justice to ourselves and a great principle, we deem it a duty to declare that this act on our part implies no sanction of, nor promise of obedience to, such of the present laws of marriage as refuse to recognize the wife as an independent, rational being, while they confer upon the husband an injurious and unnatural superiority, investing him with legal powers which no honorable man would exercise and which no man should possess': as quoted in Spender, *Women of Ideas*, 355. This protest made Stone notorious, and it is scarcely to be doubted that marital property law and suffrage were both mentioned in her Toronto address. The information regarding Stone's address to the Toronto audience is drawn from Bearden and Butler, *Shadd*, 160–1.

8 For a discussion of the activities of the Toronto Women's Literary Club, see Luke, 'Woman Suffrage in Canada,' 330.

9 'Husbands and Wives,' Toronto *Daily Mail*, 11 April 1876, 2.

10 *Canadian Law Times* 8 (1872) 266.

11 'Court of Chancery,' Toronto *Daily Telegraph*, 7 November 1867, 2.

12 In 1871 a reform commission was appointed by Blake specifically to study this question, although it was abolished by Mowat in 1872: Brown, 'Equitable Jurisdiction,' 304–5. The Blake government was a reforming regime; Mowat was also a reformer, and replaced Blake only because of legislation that forbade members to hold concurrent seats in both the national and the provincial assemblies, forcing Blake to choose between the premiership of the province and his seat in the federal house.

13 'Law and Equity,' Toronto *Globe*, 26 January 1871, 2.

14 Administration of Justice Act (1873) 36 Vict., c. 8, section 1.

15 'The Rights of Married Women,' Toronto *Globe*, 18 May 1869, 4.

16 'Woman's Rights,' Toronto *Daily Telegraph*, 19 May 1870, 2.

17 'The Rights of Married Women,' Toronto *Globe*, 18 May 1869, 4. The *Globe*, as in the 1850s, was undoubtedly the most powerful voice arguing for reform. By early 1869 the daily *Globe* had a circulation of 16,320, while the weekly version of the paper, which reached the farther areas of the province, had a circulation of 31,200. With the population of Toronto still not much over 50,000, this represented a remarkable achievement: Careless, *Brown of the Globe*, vol. 2, 269.

18 Richard Pankhurst's wife, Emmeline, and his daughters, Crystabel and Sylvia, became leading members of the suffrage movement, and Pankhurst was himself a prominent supporter of women's causes in Parliament.

19 'Married Women,' *Local Courts and Municipal Gazette*, vol. 4 (August 1868), 116; reprinted from the *Solicitors Journal*.

20 This bill was almost identical in its provisions to that introduced by Sir Erskine Perry in 1857.

21 'Married Women,' *Local Courts' and Municipal Gazette*, 116–17.

22 Holcombe, *Wives and Property*, 168.

23 'Married Women,' *Local Courts' and Municipal Gazette*, 116.

24 Holcombe, *Wives and Property*, 171.

25 This bill, in other words, would have gone no further in reform than the Upper Canadian legislation of 1859. Ullrich, 'Reform of Matrimonial Property Law,' 23.

26 Holcombe, *Wives and Property*, 178. This was just one of many examples of reforms advocated by the House of Commons that were rejected or revised beyond recognition by the conservative House of Lords. The conflict between these legislative bodies culminated in the passage of the Parliament Act of 1911, which severely limited the legislative powers of the House of Lords. Of course, no such conflict existed in Ontario after 1867 because the provincial legislature was unicameral, and the national legislature had no jurisdiction in matters of property law.

27 As quoted in Holcombe, *Wives and Property*, 179.

28 Married Women's Property Act [UK] (1870) 33 and 34 Vict., c. 93, section 1; section 7; and sections 3 and 4. This limitation with regard to the extent of inherited property that could be held by the wife as her statutory separate estate was not repeated in the Ontario act of 1872. This perhaps reflected the fact that most prudent families in Britain with larger estates would have already ensured the security of a daughter's inheritance through the use of a marriage settlement, thus rendering statutory protection for such property redundant. This was not the case in Ontario.

29 Adam Crooks was originally from Dundas, Ontario, and had been called to the bar in 1851. He was an important member of Blake's reform cabinet, and

helped draft not only the Married Women's Property Act but also the Municipal Institutions Act, the Mechanics' Lien Act, and a liquor licensing act. He was minister of education under Mowat in 1876 and helped to establish standardized teaching qualifications in the province. Forgotten today, in his own time he was a prominent member of the government. He collapsed in the House in 1883, suffering from cerebral paresis, was declared incurably insane in 1884, and died in obscurity the next year: *Benchers Files,* Archives of the Law Society of Upper Canada. See also *Dictionary of Canadian Biography,* vol. 11, 220–3.

30 'The Legal Capacity of Married Women,' Toronto *Globe,* 24 January 1872, 3.

31 'Married Women's Rights of Property,' Toronto *Globe,* 10 February 1872, 3.

32 'The Rights of Married Women,' Toronto *Globe,* 18 May 1869, 4.

33 An Act to extend the rights of property of Married Women (1872) 35 Vict., c. 16, section 2.

34 Ibid. section 1.

35 'The Rights of Married Women,' Toronto *Globe,* 25 January 1878, 2. The greatest concern expressed by the *Globe* in this article was that women were unaware of the rights they possessed under this act. The article in question was written in response to a lecture given by a foreign woman who 'complained of the grievous disabilities under which married women labour in most countries.' The lecturer did not know the state of the law in Ontario, and 'perhaps others are equally ignorant, and it may therefore be worthwhile to state in a few words what the Ontario law on the subject really is.'

36 'Woman's Rights in Ontario,' Toronto *Daily Mail,* 24 September 1872, 2.

37 In *Merrick v Sherwood* (1872) 22 UCCP 467, Gwynne J conceded that a dispositive power over real estate had been granted by the act.

38 An Act to facilitate the conveyance of Real Estate by Married Women (1873) 36 Vict., c. 18.

39 'Parliamentary Debates,' Toronto *Globe,* 23 January 1873, 4.

40 36 Vict., c. 18, sections 4 and 3.

41 Ibid. section 4.

42 Walkem, *Married Women's Property Acts,* 14. Although little information is available to suggest reasons why Walkem chose to interpret the acts in this liberal manner, it is clear that this treatise was written with an explicit political purpose in mind. The fact that this treatise, after the passage of the act of 1884, became a staple law school textbook may explain why the act of 1872 has frequently been misinterpreted by authors who take his description of the terms and intent of the acts of 1872 and 1873 at face value. Walkem was a committed reformer, more radical than most of his contemporaries, and had a long and distinguished legal career. It is interesting to note that Walkem's wife was

vice-president of the Kingston Local Council of Women, a fact which suggests that his interest in a liberal interpretation of the act was not guided merely by a concern for the rights of creditors: Henry James Morgan, *The Canadian Men and Women of the Time: A Hand-Book of Canadian Biography* (Toronto 1898).

43 Walkem, *Married Women's Property Acts*, 51.

CHAPTER 6

1 *Dynan v Walls*, RG 22, Chancery 515/19/3/4–629/1883, AO.
2 Holmested, 'Married Women's Rights of Property,' *Canadian Law Times*, vol 3. (February 1883), 64.
3 Ibid.
4 The unreported court documents for this study included all extant records for York, Wentworth, Frontenac, Lambton, Brant, and Norfolk counties for the period from 1859 to 1900.
5 *Griffin v Patterson and wife* (1881), 45 UCQB 536, at 555, Armour J in dissent.
6 *Clarke v Creighton* (1881), 45 UCQB 514, AT 531, Armour J in dissent.
7 *Corrie v Cleaver* (1870), 21 UCCP 186, at 188–9.
8 *Clarke v Creighton* (1881), 45 UCQB 514, at 526, Armour J in dissent.
9 *Griffin v Patterson and Wife*, supra note 5, 536.
10 Ibid.
11 *Wright v Garden and Wife* (1869), 28 UCQB 609, at 611.
12 An Act to extend the rights of property of Married Women (1872) 35 Vict., c. 16, section 9.
13 *Lawson v Laidlaw* (1876), 3 OAR 92.
14 *Clarke v Creighton* (1881), 45 UCQB 524, Armour J in dissent.
15 *Kerr v Stripp* (1876), 40 UCQB 125, at 126.
16 Ibid. 134.
17 Ibid. 133.
18 *Foulds v Courtlett* (1871), 21 UCCP 368.
19 Ibid. 371.
20 Ibid. 372 and 374.
21 *Berry v Zeiss et al.* (1881) 32 UCCP 231, at 239.
22 Ibid.
23 *Meakin v Samson et al.* (1878) 28 UCCP 355.
24 Ibid. 363.
25 Ibid. 365.
26 Ibid. 366.
27 Ibid. 367. This was not the first time the Meakins had attempted to shield their property from the claims of creditors in this way. Mr Meakin acknowledged in

his separate examination that at the time of his insolvency proceedings 'he had put about $4,500.00 into his wife's name into the bank': ibid. 378.

28 *Harrison v Douglas* (1877), 40 UCQB 410.

29 Ibid. 415.

30 *Watts v Mitchell*, RG 22, Brant County, Chancery, 1879, AO.

31 *Wagner v Jefferson* (1876), 37 UCQB 551, at 553.

32 Ibid. 573.

33 Ibid. 574.

34 Ibid. 578.

35 In legal terms, a gift, to be deemed valid, requires proof of both intent and delivery. In a household that is amicable, delivery can pose particular problems of proof, particularly if the gift is being used by all parties equally, and since delivery is presumed in cases in which a physical transfer cannot be expected to take place.

36 Married Women's Property Act (1872) 35 Vict., c. 16, section 7.

37 *Levine v Claflin et al.* (1881), 31 UCCP 600, at 607.

38 *Dunbar v McKinnell*, RG 22, Chancery 510/5/1/4–205/1870, AO.

39 *Allen v Brodie*, RG 22, Chancery 510/9/12/9–131/1876, AO. The defendants were awarded costs of $94.88, but the plaintiff refused to pay. In 1878 the plaintiff was called for an accounting of her goods; unfortunately, no record of this accounting is extant.

CHAPTER 7

1 RG 22, York MWPA files, 1883, AO.

2 For this study, the unreported court documents from Wentworth, York, Frontenac, Brant, Norfolk, and Lambton counties were examined. Only seventeen cases of litigation between husbands and wives were found in the documents for the period 1859–1900.

3 'Married Women,' *Local Courts and Municipal Gazette*, vol. 4 (August 1868) 116–17.

4 *Balsam v Robinson* (1869), 19 UCCP 263, at 269.

5 *Philips v Philips*, RG 22, Brant County, 1871, AO.

6 Ironically, this was the same Oliver Mowat who had been central to imposing limitations on the original act of 1859. Perhaps, however, his experience on the bench influenced his later actions in Parliament, as it was under Mowat's direction that a fusion of law and equity was finally realized and the liberal act of 1884 passed.

7 *Chamberlain v McDonald* (1868), 14 Ch. R. 450.

8 *Wright v Garden* (1869), 28 UCQB 609, at 619. Adam Wilson was a fervent

reformer. A former mayor of Toronto, Wilson was a longstanding supporter of the Brownite liberal faction in the United Canadas, and later of the Blake–Mowat regime in Ontario.

9 Ibid. 620.

10 *McGuire v McGuire* (1873), 23 UCCP 123, at 135.

11 Ibid. 123.

12 Ibid. 125–6.

13 Ibid. 135.

14 An Act to facilitate the conveyance of Real Estate by Married Women (1873) 36 Vict., c. 18, section 4.

15 Both of these counties kept separate records of the protection orders issued to married women under this act: RG 22, Huron County, Appearance Book, Married Women's Real Estate Act, 1877–1884, and RG 22, York County, Married Women's Property Act Files, 1873–98, AO. Neither of these runs is complete. All cases from before 1875 are missing in the Huron County files, and those from 1874 to 1880 are missing in the York County files. Support for individual women also came occasionally from the legislature. Between 1873 and 1897, twelve women are known to have petitioned the legislature for private empowering acts to allow them to dispose of and manage their separate property 'independently of [their] husbands'; all such petitions were granted: RG 49, Office of the Clerk of the Legislature I-7-A-6, box 142, and RG 49 I-7-A-3, vols 1–8, AO. Thirty-six further petitions from York County are preserved in the Married Women's Real Estate Act Files, York County, Archives of the Law Society of Upper Canada.

16 Interestingly, two of the women who were granted the right to dispose of their separate real estate also sued their husbands for alimony in the Court of Chancery. Unfortunately, neither of these alimony cases advanced to hearing: *Burgess v Burgess*, RG 22, Chancery 510/11/3/4–482/1878; and *Melville v Melville*, RG 22, Chancery 510/9/1/6–900/1873, AO.

17 This concern for the legal problems faced by deserted wives was echoed in 1888. In that year the legislature passed an act which attempted to force deserting husbands to support their wives: An Act respecting the Maintenance of Wives deserted by their Husbands (1888) 51 Vict., c. 23.

18 RG 22, York Matters, 110/21/2/14–58-H, AO.

19 RG 22, York County, MWPA files, 1873, AO.

20 In New York this property belonged unquestionably to the wife under the Married Women's Property Act, 1860, which granted the wife full control over any money 'she acquires by her trade, business, labor or services.' See Basch, appendix 1.

21 *Goodwin v Goodwin*, RG 22, Norfolk County, 1878, AO.

22 *Webster v Webster*, RG 22, Country Causes 58/13/1/8–W/10, AO.
23 The conveyance was probably taken in Rose McKeown's name in order to shield the property from seizure by any possible future creditors of Patrick McKeown.
24 *McKeown v McKeown*, RG 22, Chancery 515/19/3/12–706/1884, AO, and *McKeown v McKeown*, RG 22, Chancery 515/29/3/2–557/1890, AO.
25 *Webb v McArthur*, RG 22, Chancery 510/5/1/5–329/1870, AO. His wife produced a host of character witnesses to uphold her virtue; the defendant's own brother, on the other hand, referred to him as a 'worthless drunk.' This was a case in which the chancellors would have had no difficulty in determining which party was deserving of relief. Interestingly, Catherine McArthur later reneged on a legitimate debt made with respect to this separate estate. Under the deed of separation the real and personal property was given to the wife for her separate use, but with the provision that until the youngest child should reach the age of twenty-one years, the property was to be used for the support and maintenance of the children. Because of this restraint upon alienation, even the personal property of the wife could not be disposed of during the children's minority, and her contract was therefore deemed invalid and nonbinding: *Field v McArthur* (1876) 27 UCCP 15.
26 *Wage v Wage*, RG 22, Chancery 510/9/1/5–12/1873, AO.
27 *Munro v Munro*, RG 22, Chancery 510/9/1/8–260/1873, AO.
28 *Locke v Locke*, RG 22, Chancery 510/6/4/12–336/1871, AO.
29 *Johnston v Johnston*, RG 22, Chancery 510/9/1/8–225/1873, AO.
30 *Sullivan v Sullivan*, RG 22, Chancery 510/9/2/14–461/1876, AO.
31 *Wright v Garden*, supra note 8, 620.

CHAPTER 8

1 George Holmested, 'Married Women's Rights of Property,' *Canadian Law Times* (February 1883) 66.
2 'Correspondence,' *Canadian Law Times* (May 1881) 318–19.
3 'Notes of Recent Decisions,' *Canadian Law Times* (June 1881) 363.
4 Ibid. 364.
5 Holmested, 'Married Women's Rights of Property,' 76.
6 Ibid.
7 Ibid. 77.
8 See Holcombe, *Wives and Property*, chapters 9 and 10.
9 For further information on the growing 'woman movement' in Ontario during this decade, see Luke, 'Woman Suffrage in Canada,' 330; Mitchinson, 'The Women's Christian Temperance Union'; Bacchi, *Liberation Deferred?*; Light and

Parr, eds, *Canadian Women on the Move*; Prentice et al., *Canadian Women*; Ray, *Emily Stowe*.

10 'Women and their Sphere,' Toronto *World*, 11 July 1883, 2.

11 This woman wrote a series of such letters to the paper. Unfortunately, it has not yet been possible to discover her identity. However, it is clear that much of the exchange took place between this author and Goldwin Smith, a notorious opponent of woman suffrage who argued elsewhere, with much disgust, that 'about everything has been done which civil legislation could do to impress the wife with the belief that her interest and that of her husband are not only separate but adverse ... that the law regarding the property of married women in particular has been so far reformed in the interests of the wife that, instead of being unduly favourable to the husband, it seems rather inspired by a mistrust of him': Goldwin Smith, 'Woman Suffrage,' *Essays on Questions of the Day*, 1892.

12 'Political Women,' Toronto *World*, 12 February 1884, 2.

13 Ironically, however, allowing women to own property removed one of the central arguments against women having the vote. The phrase that had helped to fuel the American War of Independence – 'no taxation without representation – could be used equally effectively to argue that property-owning women had a right to political voice.

14 'Judicature Bill,' Toronto *Globe*, 15 January 1880, 3–4.

15 Ibid. 4.

16 Brown, 'Equitable Jurisdiction,' 311.

17 Holcombe, *Wives and Property*, 190.

18 Bills on the subject were presented by friends of the Married Women's Property Committee in 1873, 1877, 1878, 1880, 1881, and 1882: ibid., chapter 8 and appendix 6.

19 Ibid. 198.

20 Ibid. 199.

21 Married Women's Property Act [UK] (1884) 45 & 46 Vict., c. 75, sections 1(1), and 1(2), and 2.

22 Consortium was *not* a mutually applicable right within marriage, but a right of the husband only, which had its roots in the feudal conception of the wife as her husband's vassal. In 1887, partly on the basis of this idea of consortium, it was decided in *Scott v Morley* (1887), 20 QBD (UK) 120, that a married woman could not be imprisoned for debt, even when she had separate estate which was liable on a debt but merely refused to pay it.

23 Ullrich, 'Reform of Matrimonial Property Law,' 27. This argument certainly seems to hold true in Ontario, where separate estates in Chancery after reform were used to limit the scope for women to use their separate

property, to ensure that such property would be preserved for future generations.

24 Ibid. 32.

25 *Journals of the Legislative Assembly of Ontario* (1882–3) 31, 95, 129.

26 The bill received royal assent on 24 March 1884: Married Women's Property Act, 47 Vict., c. 19. Toronto *Globe*, Newspaper Hansard, 14 March 1884, 4. Ironically, Mowat had opposed extensive reform in 1859 and had been instrumental in limiting the provisions of the Married Women's Property Act of that year. In the interim, however, he had served as chancellor, and it is not unlikely that his new support of extensive and liberal reform was influenced by this experience on the bench and the evidence of both fraud and abuse of trust by husbands.

27 Toronto *Globe*, Newspaper Hansard, 5 March 1884.

28 An Act respecting the property of Married Women (1884), 47 Vict., c. 19, section 2(1).

29 Ibid., section 2.

30 While based on the English act of 1882, this measure also deliberately sought to avoid some of the problems that had arisen under that legislation. For example, in England no specific provision had been made to include the subsequently acquired property of a married woman as liable upon contract, an anomaly that the English legislature was forced to correct in 1893.

31 47 Vict., c. 19, section 15.

32 Ibid. section 18(1).

33 For a very interesting discussion of the importance of the wages of children for the survival of working-class families, see Bradbury, *Working Families*.

34 Holmested, *Married Women's Property Act*, 8.

35 Ibid. 7.

36 Ibid. 65.

37 Goldwin Smith, 'Woman Suffrage,' in *Essays on Questions of the Day* (Toronto: Macmillan Canada 1894), 192.

38 Ullrich, 'Reform of Matrimonial Property Law,' 32.

39 Holmested, *Married Women's Property Act*, 7.

CHAPTER 9

1 Anne Hamilton, 'Operation of the Married Women's Property Act,' *The Week*, 11 September 1891, 653.

2 'Editorial Review – Married Women's Property,' *Canadian Law Times* (February 1888) 40.

3 *Harrison v Burk*, from Mr Justice Robertson's Benchbooks, Toronto Assize, December 1892, 160–1. RG 22 483/1/14, AO.

4 *Moore v Jackson* (1889), 16 OAR 432.

5 *Moore v Jackson*, RG 22, Chancery 515/20/4/5–148/88, AO.

6 Ibid. It is interesting to note that Mary Jane Graydon was later involved in a further suit with regard to separate property. In 1894 she attempted to reclaim property, seized by creditors of her husband, which she claimed to have purchased from him. It was decided, however, that without a bill of sale affirming this transaction, 'there cannot be said to be an actual and continued change of possession open and reasonably sufficient to afford public notice thereof': *Hogaboom v Graydon* (1894), 26 OR 298 (Ch. D.).

7 *Moore v Jackson* (1889), 16 OAR 433.

8 *Moore v Jackson* (1890), 20 OR 653, at 654 (QBD).

9 Ibid.

10 Ibid. 663.

11 Ibid. 664.

12 *Moore v Jackson* (1893), 22 SCR 210, at 221.

13 'Editorial Review – Married Women's Property Law,' *Canadian Law Times* (February 1888) 41.

14 *Griffin v Patterson and Wife* (1881), 45 UCQB 548.

15 *Hamilton Lumber Co. v Jane and F.F. Appleton*, RG 22 Wentworth, 45/44/2/2, AO.

16 Anne Hamilton, *The Week*, 653.

17 *Piggott v Medley*, RG 22, Wentworth HCJ – CPD 45/44/1/11, AO.

18 *Boustead v Culverwell*, RG 22, Chancery 510/9/1/16–359/74, AO.

19 *John Kay v Lida VanWormer*, RG 22, Chancery 515/20/4/5–190/88, AO.

20 *L. Berlowitz v Clemson and Lida VanWormer*, RG 22, Chancery 515/20/4/5–287/88, AO.

21 *Lida VanWormer v Jacob Levin*, RG 22, Chancery 515/20/4/15–80/89, AO.

22 Settlements were reached in twenty-five of the extant cases from the unreported court documents.

23 *Miller v Crittenden*, RG 22, Chancery 515/29/3/6–134/91, AO.

24 *Maguire v Crittenden*, RG 22, Chancery 515/29/3/6–464/93, AO.

25 *Sheratt v The Merchants' Bank of Canada* (1894), 21 OAR 480–1.

26 *Smith v Lewis et ux.*, RG 22, Chancery 515/19/4/7–9/1886, AO.

27 This assertion is strengthened by the findings of Peter Baskerville in his microeconomic study of female land ownership in British Columbia. See Baskerville, 'Already Hinted at Board.'

CHAPTER 10

1 *Young v Young*, RG 22, Chancery 515/19/4/14–205/1887, AO.

2 Although many married women earned cash necessary for family survival

through the marketing of butter, eggs, and other small produce and through the provision of sewing, laundry, and other services for neighbours and boarders, it was difficult to take such income away from the home. Moreover, as the revenue from a joint family business, such money belonged, at law, to the husband. Outside the home, employment opportunities for women remained limited to dead-end and low-paying work, and opposition to the employment of married women remained strong, making it a daunting prospect for a woman to support herself after separation, let alone support any children who might accompany her in her flight from the marital home. For more information on women's labour, see Cohen, *Women's Work*, and Bradbury, *Working Families*.

3 *Mitchell v Lizard*, RG 22, Chancery, 515/19/3/11–462/1884, AO.
4 *Hopkins v Hopkins*, (1884) 7 OR 224, AT 227 (Ch. D.).
5 Ibid. 228.
6 *Beales v Beales*, RG 22, Chancery 515/23/4/10–501/1889, AO.
7 *Beckett v Beckett*, RG 22, Chancery 515/29/2/16–944/1892, AO.
8 Ibid. Chancery 515/29/2/7–103/92, AO.
9 47 Vict., c. 19, section 15.
10 *Donnelly v Donnelly* (1885), 9 OR 673 (CPD).
11 Ibid. 674.
12 *McGuire v McGuire*, 125–6.
13 Ibid. 135.
14 *Healy v Healy*, RG 22, Country Causes, 58/10/3/10–H-55, AO.
15 *Sandford v Sandford*, RG 22, Country Causes, 58/11/1/11–S/113, Brockville 1900, AO.

CONCLUSIONS AND EPILOGUE

1 *Watts v Watts*, RG 22, Chancery 510/9/1/10–360/1873, AO.
2 *Murdoch v Murdoch* (1973), 41 DLR (3d) (SCC) 367, at 371.
3 Preamble to An Act to secure for married women certain separate rights of property (1859) 22 Vict., c. 34.
4 Holmested, *The Married Women's Property Act*, 66.
5 Law Reform Commission of Canada, *Family Property: Working Paper 8* (Ottawa 1975), 10.
6 The 1975 Act to reform certain Laws founded upon Marital or Family Relationships attempted to deal with the results of the failure to accord economic value to women's domestic labour and the poverty of post-divorce wives, but did not make any explicit statement that such work would entitle women to a share in family property. Instead, the wording of the statute continued to give

discretion to judges to determine whether or not individual women were deserving of such relief: 'Except as agreed between them, where a husband or wife contributes work, money or money's worth in respect of the acquisition, management, maintenance, operation or improvement of a property in which the other has or had a property interest, the husband or wife shall not be disentitled to any right to compensation or other interest flowing from such contribution by reason only of the relationship of husband and wife or that the acts consitituting the contribution are those of a reasonable spouse of that sex in the circumstances.' The Family Law Reform Act (1975), 1. (3), (c). It remained, however, for judges to determine the definition of what consititituted the behaviour of a 'reasonable spouse.'

7 Family Law Act (1986) part 1, subsection 5(7). For information regarding the practical workings of this act, see Lenkinski, *Practical Guide to the Family Law Act* (Toronto 1988).

8 Hough, 'Mistaking Liberalism.'

Bibliography

NOTE ON PRIMARY SOURCES

The most important, and innovative, sources used in this work were the unre-
ported case files held at the Archives of Ontario. All records of the Court of
Chancery, 1837–1900, were used, as were Judges' Benchbooks, the Country
Causes case files, and the County Court records for Lambton, Norfolk, Grey,
Wentworth and York counties. Unreported case files at the Archives of the Law
Society of Upper Canada were also consulted. Without the help of Jack Choules it
would have been an almost impossible task sorting through the unprocessed
records at the Archives of Ontario. These cases provide the basis for the conclusions that challenge traditional legal historiography and methodology, because
the decisions in unreported cases contrast with those in the law reports. It is a
central argument of this work, therefore, that law reports, while important, are
inadequate in understanding the day-to-day operation of the law and its impact
on individuals.

STATUTES

An Act to establish a Court of Chancery in this Province (1837) 7 Wm IV, c. 2.
An Act respecting the Custody of Infants (1855) 18 Vict., c. 126.
An Act respecting the Court of Chancery, (1859) 22 Vict., c. 12.
An Act to secure for married women certain separate rights of property (1859) 22
    Vict., c. 34.

An Act to Extend the Provisions of the Act for the Abolishment of Imprisonment for Debt, (1859) 22 Vict., c. 33.
An Act to extend the rights of property of Married Women (1872) 35 Vict., c. 16.
An Act to facilitate the conveyance of Real Estate by Married Women (1873), 36 Vict., c. 18.
Administration of Justice Act (1873) 36 Vict., c. 8.
An Act respecting the property of Married Women, (1884) 47 Vict., c. 19.
An Act respecting the Maintenance of Wives deserted by their Husbands (1888) 51 Vict., c. 23.
Matrimonial Causes Act [UK] (1857) 20 and 21 Vict., c. 85.
Married Women's Property Act [UK] (1870) 33 and 34 Vict., c. 93.
Married Women's Property Act [UK] (1882) 45 and 46 Vict., c. 75.

OTHER GOVERNMENT PUBLICATIONS

Grant's Chancery Reports
Ontario Appeal Reports
Ontario Reports
Supreme Court Reports
Upper Canada Common Pleas
Upper Canada Queen's Bench
Law Reform Commission. *Family Property: Working Paper 8*. Ottawa 1975.

LEGAL TREATISES

Bingham, Peregrin. *The Law of Infancy and Coverture*. London 1816.
Bishop, Joel Prentice. *Commentaries on the Law of Married Women under the Statutes of the Several States and at Common Law and in Equity*. 2 vols. Boston 1873–5.
– *Commentaries on the Law of Marriage and Divorce and Evidence in Matrimonial Suits*. Boston, 1852.
Blackstone, William. *Commentaries on the Laws of England, in Four Books*. Ed. George Tucker. 1803; reprinted New York 1969.
Cameron, Malcolm Graeme. *A Treatise on the Law of Dower* Toronto 1882.
Clarke, S.R. *The Insolvent Act of 1875 and Amending Acts* Toronto 1877.
Cooper, Robert. *The Rules and Practice of the Court of Chancery of Upper Canada, Comprising the orders of 1850 and 1851*. Toronto 1851.
Dicey, A.V. *Lectures on the Relation between Law and Public Opinion in England During the Nineteenth Century*. London 1920.
Edgar, J.D. *The Insolvent Act of 1864*. Toronto 1864.
– *The Insolvent Act of 1869*. Toronto 1869.

Gemmill, John Alexander. *The Practice of the Parliament of Canada upon Bills of Divorce*. Toronto 1889.

Holdsworth, William. *A History of English Law*. vol. 1. London 1923.

Holmested, George. *The Married Women's Property Act of Ontario*. Toronto 1905.

Jenks, Edward. *A Short History of English Law from the Earliest Times to the End of the Year 1938*. London 1949.

Kent, James. *Commentaries on American Law* 11th ed. (4 vols). Ed. George F. Comstock. Boston 1867.

Martin, Clara Brett. 'Legal Status of Women in the Provinces of the Dominion of Canada.' in *Women of Canada: Their Life and Work* compiled by the National Council of Women of Canada. Ottawa 1900.

MacMahon, H. *The Insolvent Act of 1875*. Toronto, 1875.

Macqueen, John Fraser. *The Rights and Liabilities of Husband and Wife*, 4th ed. Ed. Wyatt Paine. London 1905.

Lenkinski, Esther. *A Practical Guide to the Family Law Act, 1986*. Toronto, 1988.

Redman, Joseph Haworth. *A Concise View of the Law of Husband and Wife as Modified by the Married Women's Property Acts*. London 1883.

Reeve, Tapping. *Law of Baron and Femme*, 3d ed. Ed. Amasa Parker and Charles Baldwin. Albany 1862.

Riddell, William. *The Bar and the Courts of the Province of Upper Canada or Ontario*. Toronto 1928.

Spragge, John. *A Letter on the Subject of the Courts of Law of Upper Canada Addressed to the Attorney-General and the Solicitor-General*. Toronto 1847.

Stevens, C.H. *Insolvent Act of 1875*. Toronto 1875.

Underhill, Sir Arthur. *The Law Reform (Married Women and Tortfeasors) Act 1935 and the Unrepealed Sections of the Married Women's Property Acts*. London 1936.

Walkem, Richard Thomas. *The Married Women's Property Acts of Ontario*. Toronto, 1874.

'Vexed Questions – Frauds.' *Upper Canada Jurist*, vol 1. Toronto 1877.

Wharton, J.J.S. *An Exposition of the Law Relating to the Women of England, Showing their Rights, Remedies and Responsibilities in Every Position in Life*. London 1853

NINETEENTH-CENTURY NEWSPAPERS AND PERIODICALS

American Law Magazine
Canada Law Journal
Canadian Law Times
Local Courts' and Municipal Gazette
Upper Canada Law Journal
Barrie *Northern Advance* 1854–71.

Hamilton *Spectator* 1858–1900.
Kingston *Daily News* 1841–7.
London *Free Press* 1855–1900.
Toronto *Daily Leader* 1853–78.
Toronto Daily Mail, 1872–80.
Toronto *Daily Telegraph* 1866–72.
Toronto *Globe* 1853–1900.
Toronto *The Week*
Toronto *World* 1880–1900.

ADVICE MANUALS AND POPULAR LEGAL COMMENTARIES

Abbot, John Stevens Cabot. *The Mother at Home; or the Principles of Maternal Duty Familiarly Illustrated*. New York 1852.
Alcott, William. *The Young Wife, or Duties of Woman in the Marriage Relationship*. New York 1837; reprinted New York 1972.
Austin, Rev. B.F., ed. *Woman – Her Character – Culture and Calling*. Brantford 1890.
Cobbe, Francis Power. 'Criminals, Idiots, Women and Minors: Is the Classification Sound?' *Fraser's Magazine* 78 (1868):777–94.
Cornwallis, Caroline Francis. 'Capabilities and Disabilities of Women.' *Westminster Review* 67 (1857):42–72.
– 'The Property of Married Women: Report of the Personal Laws Committee (of the Law Amendment Society) on the Laws Relating to the Property of Married Women.' *Westminster Review* 66 (1856):331–60.
Crawford, Mary. *Legal Status of Women in Manitoba*. Winnipeg 1912.
Edwards, Henrietta Muir. *Legal Status of Canadian Women*. Ottawa 1908.
Ellis, Sarah. *The Women of England, Their Social Duties and Domestic Habits*. London 1839.
Lefevre, G. Shaw. *Speech for 'The Bill to Amend the Law with Respect to the Property of Married Women' in the House of Commons, April 21, 1868* Manchester 1868.
Leigh Smith, Barbara (Bodichon). *A Brief Summary, in Plain Language, of the Most Important Laws Concerning Women, Together with a Few Observations Thereon*. London 1854.
MacGill, Helen Gregory. *Daughters, Wives and Mothers in British Columbia: Some Laws Regarding Them*. British Columbia 1913.
Norton, Caroline. *English Laws for Women in the Nineteenth Century*. London 1854.
'The Christian Mother.' *The Witness Weekly Review and Family Newspaper*. Montreal 1846.

SECONDARY SOURCES

Bacchi, Carol Lee. *Liberation Deferred? The Ideas of the English-Canadian Suffragists, 1877–1918*. Toronto 1983.

Backhouse, Constance. 'Married Women's Property Law in Nineteenth Century Canada.' *Law and History Review* 6 (Fall 1988):211–57.

– 'Pure Patriarchy: Nineteenth Century Canadian Marriage.' *McGill Law Journal* 31 (1986):264–312.

– 'Shifting Patterns in Nineteenth Century Custody Law,' in David H. Flaherty, ed. *Essays in the History of Canadian Law*, vol. 1. Toronto 1981.

– 'To Open the Way for Others of My Sex: Clara Brett Martin' Career as Canada's First Woman Lawyer.' *Canadian Journal of Women and the Law* 1 (1985):1–41.

– 'Nineteenth-Century Canadian Rape Law 1800–1892,' in David H. Flaherty, ed. *Essays in the History of Canadian Law*, vol. 2. Toronto 1984.

– 'Involuntary Motherhood: Abortion, Birth Control and the Law in Nineteenth-Century Canada.' *Windsor Yearbook of Access to Justice* 3 (1983):61-130.

– 'Desperate Women and Compassionate Courts: Nineteenth-Century Infanticide in Canada.' *University of Toronto Law Journal* 34 (1984):447–78.

– 'Nineteenth-Century Canadian Prostitution Law: Reflections of a Discriminatory Society.' *Social History/histoire sociale* 18(36) (1985):387–423.

– 'The Tort of Seduction: Fathers and Daughters in Nineteenth-Century Canada.' *Dalhousie Law Journal* 10 (1986):264–312.

– *Petticoats and Prejudice*. Toronto 1991.

Baker, G. Blaine. 'The Reconstitution of Upper Canadian Legal Thought in the Late-Victorian Empire.' *Law and History Review* 3 (1985): 245–97.

– 'Legal Education in Upper Canada 1785–1889: The Law Society as Educator,' in David H. Flaherty, ed. *Essays in the History of Canadian Law*, vol. 2. Toronto 1983.

Basch, Norma. *In the Eyes of the Law: Women, Marriage and Property in Nineteenth Century New York*. Ithaca 1982.

– 'Invisible Women: The Fiction of Marital Unity in Nineteenth Century America.' *Feminist Studies* 5 (Summer 1979):346–66.

– 'Equity vs. Equality: Emerging Concepts of Women's Political Status in the Age of Jackson.' *Journal of the Early Republic* 3 (1983):297–318.

Baskerville, Peter. '"She Has Already Hinted at Board": Enterprising Urban Women in British Columbia 1863–1896.' *Histoire sociale–Social History* 26 (52) 52 (novembre-November 1993):205–27.

Bearden, Jim, and Linda Jean Butler. *Shadd: The Life and Times of Mary Shadd Cary*. Toronto 1977.

Blackwell, John. 'William Hume Blake and the Judicature Acts of 1849: The Process of Legal Reform a Mid-Century in Upper Canada,' in David H. Flaherty, ed. *Essays in the History of Canadian Law*, vol. 1. Toronto 1981.

Blake, Nelson Manfred. *The Road to Reno: A History of Divorce in the United States.* Westport, Connecticut 1962.

Bonfield, Lloyd. 'Marriage, Property and the Affective Family.' *Law and History Review* 1 (1983):297–312.

– *Marriage Settlements, 1660–1740: The Adoption of the Strict Settlement.* Cambridge 1983.

Boyd, Susan B., and Elizabeth A Sheehy. 'Feminist Perspectives on Law: Canadian Theory and Practice.' *Canadian Journal of Women and the Law* 2 (1986):1–52.

Bradbury, Bettina. *Working Families: Age, Gender and Daily Survival in Industrializing Montreal.* Toronto 1993.

Brown, Elizabeth. 'Equitable Jurisdiction and the Court of Chancery in Upper Canada.' *Osgoode Hall Law Journal* 21 (1983):275–314.

Careless, J.M.S. *Brown of the Globe*, 2 vols. 1959 and 1963; reprinted Toronto 1989.

Chused, Richard. 'Married Women's Property Law: 1800–1850.' *Georgetown Law Journal* 71 (June 1983):1359–1425.

– 'Late Nineteenth Century Married Women's Property Law: Reception of the Early Married Women's Property Acts by Courts and Legislatures.' *American Journal of Legal History* 29 (1985):3–35.

Cohen, Marjorie Griffin. *Women's Work, Markets and Economic Development in Nineteenth-Century Ontario.* Toronto 1988.

Conley, Carolyn. *The Unwirtten Law: Criminal Justice in Victorian Kent.* New York 1991.

Cook, Ramsay, and Wendy Mitchinson, eds. *The Proper Sphere: Woman's Place in Canadian Society.* Toronto 1976.

Cott, Nancy. *The Bonds of Womanhood: Woman's Sphere in New England, 1780–1825.* New Haven 1977.

– 'Divorce and the Changing Status of Women in Eighteenth-Century Massachusetts.' *William and Mary Quarterly* (3d ser.) 33 (1976):586–614.

Daly, Mary. *The Church and the Second Sex.* New York 1975.

Davidoff, Leonore, and Catherine Hall. *Family Fortunes: Men and Women of the English Middle Class, 1780–1850.* Chicago 1987.

Davies, Nancy. 'Patriarchy from the Grave: Family Relations in 19th Century New Brunswick Wills.' *Acadiensis* 13 (1984): 91–100.

Dicey, A.V. *Letters on the Relation Between Law and Public Opinion in England During the Nineteenth Century.* London 1920.

Douglas, Ann. *The Feminization of American Culture.* New York 1977.

Dubinsky, Karen. *Improper Advances: Rape and Heterosexual Conflict in Ontario, 1880–1929.* Chicago 1993.

Ehrenreich, Barbara, and Deirdre English. *For Her Own Good: 150 Years of Experts' Advice to Women*. New York 1978.

Errington, Jane. *Wives and Mothers*. Toronto 1995.

Fingard, Judith. 'The Prevention of Cruelty, Marriage Breakdown and the Rights of Wives in Nova Scotia, 1880–1900.' *Acadiensis* 22, 2 (Spring 1993):84–101.

Friedman, Lawrence. *A History of American Law*. New York 1973.

Fuller, Lon. *Legal Fictions*. Stanford 1967.

Gagan, David, and Herbert Mays. 'Historical Demography and Canadian Social History: Families and Land in Peel County, Ontario.' *Canadian Historical Review* 54 (1) (1973): 27–47.

Gagan, David. *Hopeful Travellers: Families, Land and Social Change in Mid-Victorian Peel County, Canada West*. Toronto 1981.

Gee, Ellen. 'Marriage in Nineteenth-Century Canada.' *Canadian Review of Sociology and Anthropology* 19 (1982):311–25.

Girard, Philip. 'Married Women's Property, Chancery Abolition and Insolvency Law: Law Reform in Nova Scotia 1820–1867,' in Philip Girard and Jim Phillips, eds. *Essays in the History of Canadian Law, vol. iii–Nova Scotia*. Toronto 1990.

Gordon, Linda. *Heroes of Their Own Lives: The Politics and History of Family Violence* New York 1988.

Graveson, R.H., and F.E. Crane, eds. *A Century of Family Law, 1857–1957*. London 1957.

Griswold, Robert. *The Family and Divorce in California, 1850–1890*. Albany 1982.

Grossberg, Michael. *Governing the Hearth: Law and the Family in Nineteenth-Century America*. Chapel Hill 1985.

Hammerton, James. 'Victorian Marriage and the Law of Matrimonial Cruelty.' *Victorian Studies* 33 (Winter 1990):269–92.

Harvey, Kathryn. 'Amazons and Victims: Resisting Wife-Abuse in Working-Class Montreal, 1869–1879.' *Journal of the Canadian Historical Association* 2 (1991:131–47).

– 'To Love, Honour and Obey: Wife-Battering in Working-Class Montreal, 1869–1879.' *Urban History Review/Revue d'histoire urbaine* 19 (2) (October 1990):128–40.

Hay, Douglas. 'Property, Authority and the Criminal Law,' in Hay et al., eds. *Albion's Fatal Tree*. Harmondsworth 1977.

Herstein, Sheila R. *A Mid-Victorian Feminist: Barbara Leigh Smith Bodichon*. New Haven 1985.

Holcombe, Lee. *Wives and Property: Reform of the Married Women's Property Law in Nineteenth-Century England*. Toronto 1983.

Holdsworth, William Searle. *A History of English Law*, 16 Vols. London 1903–16.

Hough, Janet. 'Mistaking Liberalism for Feminism: Spousal Support in Canada.' *Journal of Canadian Studies* 29 (2) (Summer 1994):147–64.

Ingram, Martin. *Church Courts, Sex and Marriage in England, 1570–1640* New York 1987.

Jamieson, Kathleen. *Indian Women and the Law in Canada: Citizens Minus*. Ottawa 1978.

Katz, Michael. 'Social Class in North American Urban History.' *Journal of Interdisciplinary History* 2 (Spring 1981):579–606.

Katz, Stanley. 'The Politics of Law in Colonial America: Controversies over Chancery Courts and Equity Law in the Eighteenth Century.' *Perspectives in American History* 5 (1971):257–84.

Lasch, Christopher. *Haven in a Heartless World*. New York 1977.

Lebsock, Suzanne. *The Free Women of Petersburg: Status and Culture in a Southern Town, 1784–1860*. New York 1984.

Lenkinski, Esther. *A Practical Guide to the Family Law Act, 1986*. Toronto 1988.

Light, Beth, and Joy Parr, eds. *Canadian Women on the Move 1880–1920* Toronto 1983.

Luke, Edith. 'Woman Suffrage in Canada,' *Canadian Magazine* 5 (1895): 330.

Marks, Lynne, and Chad Gaffield. 'Women at Queens' University, 1895–1905: A Little Sphere All Their Own.' *Ontario History* 78(4) (December 1986):331–49.

Maynard, Kimberley Smith. 'Divorce in Nova Scotia 1750–1890,' in Philip Girard and Jim Phillips, eds. *Essays in the History of Canadian Law, vol. iii – Nova Scotia*. Toronto 1990.

Millett, Kate. *Sexual Politics*. New York 1971.

Mitchinson, Wendy. 'The Women's Christian Temperance Union: "For God, Home and Native Land,"' in Michael Cross and Gregory Kealey, eds. *Canada's Age of Industry*. Toronto 1982.

Morgan, Cecilia. 'Languages of Gender in Upper Canadian Religion and Politics 1791–1850.' PhD dissertation, University of Toronto 1993.

Morgan, Henry James. *The Canadian Men and Women of the Time: A Hand-book of Canadian Biography*. Toronto 1898.

Morse, Bradford W. 'Indian and Inuit Law and the Canadian Legal System.' *American Indian Law Review* 8 (1980):199–227.

Owen, Wendy, and J.M. Bumsted. 'Divorce in a Small Province: A History of Divorce on Prince Edward Island from 1833.' *Acadiensis* 20 (1991):86–104.

Phillips, Roderick. *Putting Asunder: A History of Divorce in Western Society*. New York 1988.

Pleck, Elisabeth. *Domestic Tyranny: The Making of American Social Policy Against Family Violence from Colonial Times to the Present*. New York 1987.

Prentice, Alison, et al. *Canadian Women: A History*. Toronto 1988.

Rabkin, Peggy. 'The Origins of Law Reform: The Social Significance of the Nineteenth Century Codification Movement and its Contribution to the Passage of

the Early Married Women's Property Acts.' *Buffalo Law Review* 24 (1974–5):683–760.
– *From Fathers to Daughters: The Legal Foundations of Female Emancipation* Westport, Connecticut 1980.
Ray, Janet. *Emily Stowe*. Toronto 1978.
Riddell, William Renwick. 'Legislative Divorce in Colonial Pennsylvania.' *Pennsylvania Magazine of History and Biography* 57 (1931):175–80.
Rifkind, Janet. 'Toward a Theory of Law and Patriarchy.' *Harvard Women's Law Journal* 3 (1980):83–95.
Rothman, Ellen. *Hands and Hearts: A History of Courtship in America*. Cambridge 1987.
Rothman, Sheila M. *Woman's Proper Place: A History of Changing Ideals and Practices, 1870 to the Present*. New York 1978.
Rundell, Oliver. 'The Chancellor's Foot: The Nature of Equity.' *University of Kansas City Law Review* 27 (1958):71–85.
Rutherford, Paul. *A Victorian Authority: The Daily Press in Late Nineteenth-Century Canada*. Toronto 1982.
Sachs, Albie, and Joan Hoff Wilson. *Sexism and the Law: Male Beliefs and Legal Bias in Britain and the United States*. New York 1978.
Salmon, Marylynn. *Women and the Law of Property in Early America*. Chapel Hill 1986.
– 'Women and Property in South Carolina: The Evidence from Marriage Settlements, 1730–1830.' *William and Mary Quarterly* 39 (1982):655–85.
– 'The Legal Status of Women in Early America: A Reappraisal.' *Law and History Review* 1 (1983):129–51.
Sears, Hal. *The Sex-Radicals: Free Love in High Victoria America*. Kansas 1977.
Shanley, Mary Lyndon. *Feminism, Marriage and the Law in Victorian England*. Princeton 1989.
Shorter, Edward. *The Making of the Modern Family*. New York 1975.
Smith, Hilda. 'Feminism and the Methodology of Women's History,' in Berenice Carroll, ed. *Liberating Women's History*. Urbana 1976.
Snell, James. *In the Shadow of the Law: Divorce in Canada, 1900–1939*. Toronto 1991.
– 'Marital Cruelty and the Nova Scotia Divorce Court, 1900–1939.' *Acadiensis* 18 (1) (Autumn 1988):3–32.
Spender, Dale. *Women of Ideas and What Men Have Done to Them*. London 1982.
Staves, Susan. *Married Women's Separate Property in England, 1660–1833* Cambridge 1990.
Stone, Lawrence. *The Family, Sex and Marriage*. London 1977.
Stouffer, Allen P. *The Light of Nature and the Law of God: Antislavery in Ontario 1833–1877*. Montreal 1992.

Strange, Carolyn. *Toronto's Girl Problem: The Perils and Pleasures of the City, 1880–1930*. Toronto 1995.

– 'The Criminal Prosecution of Rape in York County, Ontario, 1880–1930,' in Jim Phillips, Tina Loo, and Susan Lethwaite, eds. *Essays in the History of Canadian Law, vol. v: Crime and Criminal Justice*. Toronto 1994.

Thurman, Kay Ellen. 'The Married Women's Property Acts.' LLM dissertation, University of Wisconsin Law School 1966.

Tomes, Nancy. 'A Torrent of Abuse: Crimes of Violence between Working-Class Men and Women in London, 1840–1875.' *Journal of Social History* 11 (1978):328–45.

Trumbach, Randolph. *The Rise of the Egalitarian Family: Aristocratic Kinship and Domestic Relations in Eighteenth-Century England*. London 1978.

Ullrich, Vivienne. 'The Reform of Matrimonial Property Law in England during the Nineteenth Century.' *Victoria University of Wellington Law Review* 9 (1977):24–42.

Van Kirk, Sylvia. *Many Tender Ties: Women in Fur-Trade Society 1670–1870*. Winnipeg 1980.

Veinott, Rebecca. 'Child Custody and Divorce: A Nova Scotia Study, 1866–1910,' in Philip Girard and Jim Phillips, eds. *Essays in the History of Canadian Law, vol. III Nova Scotia*. Toronto 1990.

– 'The Changing Legal Status of Women in Nova Scotia, 1850–1910.' MA dissertation, Dalhousie University 1989.

Veinott, Rebecca, and Philip Girard. 'Married Women's Property Law in Nova Scotia, 1850–1900,' in Janet Guildford and Suzanne Morton, eds. *Separate Spheres: Women's Worlds in the 19th-century Maritimes*. Fredricton 1995.

Warbasse, Elizabeth Bowles. 'The Changing Legal Rights of Married Women, 1800–1861.' PhD dissertation, Radcliffe College 1966.

Ward, Peter W. 'Unwed Motherhood in Nineteenth-Century English Canada.' *Canadian Historical Association – Historical Papers* (1981).

– *Courtship, Love and Marriage in Nineteenth-Century English Canada*. Montreal 1990.

– 'Courtship and Social Space in Nineteenth-Century English Canada' *Canadian Historical Review* 68(1) (1987):35–62.

Welter, Barbara. 'The Cult of True Womanhood: 1820–1860.' *American Quarterly* 18 (1966):151–74.

Index

PUBLICATIONS OF THE OSGOODE SOCIETY FOR
CANADIAN LEGAL HISTORY